PORTUGUESE ARCHITECTURE

BY
WALTER CRUM WATSON

PREFACE

THE buildings of Portugal, with one or two exceptions, cannot be said to excel or even to come up to those of other countries. To a large extent the churches are without the splendid furniture which makes those of Spain the most romantic in the world, nor are they in themselves so large or so beautiful. Some apology, then, may seem wanted for imposing on the public a book whose subject-matter is not of first-class importance.

The present book is the outcome of visits to Portugal in April or May of three successive years; and during these visits the writer became so fond of the country and of its people, so deeply interested in the history of its glorious achievements in the past, and in the buildings which commemorate these great deeds, that it seemed worth while to try and interest others in them. Another reason for writing about Portugal instead of about Spain is that the country is so much smaller that it is no very difficult task to visit every part and see the various buildings with one's own eyes: besides, in no language does there exist any book dealing with the architecture of the country as a whole. There are some interesting monographs in Portuguese about such buildings as the palace at Cintra, or Batalha, while the Renaissance has been fully treated by Albrecht Haupt, but no one deals at all adequately with what came before the time of Dom Manoel.

Most of the plans in the book were drawn from rough measurements taken on the spot and do not pretend to minute accuracy.

For the use of that of the Palace at Cintra the thanks of the writer are due to Conde de Sabugosa, who allowed it to be copied from his book, while the plan of Mafra was found in an old magazine.

Thanks are also due to Senhor Joaquim de Vasconcellos for much valuable information, to his wife, Senhora Michaelis de Vasconcellos, for her paper about the puzzling inscriptions at Batalha, and above all the Baron and the Baroneza de Soutellinho, for their repeated welcome to Oporto and for the trouble they have taken in getting books and photographs.

That the book may be more complete there has been added a short account of some of the church plate and paintings which still survive, as well as of the tile work which is so universal and so characteristic.

As for the buildings, hardly any of any consequence have escaped notice.

EDINBURGH, 1907.

INTRODUCTION

No one can look at a map of the Iberian Peninsula without being struck by the curious way in which it is unequally divided between two independent countries. Spain occupies by far the larger part of the Peninsula, leaving to Portugal only a narrow strip on the western seaboard some one hundred miles wide and three hundred and forty long. Besides, the two countries are separated the one from the other by merely artificial boundaries. The two largest rivers of the Peninsula, the Douro and the Tagus, rise in Spain, but finish their course in Portugal, and the Guadiana runs for some eighty miles through Portuguese territory before acting for a second time as a boundary between the two countries. The same, to a lesser degree, is true of the mountains. The Gerez and the Marão are only offshoots of the Cantabrian mountains, and the Serra da Estrella in Beira is but a continuation of the Sierra de Gata which separates Leon from Spanish Estremadura. Indeed the only natural frontiers are formed by the last thirty miles of the Minho in the north, by about eighty miles of the Douro, which in its deep and narrow gorge really separates Traz os Montes from Leon; by a few miles of the Tagus, and by the Guadiana both before and after it runs through a part of Alemtejo.

If the languages of the two countries were radically unlike this curious division would be more easy to understand, but in reality Castilian differs from Portuguese rather in pronunciation than in anything else; indeed differs less from Portuguese than it does from Cataluñan.[1]

During the Roman dominion none of the divisions of the Peninsula corresponded exactly with Portugal. Lusitania, [2] which the poets of the Renaissance took to be the Roman name of their country, only reached up to the Douro, and took in a large part of Leon and the whole of Spanish Estremadura.

In the time of the Visigoths, a Suevic kingdom occupied most of Portugal to the north of the Tagus, but included also all Galicia and part of Leon; and during the Moorish occupation there was nothing which at all corresponded with the modern divisions.

It was, indeed, only by the gradual Christian re-conquest of the country from the Moors that Portugal came into existence, and only owing to the repeated failure of the attempt to unite the two crowns of Portugal and Castile by marriage that they have remained separated to the present day.

Of the original inhabitants of what is now Portugal little is known, but that they were more Celtic than Iberian seems probable from a few Celtic words which have survived, such as *Mor* meaning *great* as applied to the *Capella Mor* of a church or to the title of a court official. The name too of the Douro has probably nothing to do with gold but is connected with a Celtic word for water. The Tua may mean the 'gushing' river, and the Ave recalls the many Avons. *Ebora*, now Evora, is very like the Roman name of York, Eboracum. *Briga*, too, the common termination of town names in Roman times as in Conimbriga—Condeixa a Velha—or Cetobriga, near Setubal—in Celtic means *height* or *fortification*. All over the country great rude stone monuments are to be found, like those erected by primitive peoples in almost every part of Europe, and the most interesting, the curious buildings found at various places near Guimarães, seem to belong to a purely Celtic civilisation.

The best-known of these places, now called Citania—from a name of a native town mentioned by ancient writers—occupies the summit of a hill about nine hundred feet above the road and nearly half-way between Guimarães and Braga. The top of this hill is covered with a number of structures, some round from fifteen to twenty feet across, and some square, carefully built of well-cut blocks of granite. The only opening is a door which is often surrounded by an architrave adorned with rough carving; the roofs seem to have been of wood and tiles.

Some, not noticing the three encircling walls and the well-cut 3 water-channels, and thinking that the round buildings far exceeded the rectangular in number, have thought that they might have been intended for granaries where corn might be stored against a time of war. But it seems far more likely that Citania was a town placed on this high hill for safety. Though the remains show no other trace of Roman civilisation, one or two of the houses are inscribed with their owner's names in Roman character, and from coins found there they seem to have been inhabited long after the surrounding valleys had been subdued by the Roman arms, perhaps even after the great baths had been built not far off at the hot springs of Taipas. Uninfluenced by Rome, Citania was also untouched by Christianity, though it may have been inhabited after St. James—if indeed he ever preached in Bracara Augusta, now Braga—and his disciple São Pedro de Rates had begun their mission.

But if Citania knew nothing of Christianity there still remains one remarkable monument of the native religion. Among the ruins there long lay a huge thin slab of granite, now in the museum of Guimarães, which certainly has the appearance of having been a sacrificial stone. It is a rough pentagon with each side measuring about five feet. On one side, in the middle, a semicircular hollow has been cut out as if to leave room for the sacrificing priest, while on the surface of the stone a series of grooves has been cut, all draining to a hole near this hollow and arranged as if for a human body with outstretched legs and arms. The rest of the surface is covered with an intricate pattern like what may often be found on Celtic stones in Scotland. Besides this so-called Citania similar buildings have been found elsewhere, as at Sabrosa, also near Guimarães, but there the Roman influence seems usually to have been greater. (Fig. 1.)

The Romans began to occupy the Peninsula after the second Punic war, but the conquest of the west and north was not completed till the reign of Augustus more than two hundred years later. The Roman dominion over what is now Portugal lasted for over four hundred years, and the chief monument of their occupation is found in the language. More material memorials are the milestones which still stand in the Gerez, some tombstones, and some pavements and other remains at Condeixa a Velha, once Conimbriga, near Coimbra and at the place now called Troya, perhaps the 4 original Cetobriga, on a sandbank opposite Setubal, a town whose founders were probably Phœnicians.

But more important than any of these is the temple at Evora, now without any reason called the temple of Diana. During the middle ages, crowned with battlements, with the spaces between the columns built up, it was later degraded by being turned into a slaughter-house, and was only cleared of such additions a few years since. Situated near the cathedral, almost on the highest part of the town, it stands on a terrace whose great retaining wall still shows the massiveness of Roman work.

Of the temple itself there remains about half of the podium, some eleven feet high, fourteen granite columns, twelve of which still retain their beautiful Corinthian capitals, and the architrave and part of the frieze resting on these twelve capitals. Everything is of granite except the capitals and bases which are of white marble; but instead of the orthodox twenty-four flutes each column has only twelve, with a distinctly unpleasing result. The temple seems to have been hexastyle peripteral, but all trace of the cella has disappeared. Nothing is known of the temple or who it was that built it, but in Roman times Evora was one of the chief cities of Lusitania; nothing else is left but the temple, for the aqueduct has been rebuilt and the so-called Tower of Sertorius was mediæval. Yet, although it may have less to show than Merida, once Augusta Emerita and the capital of the province, this temple is the best-preserved in the whole peninsula. (Fig. 2.)

Before the Roman dominion came to an end, in the first quarter of the fifth century, Christianity had been for some time firmly established. Religious intolerance also, which nearly a thousand years later made Spain the first home of the Inquisition, had already made itself manifest in the burning of the heretical Priscillianists by Idacius, whose see was at or near Lamego.

Soon, however, the orthodox were themselves to suffer, for the Vandals, the Goths, and the Suevi, who swept across the country from 417 A.D., were Arians, and it was only after many years had passed that the ruling Goths and Suevi were converted to the Catholic faith.

The Vandals soon passed on to Africa, leaving their name in Andalucia and the whole land to the Goths and Suevi, the

FIG. 1.
HOUSE FROM SABROSA.
NOW IN MUSEUM, GUIMARÃES.
FIG. 2.
EVORA.
TEMPLE OF "DIANA."

5 Suevi at first occupying the whole of Portugal north of the Tagus as well as Galicia and part of Leon. Later they were expelled from the southern part of their dominion, but they as well as the Goths have left practically no mark on the country, for the church built at Oporto by the Suevic king, Theodomir, on his conversion to orthodoxy in 559, has been rebuilt in the eleventh or twelfth century.

These Germanic rulers seem never to have been popular with those they governed, so that when the great Moslem invasion crossed from Morocco in 711 and, defeating King Roderick at Guadalete near Cadiz, swept in an incredibly short time right up to the northern mountains, the whole country submitted with scarcely a struggle.

A few only of the Gothic nobles took refuge on the seaward slopes of the Cantabrian mountains in the Asturias and there made a successful stand, electing Don Pelayo as their king.

As time went on, Pelayo's descendants crossed the mountains, and taking Leon gradually extended their small kingdom southwards.

Meanwhile other independent counties or principalities further east were gradually spreading downwards. The nearest was Castile, so called from its border castles, then Navarre, then Aragon, and lastly the county of Barcelona or Cataluña.

Galicia, in the north-west corner, never having been thoroughly conquered by the invaders, was soon united with the Asturias and then with Leon. So all these Christian realms, Leon—including Galicia and Asturias—Castile, and Aragon, which was soon united to Cataluña, spread southwards, faster when the Moslems were weakened by division, slower when they had been united and strengthened by a fresh wave of fanaticism from Africa. Navarre alone was unable to grow, for the lower Ebro valley was won by the kings of Aragon, while Castile as she grew barred the way to the south-west.

At last in 1037 Fernando I. united Castile and Leon into one kingdom, extending from the sea in the north to the lower course of the Douro and to the mountains dividing the upper Douro from the Tagus valley in the south. Before Fernando died in 1065 he had extended his frontier on the west as far south as the Mondego, making Sesnando, a converted Moslem, count of this important marchland. Then 6 followed a new division, for Castile went to King Sancho, Leon to Alfonso VI., and Galicia, including the two counties of Porto and of Coimbra, to Garcia.

Before long, however, Alfonso turned out his brothers and also extended his borders even to the Tagus by taking Toledo in 1085. But his successes roused the Moslem powers to fresh fanaticism. A new and stricter dynasty, the Almoravides,[2] arose in Africa and crossing the straits inflicted a crushing defeat on the Christians at Zalaca. In despair at this disaster and at the loss of Santarem and of Lisbon, Alfonso appealed to Christendom for help. Among those who came were Count Raymond of Toulouse, who was rewarded with the kingdom of Galicia and the hand of his daughter and heiress Urraca, and Count Henry of Burgundy, who was granted the counties of Porto and of Coimbra and who married another daughter of Alfonso's, Theresa.

This was really the first beginning of Portugal as an independent state; for Portugal, derived from two towns Portus and Cales, which lie opposite each other near the mouth of the Douro, was the name given to Henry's county. Henry did but little to make himself independent as he was usually away fighting elsewhere, but his widow Theresa refused to acknowledge her sister Urraca, now queen of Castile, Leon and Galicia, as her superior, called herself Infanta and behaved as if she was no one's vassal. Fortunately for her and her aims, Urraca was far too busy fighting with her second husband, the king of Aragon, to pay much attention to what was happening in the west, so that she had time to consolidate her power and to accustom her people to think of themselves as being not Galicians but Portuguese.

The breach with Galicia was increased by the favour which Theresa, after a time, began to show to her lover, Don Fernando Peres de Trava, a Galician noble, and by the grants of lands and of honours she made to him. This made her so unpopular that when Alfonso Raimundes, Urraca's son, attacked Theresa in 1127, made her acknowledge him as suzerain, and give up Tuy and Orense, Galician towns she had taken, the people rose against her and declared her son Affonso Henriques old enough to reign. 7

Then took place the famous submission of Egas Moniz, Affonso's governor, who induced the king to retire from the siege of Guimarães by promising that his pupil would agree to the terms forced on his mother. This, though but seventeen, Affonso refused to do, and next year raising an army he expelled his mother and Don Fernando, and after four wars with his cousin of Castile finally succeeded in maintaining his independence, and even in assuming the title of King.

These wars with Castile taught him at last that the true way to increase his realm was to leave Christian territory alone and to direct his energies southwards, gaining land only at the expense of the Moors.

So did the kingdom of Portugal come into existence, almost accidentally and without there being any division of race or of language between its inhabitants and those of Galicia.

The youngest of all the Peninsular kingdoms, it is the only one which still remains separate from the rest of the Spains, for when in 1580 union was forced on her by Philip II., Portugal had had too glorious a past, and had become too different in language and in custom easily to submit to so undesired a union, while Spain, already suffering from coming weakness and decay, was not able long to hold her in such hated bondage.

It is not necessary here to tell the story of each of Affonso Henriques' descendants. He himself permanently extended the borders of his kingdom as far as the Tagus, and even

4

raided the Moslem lands of the south as far as Ourique, beyond Beja. His son, Sancho I., finding the Moors too strong to make any permanent conquests beyond the Tagus, devoted himself chiefly—when not fighting with the king of Castile and Leon—to rebuilding and restoring the towns in Beira, and it was not till the reign of his grandson, Affonso III., that the southern sea was reached by the taking of the Algarve in the middle of the thirteenth century.

Dom Diniz, Affonso III.'s son, carried on the work of settling the country, building castles and planting pine-trees to stay the blowing sands along the west coast.

From that time on Portugal was able to hold her own, and was strong enough in 1387 to defeat the king of Castile at Aljubarrota when he tried to seize the throne in right of his wife, only child of the late Portuguese king, Fernando.[8]

Under the House of Aviz, whose first king, João I., had been elected to repel this invasion, Portugal rose to the greatest heights of power and of wealth to which the country was ever to attain. The ceaseless efforts of Dom Henrique, the Navigator, the third son of Dom João, were crowned with success when Vasco da Gama landed at Calicut in May 1498, and when Pedro Alvares Cabral first saw the coasts of Brazil in 1500.

To-day one is too ready to forget that Portugal was the pioneer in geographical discovery, that the Portuguese were the first Westerns to reach Japan, and that, had João II. listened to Columbus, it would have been to Portugal and not to Spain that he would have given a new world.

It was, too, under the House of Aviz that the greatest development in architecture took place, and that the only original and distinctive style of architecture was formed. That was also the time when the few good pictures which the country possesses were painted, and when much of the splendid church plate which still exists was wrought.

The sixty years of the Spanish captivity, as it was called, from 1580 to 1640, were naturally comparatively barren of all good work. After the restoration of peace and a revival of the Brazilian trade had brought back some of the wealth which the country had lost, the art of building had fallen so low that of the many churches rebuilt or altered during the eighteenth century there is scarcely one possessed of the slightest merit.

The most important events of the eighteenth century were the great earthquakes of 1755 and the ministry of the Marques de Pombal.

Soon after the beginning of the nineteenth century came the invasion led by Junot, 1807, the flight of the royal family to Brazil, and the Peninsular War. Terrible damage was done by the invaders, cart-loads of church plate were carried off, and many a monastery was sacked and burned. Peace had not long been restored when the struggle broke out between the constitutional party under Pedro of Brazil, who had resigned the throne of Portugal in favour of his daughter, Maria da Gloria, and the absolutists under Dom Miguel, his brother.

The civil war lasted for several years, from May 1828, when Dom Miguel, then regent for his niece, summoned the Cortes and caused himself to be elected king, till May 1834,[9] when he was finally defeated at Evora Monte and forced to leave the country. The chief events of his usurpation were the siege of Oporto and the defeat of his fleet off Cape St. Vincent in 1833 by Captain Charles Napier, who fought for Dona Maria under the name of Carlos de Ponza.

One of the first acts of the constitutional Cortes was to suppress all the monasteries in the kingdom in 1834. At the same time the nunneries were forbidden to receive any new nuns, with the result that in many places the buildings have gradually fallen into decay, till the last surviving sister has died, solitary and old, and so at length set free her home to be turned to some public use.[3]

Since then the history of Portugal has been quiet and uneventful. Good roads have been made—but not always well kept up—railways have been built, and Lisbon, once known as the dirtiest of towns, has become one of the cleanest, with fine streets, electric lighting, a splendidly managed system of electric tramways, and with funiculars and lifts to connect the higher parts of the town with its busy centre.

It is not uninteresting to notice in how many small matters Portugal now differs from Spain. Portugal drinks tea, Spain chocolate or coffee; it lunches and dines early, Spain very

5

late; its beds and pillows are very hard, in Spain they are much softer. Travelling too in Portugal is much pleasanter; as the country is so much smaller, trains leave at much more reasonable hours, run more frequently, and go more quickly. The inns also, even in small places, are, if not luxurious, usually quite clean with good food, and the landlord treats his guests with something more pleasing than that lofty condescension which is so noticeable in Spain.

Of the more distant countries of Europe, Portugal is now one of the easiest to reach. Forty-eight hours from Southampton in a boat bound for South America lands the traveller at Vigo, or three days at Lisbon, where the brilliant sun and blue sky, the judas-trees in the Avenida, the roses, the palms, and the sheets of bougainvillia, are such an unimaginable change from the cold March winds and pinched buds of England.

There is perhaps no country in Europe which has so interesting a flora, especially in spring. In March in the granite north the ground under the pine-trees is covered 10 with the exquisite flowers of the narcissus triandrus,[4] while the wet water meadows are yellow with petticoat daffodils. Other daffodils too abound, but these are the commonest.

Later the granite rocks are hidden by great trees of white broom, while from north to south every wild piece of land is starred with the brilliant blue flowers of the lithospermum. There are also endless varieties of cistus, from the small yellow annual with rich brown heart to the large gum cistus that covers so much of the poor soil in the Alemtejo. These plains of the Alemtejo are supposed to be the least beautiful part of the country, but no one can cross them in April without being almost overcome with the beauty of the flowers, cistus, white, yellow, or red, tall white heaths, red heaths, blue lithospermum, yellow whin, and most brilliant of all the large pimpernel, whose blue flowers almost surpass the gentian. A little further on where there is less heath and cistus, tall yellow and blue Spanish irises stand up out of the grass, or there may be great heads of blue scilla peruviana or sheets of small iris of the brightest blue.

Indeed, sheets of brilliant colour are everywhere most wonderful. There may be acres of rich purple where the bugloss hides the grass, or of brilliant yellow where the large golden daisies grow thickly together, or of sky-blue where the convolvulus has smothered a field of oats.

PAINTING IN PORTUGAL.[5]

From various causes Portugal is far less rich in buildings of interest than is Spain. The earthquake has destroyed many, but more have perished through tasteless rebuilding during the eighteenth century when the country again regained a small part of the trade and wealth lost during the Spanish usurpation.

But if this is true of architecture, it is far more true of painting. During the most flourishing period of Spanish painting, the age of Velasquez and of Murillo, Portugal was, before 1640, a despised part of the kingdom, treated as a conquered province, while after the rebellion the long struggle, which lasted for twenty-eight years, was enough to prevent 11 any of the arts from flourishing. Besides, many good pictures which once adorned the royal palaces of Portugal were carried off to Madrid by Philip or his successors.

And yet there are scattered about the country not a few paintings of considerable merit. Most of them have been terribly neglected, are very dirty, or hang where they can scarcely be seen, while little is really known about their painters.

From the time of Dom João I., whose daughter, Isabel, married Duke Philip early in the fifteenth century, the two courts of Portugal and of Burgundy had been closely united. Isabel sent an alabaster monument for the tomb of her father's great friend and companion, the Holy Constable, and one of bronze for that of her eldest brother; while as a member of the embassy which came to demand her hand, was J. van Eyck himself. However, if he painted anything in Portugal, it has now vanished.

There was also a great deal of trade with Antwerp where the Portuguese merchants had a *lonja* or exchange as early as 1386, and where a factory was established in 1503. With the heads of this factory, Francisco Brandão and Rodrigo Ruy de Almada, Albert Dürer was on friendly terms, sending them etchings and paintings in return for wine and southern rarities. He also drew the portrait of Damião de Goes, Dom Manoel's friend and chronicler.

It is natural enough, therefore, that Flanders should have had a great influence on Portuguese painting, and indeed practically all the pictures in the country are either by Netherland masters, painted at home and imported, or painted in Portugal by artists who had been attracted there by the fame of Dom Manoel's wealth and generosity, or else by Portuguese pupils sent to study in Flanders.

During the seventeenth century all memory of these painters had vanished. Looking at their work, the writers of that date were struck by what seemed to them, in their natural ignorance of Flemish art, a strange and peculiar style, and so attributed them all to a certain half-mythical painter of Vizeu called Vasco, or Grão Vasco, who is first mentioned in 1630.

Raczynski,[6] in his letters to the Berlin Academy, says that he had found Grão Vasco's birth in a register of Vizeu; but 12 Vasco is not an uncommon name, and besides this child, Vasco Fernandes, was born in 1552—far too late to have painted any of the so-called Grão Vasco's pictures.

It is of course possible that some of the pictures now at Vizeu were the work of a man called Vasco, and one of those at Coimbra, in the sacristy of Santa Cruz, is signed Velascus—which is only the Spanish form of Vasco—so that the legendary personage may have been evolved from either or both of these, for it is scarcely possible that they can have been the same.

Turning now to some of the pictures themselves, there are thirteen representing scenes from the life of the Virgin in the archbishop's palace at Evora, which are said by Justi, a German critic, to be by Gerhard David. Twelve of these are in a very bad state of preservation, but one is still worthy of some admiration. In the centre sits the Virgin with the Child on her knee: four angels are in the air above her holding a wreath. On her right three angels are singing, and on her left one plays an organ while another behind blows the bellows. Below there are six other angels, three on each side with a lily between them, playing, those on the right on a violin, a flute, and a zither, those on the left on a harp, a triangle, and a guitar. Once part of the cathedral reredos, it was taken down when the new Capella Mor was built in the eighteenth century.

Another Netherlander who painted at Evora was Frey Carlos, who came to Espinheiro close by in 1507. Several of his works are in the Museum at Lisbon.[7]

When Dom Manoel was enriching the old Templar church at Thomar with gilding and with statues of saints, he also caused large paintings to be placed round the outer wall. Several still remain, but most have perished, either during the French invasion or during the eleven years after the expulsion of the monks in 1834 when the church stood open for any one to go in and do what harm he liked. Some also, including the 'Raising of Lazarus,' the 'Entry into Jerusalem,' the 'Resurrection,' and the 'Centurion,' are now in Lisbon. Four—the 'Nativity,' the 'Visit of the Magi,' the 'Annunciation,' and a 'Virgin and Child'—are known to have been given by Dom 13 Manoel; twenty others, including the four now at Lisbon, are spoken of by Raczynski in 1843,[8] and some at least of these, as well as the angels holding the emblems of the Passion, who stand above the small arches of the inner octagon, may have been painted by Johannes Dralia of Bruges, who died and was buried at Thomar in 1504.[9]

Also at Thomar, but in the parish church of São João Baptista, are some pictures ascribed by Justi to a pupil of Quentin Matsys. Now it is known that a Portuguese called *Eduard* became a pupil of Matsys in 1504, and four years later a Vrejmeester of the guild. So perhaps they may be by this Eduard or by some fellow-pupil.

The Jesus Church at Setubal, built by Justa Rodrigues, Dom Manoel's nurse, has fifteen paintings in incongruous gilt frames and hung high up on the north wall of the church, which also have something of the same style.[10]

More interesting than these are two pictures in the sacristy of Santa Cruz at Coimbra, an 'Ecce Homo' and the 'Day of Pentecost.' It is the 'Pentecost' which is signed Velascus, and in it the Apostles in an inner room are seen through an arcade of three arches like a chapter-house entrance. Perhaps once part of the great reredos, this picture has suffered terribly from neglect; but it must once have been a fine work, and the way in which the

Apostles in the inner room are separated by the arcade from the two spectators is particularly successful.

In Oporto there exists at least one good picture, 'The Fountain of Mercy,' now in the board-room of the Misericordia,[11] but painted to be the reredos of the chapel of São Thiago in the Sé where the brotherhood was founded by Dom Manoel in 1499. (Fig. 3.)

In the centre above, between St. John and the Virgin, stands a crucifix from which blood flows down to fill a white marble well.

Below, on one side there kneels Dom Manoel with his [14] six sons—João, afterwards king; Luis, duke of Beja; Fernando, duke of Guarda; Affonso, afterwards archbishop of Lisbon, with his cardinal's hat; Henrique, later cardinal archbishop of Evora, and then king; and Duarte, duke of Guimarães and ancestor of the present ruling house of Braganza.

On the other side are Queen Dona Leonor,[12] granddaughter of Ferdinand and Isabella, Dom Manoel's third wife[13] and her two stepdaughters, Dona Isabel, the wife of Charles V. and mother of Philip II., who through her claimed and won the throne of Portugal when his uncle, the cardinal king, died in 1580, and Dona Beatriz, who married Charles III.. of Savoy.

The date of the picture is fixed as between 1518 when Dom Affonso, then aged nine, received his cardinal's hat, and 1521 when Dom Manoel died.[14]

Unfortunately the picture has been somewhat spoiled by restoration, but it is undoubtedly a very fine piece of work—especially the portraits below—and would be worthy of admiration anywhere, even in a country much richer in works of art.

It has of course been attributed to Grão Vasco, but it is quite different from either the Velascus pictures at Coimbra or the paintings at Vizeu; besides, some of the beautifully painted flowers, such as the columbines, which enrich the grass on which the royal persons kneel, are not Portuguese flowers, so that it is much more likely to have been the work of some one from Flanders.

Equally Flemish are the pictures at Vizeu, whether any of them be by the Grão Vasco or not. Tradition has it that he was born at a mill not far off, still called *Moinho do Pintor,* the *Painter's Mill,* and that Dom Manoel sent him to study in Italy. Now, wherever the painter of the Vizeu pictures had studied it can scarcely have been in Italy, as they are all surely much nearer to the Flemish than to any Italian school.

FIG. 3.
THE FOUNTAIN OF MERCY.
MISERICORDIA, OPORTO.
FROM A PHOTOGRAPH BY E. BIEL & CO., OPORTO.

[15] There are still in the precincts of the cathedral some thirty-one pictures of very varied merit, and not all by the same hand. Of these there are fourteen in the chapter-house, a room opening off the upper cloister. They are all scenes from the life of Our Lord from the Annunciation to the day of Pentecost. Larger than any of these is a damaged 'Crucifixion' in the Jesus Chapel under the chapter-house. The painting is full, perhaps too full, of movement and of figures. Besides the scenes usually portrayed in a picture of the Crucifixion, others are shown in the background, Judas hanging himself on one side, and Joseph of Arimathea and Nicodemus on the other, coming out from Jerusalem with their spices. Lastly, in the sacristy there are twelve small paintings of the Apostles and other saints of no great merit, and four large pictures, 'St. Sebastian,' the 'Day of Pentecost,' where the room is divided by three arches, with the Virgin and another saint in the centre, and six of the Apostles on each side; the 'Baptism of Our Lord,' and lastly 'St. Peter.' The first three are not very remarkable, but the 'St. Peter' is certainly one of the finest pictures in the country, and is indeed worthy of ranking among the great pictures of the world.[15] (Fig. 4.)

As in the 'Day of Pentecost' there is a triple division; St. Peter's throne being in the middle with an arch on each side open to show distant scenes. The throne seems to be of stone, with small boys and griffins holding shields charged with the Cross Keys on the arms. On the canopy two other shields supporting triple crowns flank an arch whose classic ornaments and large shell are more Italian than is any other part of the painting. On the throne sits St. Peter pontifically robed, and with the triple crown on his head. His right hand is raised in blessing, and in his left he holds one very long key while he keeps a book open upon his knee.

The cope is of splendid gold brocade of a fine Gothic pattern, with orfreys or borders richly embroidered with figures of saints, and is fastened in front by a great square gold and jewelled morse. All the draperies are very finely modelled and richly coloured, but finest of all is St. Peter's [16] face, solemn and stern and yet kindly, without any of that pride and arrogance which would seem but natural to the wearer of such vestments; it is, with its grey hair and short grey beard, rather the face of the fisherman of Galilee than that of a Pope.

Through the arches to the right and left above a low wall are seen the beginning and the end of his ministry. On the one side he is leaving his boat and his nets to become a fisher of men, and on the other he kneels before the vision of Our Lord, when fleeing from Rome he met Him at the place now called 'Quo Vadis' on the Appian way, and so was turned back to meet his martyrdom.

Fortunately this painting has suffered from no restoration, and is still wonderfully clean, but the wood on which it is painted has split rather badly in places, one large crack running from top to bottom just beyond the throne on St. Peter's right.

This 'St. Peter,' then, is entirely Flemish in the painting of the drapery and of the scenes behind; especially of the turreted Gothic walls of Rome. The details of the throne may be classic, but French renaissance forms were first introduced into the country at Belem in 1517, just the time when the cathedral here was being built by Bishop Dom Diogo Ortiz de Vilhegas. This, and the other pictures in the sacristy, were doubtless once parts of the great reredos, which would not be put up till the church was quite finished, and so may not have been painted till some time after 1520, or even later. Already in 1522 much renaissance work was being done at Coimbra, not far off, so it is possible that the painter of these pictures may have adopted his classic detail from what he may have seen there.

It is worth noting, too, that preserved in the sacristy at Vizeu there is, or was,[16] a cope so like that worn by St. Peter, that the painting must almost certainly have been copied from it.

We may therefore conclude that these pictures are the work of some one who had indeed studied abroad, probably at Antwerp, but who worked at home.

Not only to paint religious pictures and portraits did Flemish artists come to Portugal. One at least, Antonio de

FIG. 4.
ST. PETER.
IN THE CATHEDRAL SACRISTY.
VIZEU.

[17] Hollanda, was famous for his illuminations. He lived and worked at Evora, and is said by his son Francisco to have been the first in Portugal 'to make known a pleasing manner of painting in black and white, superior to all processes known in other countries.'[17]

When the convent of Thomar was being finished by Dom João III., some large books were in November 1533 sent on a mule to Antonio at Evora to be illuminated. Two of these books were finished and paid for in February 1535, when he received 63 795 or about £15. The books were bound at Evora for 4 000 or sixteen shillings.

By the end of the next year a Psalter was finished which cost 54 605 or £12, at the rate of 6 000, £1, 6s. 8d. for each of four large headings, forty illuminated letters with vignettes at 2s. 2d. each, a hundred and fifteen without vignettes at fivepence-halfpenny, two hundred and three in red, gold, and blue at fourpence-farthing, eighty-four drawn in black at twopence, and 2846 small letters at the beginning of each verse at less than one farthing. Next March this Psalter was brought back to Thomar on a mule whose hire was two shillings and twopence—a sum small enough for a journey of well over a hundred miles,[18] but which may help us the better to estimate the value of the money paid to Antonio.[19]

CHURCH PLATE.

9

A very great part of the church plate of Portugal has long since disappeared, for few chapters had the foresight to hide all that was most valuable when Soult began his devastating march from the north, and so he and his men were able to encumber their retreat with cart-loads of the most beautiful gold and silver ornaments.

Yet a good deal has survived, either because it was hidden away as at Guimarães or at Coimbra—where it is said to have been only found lately—or because, as at Evora, it lay apart from the course of this famous plunderer.

The richest treasuries at the present day are those of 18 Nossa Senhora da Oliveira at Guimarães, and of the Sés at Braga, at Coimbra, and at Evora.

A silver-gilt chalice and a pastoral staff of the twelfth century in the sacristy at Braga are among the oldest pieces of plate in the country. The chalice is about five inches high. The cup, ornamented with animals and leaves, stands on a plain base inscribed, 'In nme Dmi Menendus Gundisaluis de Tuda domna sum.' It is called the chalice of São Giraldo, and is supposed to have belonged to that saint, who as archbishop of Braga baptized Affonso Henriques.

The staff of copper-gilt is in the form of a snake with a cross in its mouth, and though almost certainly of the twelfth century is said to have been found in the tomb of Santo Ovidio, the third archbishop of the see.

Another very fine chalice of the same date is in the treasury at Coimbra. Here the round cup is enriched by an arcade, under each arch of which stands a saint, while on the base are leaves and medallions with angels. It is inscribed, 'Geda Menendis me fecit in onore sci. Michaelis e. MCLXXXX.', that is A.D. 1152.

It was no doubt given by Dom Miguel, who ruled the see from 1162 to 1176 and who spent so much on the old cathedral and on its furniture. For him Master Ptolomeu made silver altar fronts, and the goldsmith Felix a jug and basin for the service of the altar. He also had a gold chalice made weighing 4 marks, probably the one made by Geda Menendis, and a gold cross to enclose some pieces of the Holy Sepulchre and two pieces of the True Cross.

At Guimarães the chalice of São Torquato is of the thirteenth century. The cup is quite plain and small, but on the wide-spreading base are eight enamels of Our Lady and of seven of the Apostles.

The finest of all the objects in the Guimarães treasury is the reredos, taken by Dom João I. from the Spanish king's tent after the victory of Aljubarrota, and one of the angels which once went with it.

The same king also gave to the small church of São Miguel a silver processional cross, all embossed with oak leaves, and ending in fleurs-de-lys, which rises from two superimposed octagons, covered with Gothic ornament.

Another beautiful cross now at Coimbra has a 'Virgin and Child' in the centre under a rich canopy, and enamels of the 19 four Evangelists on the arms, while the rest of the surface including the foliated ends is covered with exquisitely pierced flowing tracery. (Fig. 5.)

Earlier are the treasures which once belonged the Queen St. Isabel who died in 1327, and which are still preserved at Coimbra. These include a beautiful and simple cross of agate and silver, a curious reliquary made of a branch of coral with silver mountings, her staff as abbess of St. Clara, shaped like the cross of an Eastern bishop, and with heads of animals at the ends of the arms, and a small ark-shaped reliquary of silver and coral now set on a high renaissance base.

But nearly all the surviving church plate dates from the time of Dom Manoel or his son.

To Braga Archbishop Diogo de Souza gave a splendid silver-gilt chalice in 1509. Here the cup is adorned above by six angels holding emblems of the Passion, and below by six others holding bells. Above them runs an inscription, *Hic est calix sanguinis mei novi et eter.* The stem is entirely covered with most elaborate canopy work, with six Apostles in niches, while on the base are five other Apostles in relief, the archbishop's arms, and six pieces of enamel.

Very similar is a splendid chalice in the Misericordia at Oporto, probably of about the same date, and two at Coimbra. In both of these the cup is embossed with angels and leafage—in one the angels hold bells—and the stem is covered with tabernacle work. On the base of the one is a *pietà* with mourning angels and other emblems of the Passion in relief, while that of the other is enriched with filigree work. (Fig. 6.)

Another at Guimarães given by Fernando Alvares is less well proportioned and less beautiful.

So far the architectural details of the chalices mentioned have been entirely national, but there is a custodia at Evora, whose interlacing canopy work seems to betray the influence of the Netherlands. The base of this custodia[20] or monstrance, in the shape of a chalice seems later than the upper part, which is surmounted by a rounded canopy whose hanging cusps and traceried panels strongly recall the Flemish work of the great reredos in the old cathedral at Coimbra.

Even more Flemish are a pastoral staff made for Cardinal 20 Henrique, son of Dom Manoel and afterwards king, a monstrance or reliquary at Coimbra,[21] and another at Guimarães.[22]

Much splendid plate was also given to Santa Cruz at Coimbra by Dom Manoel, but all—candlesticks, lamps, crosses and a monstrance—have since vanished, sent to Gôa in India when the canons in the eighteenth century wanted something more fashionable.

Belem also possessed splendid treasures, among them a cross of silver filigree and jewels which is still preserved.

Much filigree work is still done in the north, where the young women invest their savings in great golden hearts or in beautiful earrings, though now bunches of coloured flowers on huge lockets of coppery gold are much more sought after.

Curiously, many of the most famous goldsmiths of the sixteenth century were Jews. Among them was the Vicente family, a member of which made a fine monstrance for Belem in 1505, and which, like other families, was expelled from Coimbra to Guimarães between the years 1532 and 1537, and doubtless wrought some of the beautiful plate for which the treasury of Nossa Senhora is famous.

The seventeenth century, besides smaller works, has left the great silver tomb of the Holy Queen St. Isabel in the new church of Santa Clara. Made by order of Bishop Dom Affonso de Castello Branco in 1614, it weighs over 170 lbs., has at the sides and ends Corinthian columns, leaving panels between them with beautifully chased framing, and a sloping top.

Later and less worthy of notice are the coffins of the two first sainted abbesses of the convent of Lorvão, near Coimbra, in which elaborate acanthus scrolls in silver are laid over red velvet.

TILE WORK OR AZULEJOS.

The Moors occupied most of what is now Portugal for a considerable length of time. The extreme north they held for rather less than two hundred years, the extreme south for more than five hundred. This occupation by a governing class, so different in religion, in race, and in customs from

FIG. 5.   **FIG. 5.**   **FIG. 7.**
CHALICE AT COIMBRA.CROSS AT COIMBRA.MONSTRANCE AT COIMBRA.

21 those they ruled, has naturally had a strong influence, not only on the language of Portugal, but also on the art. Though there survive no important Moorish buildings dating from before the re-conquest—for the so-called mosque at Cintra is certainly a small Christian church—many were built after it for Christians by Moorish workmen.

These, as well as the Arab ceilings, or those derived therefrom, will be described later, but here must be mentioned the tilework, the most universally distributed legacy of the Eastern people who once held the land. There is scarcely a church, certainly scarcely one of any size or importance which even in the far north has not some lining or dado of tiles, while others are entirely covered with them from floor to ceiling or vault.

The word *azulejo* applied to these tiles is derived from the Arabic *azzallaja* or *azulaich*, meaning *smooth*, or else through the Arabic from a Low Latin word *azuroticus* used by a Gaulish writer of the fifth century to describe mosaic[23] and not from the word *azul* or *blue*. At first each different piece or colour in a geometric pattern was cut before firing to the

11

shape required, and the many different pieces when coloured and fired were put together so as to form a regular mosaic. This method of making tiles, though soon given up in most places as being too troublesome, is still employed at Tetuan in Morocco, where in caves near the town the whole process may still be seen; for there the mixing of the clay, the cutting out of the small pieces, the colouring and the firing are still carried on in the old primitive and traditional manner.[24]

Elsewhere, though similar designs long continued to be used in Spain and Portugal, and are still used in Morocco, the tiles were all made square, each tile usually forming one quarter of the pattern. In them the pattern was formed by lines slightly raised above the surface of the tile so that there was no danger during the firing of the colour running beyond the place it was intended to occupy.

For a long time, indeed right up to the end of the fifteenth century, scarcely anything but Moorish geometric patterns seem to have been used. Then with the renaissance their 22 place was taken by other patterns of infinite variety; some have octagons with classic mouldings represented in colour, surrounding radiating green and blue leaves;[25] some more strictly classical are not unlike Italian patterns; some again are more naturalistic, while in others the pattern, though not of the old geometric form, is still Moorish in design.

Together with the older tiles of Moorish pattern plain tiles were often made in which each separate tile, usually square, but at times rhomboidal or oblong, was of one colour, and such tiles were often used from quite early times down at least to the end of the seventeenth century.

More restricted in use were the beautiful embossed tiles found in the palace at Cintra, in which each has on it a raised green vine-leaf and tendril, or more rarely a dark bunch of grapes.

Towards the middle of the sixteenth century the Moorish technique of tilemaking, with its patterns marked off by raised edges, began to go out of fashion, and instead the patterns were outlined in dark blue and painted on to flat tiles. About the same time large pictures painted on tiles came into use, at first, as in the work of Francisco de Mattos, with scenes more or less in their natural colours, and later in the second half of the seventeenth century, and in the beginning of the eighteenth in blue on a white ground.

Towards the end of the eighteenth century blue seems to have usurped the place of all other colours, and from that time, especially in or near Oporto, tiles were used to mask all the exterior rubble walls of houses and churches, even spires or bulbous domes being sometimes so covered.

Now in Oporto nearly all the houses are so covered, usually with blue-and-white tiles, though on the more modern they may be embossed and pale green or yellow, sometimes even brown. But all the tiles from the beginning of the nineteenth century to the present day are marked by the poverty of the colour and of the pattern, and still more by the hard shiny glaze, which may be technically more perfect, but is infinitely inferior in beauty to the duller and softer glaze of the previous centuries.

When square tiles were used they were throughout 23 singularly uniform in size, being a little below or a little above five inches square. The ground is always white with a slightly blueish tinge. In the earlier tiles of Arab pattern the colours are blue, green, and brown; very rarely, and that in some of the oldest tiles, the pattern may be in black; yellow is scarcely ever seen. In those of Moorish technique but Western pattern, the most usual colours are blue, green, yellow and, more rarely, brown.

Later still in the flat tiles scarcely anything but blue and yellow are used, though the blue and the yellow may be of two shades, light and dark, golden and orange. Brown and green have almost disappeared, and, as was said above, so did yellow at last, leaving nothing but blue and white.

Although there are few buildings which do not possess some tiles, the oldest, those of Moorish design, are rare, and, the best collection is to be found in the old palace at Cintra, of which the greater part was built by Dom João I. towards the end of the fourteenth and the beginning of the fifteenth century.

12

Formerly all the piers of the old cathedral of Coimbra were covered with such tiles, but they have lately been swept away, and only those left which line the aisle walls.

At Cintra there are a few which it is supposed may have belonged to the palace of the Walis, or perhaps it would be safer to say to the palace before it was rebuilt by Dom João. These are found round a door leading out of a small room, called from the mermaids on the ceiling the *Sala das Sereias*. The pointed door is enclosed in a square frame by a band of narrow dark and light tiles with white squares between, arranged in checks, while in the spandrels is a very beautiful arabesque pattern in black on a white ground.

Of slightly later date are the azulejos of the so-called *Sala dos Arabes*, where the walls to a height of about six feet are lined with blue, green, and white tiles, the green being square and the other rhomboidal. Over the doors, which are pointed, a square framing is carried up, with tiles of various patterns in the spandrels, and above these frames, as round the whole walls, runs a very beautiful cresting two tiles high. On the lower row are interlacing semicircles in high relief forming foliated cusps and painted blue. In the spandrels formed by the interlacing of the semicircles are three green leaves growing out from a brown flower; in short the 24 design is exactly like a Gothic corbel table such as was used on Dom João's church at Batalha turned upside down, and so probably dates from his time. On the second row of tiles there are alternately a tall blue fleur-de-lys with a yellow centre, and a lower bunch of leaves, three blue at the top and one yellow on each side; the ground throughout is white. (Fig. 8.)

Also of Dom João's time are the tiles in the *Sala das Pegas*, where they are of the regular Moorish pattern—blue, green and brown on a white ground, and where four go to make up the pattern. The cresting of green scrolls and vases is much later.

Judging from the cresting in the dining-room or *Sala de Jantar*, where, except that the ground is brown relieved by large white stars, and that the cusps are green and not blue, the design is exactly the same as in the *Sala dos Arabes*, the tiles there must be at least as old as these crestings; for though older tiles might be given a more modern cresting, the reverse is hardly likely to occur, and if as old as the crestings they may possibly belong to Dom João's time, or at least to the middle of the fifteenth century. (Fig. 9.)

These dining-room tiles, and also those in the neighbouring *Sala das Sereias*, are among the most beautiful in the palace. The ground is as usual white, and on each is embossed a beautiful green vine-leaf with branches and tendril. Tiles similar, but with a bunch of grapes added, line part of the stair in the picturesque little *Pateo de Diana* near at hand, and form the top of the back of the tiled bench and throne in the *Sala do Conselho*, once an open veranda. Most of this bench is covered with tiles of Moorish design, but on the front each is stamped with an armillary sphere in which the axis is yellow, the lines of the equator and tropics green, and the rest blue. These one would certainly take to be of Dom Manoel's time, for the armillary sphere was his emblem, but they are said to be older.

Most of the floor tiles are of unglazed red, except some in the chapel, which are supposed to have formed the paving of the original mosque, and some in an upper room, worn smooth by the feet of Dom Affonso VI., who was imprisoned there for many a year in the seventeenth century.

When Dom Manoel was making his great addition to the palace in the early years of the sixteenth century he lined the walls of the *Sala dos Cysnes* with tiles forming a check of green and white. These are carried up over the doors and windows, and in places have a curious cresting of green cones like Moorish battlements, and of castles.

FIG. 8.
SALA DOS ARABES.
PALACE, CINTRA.
FROM A PHOTOGRAPH BY L. ORAM, CINTRA.
FIG. 9.
DINING-ROOM, OLD PALACE.
CINTRA.
FROM A PHOTOGRAPH BY L. ORAM, CINTRA.

25

13

Much older are the tiles in the central *Pateo*, also green and white, but forming a very curious pattern.

Of later tiles the palace also has some good examples, such as the hunting scenes with which the walls of the *Sala dos Brazões* were covered probably at the end of the seventeenth century, during the reign of Dom Pedro II.

The palace at Cintra may possess the finest collection of tiles, Moorish both in technique and in pattern, but it has few or none of the second class where the technique remains Moorish but the design is Western. To see such tiles in their greatest quantity and variety one must cross the Tagus and visit the Quinta de Bacalhôa not far from Setubal.

There a country house had been built in the last quarter of the fifteenth century by Dona Brites, the mother of Dom Manoel.[26] The house, with melon-roofed corner turrets, simple square windows and two loggias, has an almost classic appearance, and if built in its present shape in the time of Dona Brites, must be one of the earliest examples of the renaissance in the country. It has therefore been thought that Bacalhôa may be the mysterious palace built for Dom João II. by Andrea da Sansovino, which is mentioned by Vasari, but of which all trace has been lost. However, it seems more likely that it owes its classic windows to the younger Affonso de Albuquerque, son of the great Indian Viceroy, who bought the property in 1528. The house occupies one corner of a square garden enclosure, while opposite it is a large square tank with a long pavilion at its southern side. A path runs along the southern wall of the garden leading from the house to the tank, and all the way along this wall are tiled seats and tubs for orange-trees. It is on these tubs and seats that the greatest variety of tiles are found.

It would be quite impossible to give any detailed description of these tiles, the patterns are so numerous and so varied. In some the pattern is quite classical, in others it still shows traces of Moorish influence, while in some again the design is entirely naturalistic. This is especially the case in a pattern used in the lake pavilion, where eight large green leaves are arranged pointing to one centre, and four smaller brown ones 26 to another, and in a still more beautiful pattern used on an orange tub in the garden, where yellow and dark flowers, green and blue leaves are arranged in a circle round eight beautiful fruits shaped like golden pomegranates with blue seeds set among green leaves and stalks.

But these thirty or more patterns do not exhaust the interest of the Quinta. There are also some very fine tile pictures, especially one of 'Susanna and the Elders,' and a fragment of the 'Quarrel of the Lapithæ and Centaurs' in the pavilion overlooking the tank. 'Susanna and the Elders' is particularly good, and is interesting in that on a small temple in the background is the date 1565.[27] Rather later seem the five river gods in the garden loggia of the house, for their strapwork frames of blue and yellow can hardly be as early as 1565; besides, a fragment with similar details has on it the letters TOS, no doubt the end of the signature 'Francisco Mattos,' who also signed some beautiful tiles in the church of São Roque at Lisbon in 1584.

It is known that the entrance to the convent of the Madre de Deus at Lisbon was ornamented by Dom Manoel with some della Robbia reliefs, two of which are now in the Museum.

On the west side of the tank at Bacalhôa is a wall nearly a hundred feet long, and framed with tiles. In the centre the water flows into the tank from a dolphin above which is an empty niche. There are two other empty niches, one inscribed *Tempora labuntur more fluentis aquae*, and the other *Vivite victuri moneo mors omnibus instat*. These niches stand between four medallions of della Robbia ware, some eighteen inches across. Two are heads of men and two of women, only one of each being glazed. The glazed woman's head is white, with yellow hair, a sky-blue veil, and a loose reddish garment all on a blue ground. All are beautifully modelled and are surrounded by glazed wreaths of fruit and leaves. These four must certainly have come from the della Robbia factory in Florence, for they, and especially the surrounding wreaths, are exactly like what may be seen so often in North Italy.

Much less good are six smaller medallions, four of which are much destroyed, on the wall leading north from the tank to a pavilion named the *Casa da India*, so called from the [27] beautiful Indian hangings with which its walls were covered by Albuquerque. In them the modelling is less good and the wreaths are more conventional.

Lastly, between the tank and the house are twelve others, one under each of the globes, which, flanked by obelisks, crown the wall. They are all of the same size, but in some the head and the blue backing are not in one place. The wreaths also are inferior even to those of the last six, though the actual heads are rather better. They all represent famous men of old, from Alexander the Great to Nero. Two are broken; that of Augustus is signed with what may perhaps be read Doñus Vilhelmus, 'Master William,' who unfortunately is otherwise unknown.

It seems impossible now to tell where these were made, but they were certainly inspired by the four genuine Florentine medallions on the tank wall, and if by a native artist are of great interest as showing how men so skilled in making beautiful tiles could also copy the work of a great Italian school with considerable success.

Of the third class of tiles, those where the patterns are merely painted and not raised, there are few examples at Bacalhôa—except when some restoration has been done—for this manner of tile-painting did not become common till the next century, but there are a few with very good patterns in the house itself, and close by, the walls of the church of São Simão are covered with excellent examples. These were put up by the heads of a brotherhood in 1648, and are almost exactly the same as those in the church of Alvito; even the small saintly figures over the arches occur in both. The pattern of Alvito is one of the finest, and is found again at Santarem in the church of the Marvilla, where the lower tiles are all of singular beauty and splendid colouring, blue and yellow on a white ground. Other beautiful tiled interiors are those of the Matriz at Caldas da Rainha, and at Caminha on the Minho. Without seeing these tiled churches it is impossible to realise how beautiful they really are, and how different are these tiles from all modern ones, whose hard smooth glaze and mechanical perfection make them cold and anything but pleasing. (Figs. 10 and 11, *frontispiece*.)

Besides the picture-tiles at Bacalhôa there are some very good examples of similar work in the semicircular porch which surrounds the small round chapel of Sant' Amaro at [28] Alcantara close to Lisbon. The chapel was built in 1549, and the tiles added about thirty years later. Here, as in the Dominican nunnery at Elvas, and in some exquisite framings and steps at Bacalhôa, the pattern and architectural details are spread all over the tiles, often making a rich framing to a bishop or saint. Some are not at all unlike Francisco Mattos' work in São Roque, which is also well worthy of notice.

Of the latest pictorial tiles, the finest are perhaps those in the church of São João Evangelista at Evora, which tell of the life of San Lorenzo Giustiniani, Venetian Patriarch, and which are signed and dated 'Antoninus ab Oliva fecit 1711.'[28] But these blue picture-tiles are almost the commonest of all, and were made and used up to the end of the century.[29]

Now although some of the patterns used are found also in Spain, as at Seville or at Valencia, and although tiles from Seville were used at Thomar by João de Castilho, still it is certain that many were of home manufacture.

As might be expected from the patterns and technique of the oldest tiles, the first mentioned tilers are Moors.[30] Later there were as many as thirteen tilemakers in Lisbon, and many were made in the twenty-eight ovens of *louça de Veneza*, 'Venetian faience.' The tiles used by Dom Manoel at Cintra came from Belem, while as for the picture tiles the novices of the order of São Thiago at Palmella formed a school famous for such work.

Indeed it may be said that tilework is the most characteristic feature of Portuguese buildings, and that to it many a church, otherwise poor and even mean, owes whatever interest or beauty it possesses. Without tiles, rooms like the *Sala das Sereias* or the *Sala dos Arabes* would be plain whitewashed featureless apartments, with them they have a charm and a romance not easy to find anywhere but in the East. [29]

CHAPTER I
THE EARLY BUILDINGS IN THE NORTH

PORTUGAL, like all the other Christian kingdoms of the Peninsula, having begun in the north, first as a county or march land subject to the king of Galicia or of Leon, and later, since 1139, as an independent kingdom, it is but natural to find nearly all the oldest buildings in those parts of the country which, earliest freed from the Moslem dominion, formed the original county. The province of Entre Minho-e-Douro has always been held by the Portuguese to be the most beautiful part of their country, and it would be difficult to find anywhere valleys more beautiful than those of the Lima, the Cavado, or the Ave. Except the mountain range of the Marão which divides this province from the wilder and drier Tras-os-Montes, or the Gerez which separates the upper waters of the Cavado and of the Lima, and at the same time forms part of the northern frontier of Portugal, the hills are nowhere of great height. They are all well covered with woods, mostly of pine, and wherever a piece of tolerably level ground can be found they are cultivated with the care of a garden. All along the valleys, and even high up the hillsides among the huge granite boulders, there is a continuous succession of small villages. Many of these, lying far from railway or highroad, can only be reached by narrow and uneven paths, along which no carriage can pass except the heavy creaking carts drawn by the beautiful large long-horned oxen whose broad and splendidly carved yokes are so remarkable a feature of the country lying between the Vouga and the Cavado.[31] In many of these villages may still be seen churches 30 built soon after the expulsion of the Moors, and long before the establishment of the Monarchy. Many of them originally belonged to some monastic body. Of these the larger part have been altered and spoiled during the seventeenth or eighteenth centuries, when, after the expulsion of the Spaniards, the country began again to grow rich from trade with the recovered colony of Brazil. Still enough remains to show that these old romanesque churches differed in no very striking way from the general romanesque introduced into Northern Spain from France, except that as a rule they were smaller and ruder, and were but seldom vaulted.

That these early churches should be rude is not surprising. They are built of hard grey granite. When they were built the land was still liable to incursions, and raids from the south, such as the famous foray of Almansor, who harried and burned the whole land not sparing even the shrine of Santiago far north in Galicia. Their builders were still little more than a race of hardy soldiers with no great skill in the working of stone. Only towards the end of the twelfth century, long after the border had been advanced beyond the Mondego and after Coimbra had become the capital of a new county, did the greater security as well as the very fine limestone of the lower Mondego valley make it possible for churches to be built at Coimbra which show a marked advance in construction as well as in elaboration of detail. Between the Mondego and the Tagus there are only four or five churches which can be called romanesque, and south of the Tagus only the cathedral of Evora, begun about 1186 and consecrated some eighteen years later, is romanesque, constructively at least, though all its arches have become pointed.

But to return north to Entre Minho-e-Douro, where the oldest and most numerous romanesque churches exist and where three types may be seen. Of these the simplest and probably the oldest is that of an aisleless nave with simple square chancel. In the second the nave has one or two aisles, and at the end of these aisles a semicircular apse, but with the chancel still square: while in the third and latest the plan has been further developed and enlarged, though even here the main chancel generally still remains square. 31

Villarinho.

There yet exist, not far from Oporto, a considerable number of examples of the first type, though several by their pointed doorways show that they actually belong, in part at least, to the period of the Transition. One of the best-preserved is the small church of Villarinho, not far from Vizella in the valley of the Ave. Originally the church of a small monastery, it has long been the parish church of a mountain hamlet, and till it was lately whitewashed inside had scarcely been touched since the day it was finished some time before the end of the twelfth century. It consists of a rather high and narrow nave, a square-ended chancel, and to the west a lower narthex nearly as large as the chancel. The church is lit by very small windows which are indeed mere slits, and by a small round opening in the gable above the narthex.[32] The narthex is entered by a perfectly plain round-headed door with strong impost and drip-mould, while above the corbels which once carried the roof of a lean-to porch, a small circle enclosing a rude unglazed quatrefoil serves as the only window. The door leading from the narthex to the nave is much more elaborate; of four orders of mouldings, the two inner are plain, the two outer have a big roll at the angle, and all are slightly pointed. Except the outermost, which springs from square jambs, they all stand on the good romanesque capitals of six shafts, four round and two octagonal. (Fig. 12.)

São Miguel, Guimarães.

Exactly similar in plan but without a narthex is the church of São Miguel at Guimarães, famous as being the church in which Affonso Henriques, the first king of Portugal, was baptized in 1111. It claims to have been the *Primaz* or chief church of the whole archdiocese of Braga. It is, like Villarinho, a small and very plain church built of great blocks of granite, with a nave and square chancel lit by narrow window slits. On the north side there are a plain square-headed doorway and two bold round arches let into the outer wall over the graves of some great men of these distant times. The drip-mould of one of these arches is carved with a shallow zigzag ornament which is repeated on the western door, a door whose slightly pointed arch may mean a rather later date than the rest of the church. The wooden roof, as at Villarinho, has a very gentle slope with eaves of considerable projection[32] resting on very large plain corbels, while other corbels lower down the wall seem to show that at one time a veranda or cloister ran round three sides of the building. The whole is even ruder and simpler than Villarinho, but has a certain amount of dignity due to the great size of the stones of which it is built and to the severe plainness of the walling.

Cedo Feita, Oporto.

Only one other church of this type need be described, and that because it is the only one which is vaulted throughout. This is the small church of São Martim de Cedo Feita or 'Early made' at Oporto itself. It is so called because it claims, wrongly indeed, to be the very church which Theodomir, king of the Suevi, who then occupied the north-west of the Peninsula, hurriedly built in 559 A.D. This he did in order that, having been converted from the Arian beliefs he shared with all the Germanic invaders of the Empire, he might there be baptized into the Catholic faith, and also that he might provide a suitable resting-place for some relic of St. Martin of Tours which had been sent to him as a mark of Orthodox approval. This story[33] is set forth in a long inscription on the tympanum of the west door stating that it was put there in 1767, a copy taken in 1557 from an old stone having then been found in the archives of the church. As a matter of fact no part of the church can be older than the twelfth century, and it has been much altered, probably at the date when the inscription was cut. It is a small building, a barrel-vaulted nave and chancel, with a door on the north side and a larger one to the west now covered by a large porch. The six capitals of this door are very like those at Villarinho, but the moulded arches are round and not as there pointed.

Other churches of this type are Gandara and Boelhe near Penafiel, and Eja not far off—a building of rather later date with a fine pointed chancel arch elaborately carved with foliage—São Thiago d'Antas, near Familicão, a slightly larger church with good capitals to the chancel arch, a good south door and another later west door with traceried round window above; and São Torquato, near Guimarães, rather larger, having once had transepts of which one survives, with square chancel and square chapels to the east; one of the simplest of all having no ornament beyond the corbel table and the small slitlike windows.

FIG. 12.	FIG. 13.
CHURCH AT VILLARINHO.	VILLAR DE FRADES. W. DOOR.

[33] South of the Douro, but still built of granite, are a group of three or four small churches at Trancoso. Another close to Guarda has a much richer corbel table with a large ball ornament on the cornice and a round window filled with curiously built-up tracery above the plain, round-arched west door, while further south on the castle hill at Leiria are the ruins of the small church of São Pedro built of fine limestone with a good west door.

Aguas Santas.

Of the second and rather larger type there are fewer examples still remaining, and of these perhaps the best is the church of Aguas Santas some seven miles north-east of Oporto.

Originally the church consisted of a nave with rectangular chancel and a north aisle with an eastern apse roofed with a semi-dome. Later a tower with battlemented top and low square spire was built at the west end of the aisle, and some thirty years ago another aisle was added on the south side. As in most of the smaller churches the chancel is lower than the nave, leaving room above its roof for a large round window, now filled up except for a small traceried circle in the centre. The most highly decorated part is the chancel, which like all the rest of the church has a good corbel table, and about two-thirds of the way up a string course richly covered with billet moulding. Interrupting this on the south side are two round-headed windows, still small but much larger than the slits found in the older churches. In each case, in a round-headed opening there stand two small shafts with bases and elaborately carved capitals but without any abaci, supporting a large roll moulding, and these are all repeated inside at the inner face of a deep splay. In one of these windows not only are the capitals covered with intertwined ribbon-work, but each shaft is covered with interknotted circles enclosing flowers, and there is a band of interlacing work round the head of the actual window opening. Inside the church has been more altered. Formerly the aisle was separated from the nave by two arches, but when the south aisle was built the central pier was taken out and the two arches thrown into one large and elliptical arch, but the 34 capitals of the chancel arch and the few others that remain are all well wrought and well designed. The west door is a good simple example of the first pointed period, with plain moulded arches and shafts which bear simple French-looking capitals. Other churches of the same class are those of São Christovão do Rio Mau not far from Villo do Conde, and São Pedro de Rates, a little further up the Ave at the birthplace of the first bishop of Braga and earliest martyr of Portugal. São Pedro is a little later, as the aisle arches are all pointed, and is a small basilica of nave and aisles with short transepts, chancel and eastern chapels.

Villar de Frades.

The two earliest examples of the third and most highly developed type, the church of Villar de Frades and the cathedral of Braga, have unfortunately both suffered so terribly, the one from destruction and the other from rebuilding, that not much has been left to show what they were originally like—barely enough to make it clear that they were much more elaborately decorated, and that their carved work was much better wrought than in any of the smaller churches already mentioned. A short distance to the south of the river Cavado and about half-way between Braga and Barcellos, in a well-watered and well-wooded region, there existed from very early Christian times a monastery called Villar, and later Villar de Frades. During the troubles and disorders which followed the Moslem invasion, this Benedictine monastery had fallen into complete decay and so remained till it was restored in 1070 by Godinho Viegas. Although again founded some centuries later and refounded in 1425 as the mother house of a new order—the Loyos—the fifteenth-century church was so built as to leave at least a part of the front of the old ruined church standing between itself and the monastic building, as well as the ruins of an apse behind. Probably this old west front was the last part of Godinho's church to be built, but it is certainly more or less contemporary with some portions of the cathedral of Braga.

At some period, which the legend leaves quite uncertain, one of the monks of this monastery was one day in the choir at matins, when they came to that Psalm where it is said that 'a thousand years in the sight of God are but as yesterday when it is gone,' and the old monk wondered greatly and began to think what that could mean. When matins were over he remained praying as was his wont, and begged Our Lord to 35 give him some understanding of that verse. Then there appeared to him a little bird which, singing most sweetly, flew this way and that, and so little by little drew him towards a wood which grew near the monastery, and there rested on a tree while the servant of God stood below to listen. After what seemed to the monk a short time it took flight, to the great sorrow of God's servant, who said, 'Bird of my Soul, where art thou gone so soon?' He waited, and when he saw that it did not return he went back to the monastery thinking it still that same morning on which he had come out after matins. When he arrived he found the door, through which he had come, built up and a new one opened in another place. The porter asked who he was and what he wanted, and he answered, 'I am the sacristan who a few

18

hours ago went out, and now returning find all changed.' He gave too the names of the Abbot and of the Prior, and wondered much that the porter still would not let him in, and seemed not to remember these names. At last he was led to the Abbot, but they did not know one another, so that the good monk was all confused and amazed at so strange an event. Then the Abbot, enlightened of God, sent for the annals and histories of the order, found there the names the old man had given, so making it clear that more than three hundred years had passed since he had gone out. He told them all that had happened to him, was received as a brother; and after praising God for the great marvel which had befallen him, asked for the sacraments and soon passed from this life in great peace.[34]

Whether the ruined west front of the older church be that which existed when the bird flew out through the door or not, it is or has been of very considerable beauty. Built, like everything else in the north, of granite, all that is now left is a high wall of carefully wrought stone. Below is a fine round arched door of considerable size, now roughly blocked up. It has three square orders covered with carving and a plain inner one. First is a wide drip-mould carved on the outer side with a zigzag threefold ribbon, and on the inner with three rows of what looks like a rude attempt to copy the classic bead-moulding; then the first order, of thirteen voussoirs, each with the 36 curious figure of a strangely dressed man or with a distorted monster. This with the drip-mould springs from a billet-moulded abacus resting on broad square piers. Of the two inner carved orders, the outer is covered on both faces with innumerable animals and birds, and the other with a delicate pattern of interlacing bands. These two spring from strange square abaci resting on the carved capitals of round shafts, two on each side. A few feet above the door runs a billet-moulded string course, and two or three feet higher another and slighter course. On this stands a large window of two orders. Of these the outer covered with animals springs from shafts and capitals very like those of the doorway, and the inner has a billet-moulded edge and an almost Celtic ornament on the face. Now whether Villar be older than the smaller buildings in the neighbourhood or not, it is undoubtedly quite different not only in style but in execution. It is not only much larger and higher, but it is better built and the carving is finer and more carefully wrought. (Fig. 13.)

It is known that the great cathedral of Santiago in Galicia was begun in 1078, just about the time Villar must have been building, and Santiago is an almost exact copy in granite of what the great abbey church of S. Sernin at Toulouse was intended to be, so that it may be assumed that Bernardo who built the cathedral was, if not a native of Toulouse, at any rate very well acquainted with what was being done there. If, then, a native of Languedoc was called in to plan so important a church in Galicia, it is not unlikely that other foreigners were also employed in the county of Portugal—at that time still a part of Galicia; and in fact many churches in the south-west of what is now France have doorways and windows whose general design is very like that at Villar de Frades, if allowance be made for the difference of material, granite here, fine limestone there, and for a comparative want of skill in the workmen.[35]

Sé, Braga.

Probably these foreigners were not invited to Portugal for the sake of the church of a remote abbey like Villar, but to work at the metropolitan cathedral of Braga. The see of Braga is said to have been founded by São Pedro de Rates, a disciple of St. James himself, and in consequence of so distinguished an origin its archbishops claim the primacy not only 37 of all Portugal, but even of all the Spains, a claim which is of course disputed by the patriarch of Lisbon, not to speak of the archbishops of Toledo and of Tarragona. However that may be, the cathedral of Braga is not now, and can never have been, quite worthy of such high pretensions. It is now a church with a nave and aisles of six bays, a transept with four square chapels to the east, a chancel projecting beyond the chapels, and at the west two towers with the main door between and a fine porch beyond.

Count Henry of Burgundy married Dona Theresa and received the earldom of Portugal from his father-in-law, Alfonso VI. of Castile and Leon, in 1095, and he and his wife rebuilt the cathedral—where they now lie buried—before the end of the century. By that time it may well have become usual, if the churches were important, to call in a

19

foreigner to oversee its erection. Of the original building little now remains but the plan and two doorways, the chancel having been rebuilt and the porch added in the sixteenth, and the whole interior beplastered and bepainted in the worst possible style in the seventeenth, century. Of the two doors the western has been very like that at Villar. It has only two orders left, of which the outer, though under a deep arch, has a billet-moulded drip-mould, and its voussoirs each carved with a figure on the outer and delicate flutings on the under side, while the inner has on both faces animals and monsters which, better wrought than those at Villar, are even more like so many in the south-west of France. The other doorway, on the south side next the south-west tower, is far better preserved. It has three shafts on each side, all with good capitals and abaci, from which spring two carved and one plain arch. The outer has a rich drip-mould covered with a curious triple arrangement of circles, has flutings on the one face and a twisting ribbon on the other, while the next has leaf flutings on both faces, and both a roll-moulding on the angle. The inner order is quite plain, but the tympanum has in the centre a circle enclosing a cross with expanding arms, the spaces between the arms and the circle being pierced and the whole surrounded with intertwining ribbons.

Sé, Oporto.

Another foundation of Count Henry's was the cathedral of Oporto, which, judging from its plan, must have been very like that of Braga, but it has been so horribly transformed during the seventeenth and eighteenth centuries that nothing now remains of the original building but part of the walls;[38] for the fine western rose window must have been inserted about the middle of the thirteenth century.

Paço de Souza.

Except the tragedy of Inez de Castro, there is no story in Portuguese history more popular or more often represented in the engravings which adorn a country inn dining-room than that of the surrender of Egas Moniz to Alfonso VII. of Castile and Leon, when his pupil Affonso Henriques, beginning to govern for himself, refused to fulfil the agreement[36] whereby Egas had induced Alfonso to raise the siege of the castle of Guimarães. And it is the fact that the church of São Salvador at Paço de Souza contains his tomb, which adds not a little to the interest of the best-preserved of the churches of the third type. Egas Moniz died in 1144, and at least the eastern part of the church may have existed before then. The chancel, where the tomb first stood, is rather long and has as usual a square east end while the two flanking chapels are apsidal. The rest of the church, which may be a little later, as all the larger arches are pointed, consists of a nave and aisles of three bays, a transept, and a later tower standing on the westernmost bay of the south aisle. The constructive scheme of the inside is interesting, though a modern boarded vault has done its best to hide what it formerly was. The piers are cross-shaped with a big semicircular shaft on each face, and a large roll-moulding on each angle which is continued up above the abacus to form an outer order for both the aisle and the main arches, for large arches are carried across the nave and aisles from north to south as if it had been intended to roof the church with an ordinary groined vault. However, it is clear that this was not really the case, and indeed it could hardly have been so as practically no vaults had yet been built in the country except a few small barrels. Indeed, though later the Portuguese became very skilful at vaulting, they were at no time fond of a nave with high groined vault upheld by flying buttresses, and low aisles, for there seems to have been never more than three or four in the country, one of which, the choir of Lisbon Cathedral, fell in 1755. Instead of groined vaults, barrel vaults continued to be used where a stone roof was wanted, even till the middle of the fourteenth century and later, long after they had been given up elsewhere, but usually a roof of wood was thought sufficient, sometimes resting, as was formerly the[39] case here, on transverse arches thrown across the nave and aisles. This was the system adopted in the cathedrals of Braga and of Oporto before they were altered, in this church and in that of Pombeiro not far off, and in that of Bayona near Vigo in Galicia.[37] (Fig. 14.)

All the details are extremely refined—almost Byzantine in their delicacy—especially the capitals, and the abaci against the walls, which are carried along as a beautiful string course from pier to pier. The bases too are all carved, some with animals' heads and some with small seated figures at the angles, while the faces of the square blocks below are covered with beautiful leaf ornament. But the most curious thing in the whole church is the tomb of Egas Moniz himself.[38] (Fig. 15.) Till the eighteenth century it stood in the middle of the chancel, then it was cut in two and put half against the wall of the south aisle, and half against that of the north. It has on it three bands of ornament. Of these the lowest is a rudely carved chevron with what are meant for leaves between, the next, a band of small figures including Egas on his deathbed and what is supposed to be three of his children riding side by side on an elongated horse with a camel-like head, and that on the top, larger figures showing him starting on his fateful journey to the court of Alfonso of Castile and Leon and parting from his weeping wife. Although very rude,—all the horses except that of Egas himself having most unhorselike heads and legs,—some of the figures are carved with a certain not unpleasing vigour, especially that of a spear-bearing attendant who marches with swinging skirts behind his master's horse. Outside the most remarkable feature is the fine west door, with its eight shafts, four on each side, some round and some octagonal, the octagonal being enriched with an ornament like the English dog-tooth, with their finely carved cubical capitals and rich abaci, and with the four orders of mouldings, two of which are enriched with ball ornament. Outside, instead of a drip-mould, runs a broad band covered with plaited ribbon. On the tympanum, 40 which rests on corbels supported on one side by the head of an ox and on the other by that of a man, are a large circle enclosing a modern inscription, and two smaller circles in which are the symbols of the Sun and Moon upheld by curious little half-figures. The two apses east of the transept are of the pattern universal in Southern Europe, being divided into three equal parts by half-shafts with capitals and crowned with an overhanging corbel table.

Pombeiro.

The abbey church of Pombeiro, near Guimarães, must once have been very similar to São Salvador at Paço de Souza, except that the nave is a good deal longer, and that it once had a large narthex, destroyed about a hundred and fifty years ago by an abbot who wished to add to the west front the two towers and square spires which still exist. So full was this narthex of tombs that from the arms on them it had become a sort of Heralds' College for the whole of the north of Portugal, but now only two remain in the shallow renaissance porch between the towers. As at Paço de Souza, the oldest part of the church is the east end, where the two apses flanking the square chancel remain unaltered. They are divided as usual by semicircular shafts bearing good romanesque capitals, and crowned by a cornice of three small arches to each division, each cut out of one stone, and resting on corbels and on the capitals. Of the west front only the fine doorway is left unchanged; pointed in shape, but romanesque in detail; having three of the five orders, carved one with grotesque animals and two with leafage. Above the shallow porch is a large round window with renaissance tracery, but retaining its original framing of a round arch resting on tall shafts with romanesque capitals. Everything else has been altered, the inside being covered with elaborate rococo painted and gilt plaster-work, and the outside disfigured by shapeless rococo windows.

Although some, and especially the last two of the buildings described above belong, in part at least, to the time of transition from romanesque to first pointed, and although the group of churches at Coimbra are wholly romanesque, it would be better to have done with all that can be ascribed to a period older than the beginning of the Portuguese monarchy before following Affonso Henriques in his successful efforts to extend his kingdom southwards to the Tagus.

FIG. 14.	FIG. 15.
CHURCH, PAÇO DE SOUZA. NAVE.	PAÇO DE SOUZA. TOMB OF EGAS MONIZ.
Guimarães, Castle.	

Although Braga was the ecclesiastical capital of their fief, 41 Count Henry and his wife lived usually at Guimarães, a small town some fifteen miles to the south. Towards the beginning of the tenth century there died D. Hermengildo Gonçalves Mendes, count of Tuy and Porto, who by his will left Vimaranes, as it was then called, to his widow, Mumadona. About 927 she there founded a monastery and built a castle for its defence, and this castle, which had twice suffered from Moslem invaders, was restored or rebuilt by Count Henry, and there in 1111 was born his son Affonso Henriques, who was later to become the first king of the new and independent kingdom of Portugal. Henry died soon after, in 1114, at Astorga, perhaps poisoned by his sister-in-law, Urraca, queen of Castile and Leon, and for several years his widow governed his lands as guardian for their son.

Thirteen years after Count Henry's death, in 1127, the castle was the scene of the famous submission of Egas Moniz to the Spanish king, and this, together with the fact that Affonso Henriques was born there, has given it a place in the romantic history of Portugal which is rather higher than what would seem due to a not very important building. The castle stands to the north of the town on a height which commands all the surrounding country. Its walls, defended at intervals by square towers, are built among and on the top of enormous granite boulders, and enclose an irregular space in which stands the keep. The inhabited part of the castle ran along the north-western wall where it stood highest above the land below, but it has mostly perished, leaving only a few windows which are too large to date from the beginning of the twelfth century. The square keep stands within a few feet of the western wall, rises high above it, and was reached by a drawbridge from the walk on the top of the castle walls. Its wooden floors are gone, its windows are mere slits, and like the rest of the castle it owes its distinctive appearance to the battlements which crown the whole building, and whose merlons are plain blocks of stone brought to a sharp point at the top. This feature, which is found in all the oldest Portuguese castles such as that of Almourol on an island in the Tagus near Abrantes, and even on some churches such as the old cathedral at Coimbra and the later church at Leça de Balio, is one of the most distinct legacies left by the Moors: here the front of each merlon is perpendicular to the top, but more usually it is finished in a small sharp pyramid. 42

Church.

The other foundation of Mumadona, the monastery of Nossa Senhora and São Salvador in the town of Guimarães, had since her day twice suffered destruction at the hands of the Moors, once in 967 when the castle was taken by Al-Coraxi, emir of Seville, and thirty years later when Almansor[39] in 998 swept northwards towards Galicia, sacking and burning as he went. At the time when Count Henry and Dona Teresa were living in the castle, the double Benedictine monastery for men and women had fallen into decay, and in 1109 Count Henry got a Papal Bull changing the foundation into a royal collegiate church under a Dom Prior, and at once began to rebuild it, a restoration which was not finished till 1172. Since then the church has been wholly and the cloisters partly rebuilt by João I. at the end of the fourteenth century, but some arches of the cloister and the entrance to the chapter-house may very likely date from Count Henry's time. These cloisters occupy a very unusual position. Starting from the north transept they run round the back of the chancel, along the south side of the church outside the transept, and finally join the church again near the west front. The large round arches have chamfered edges; the columns are monoliths of granite about eighteen inches thick; the bases and the abaci all romanesque in form, though many of the capitals, as can be seen from their shape and carving, are of the fourteenth or even fifteenth century, showing how Juan Garcia de Toledo, who rebuilt the church for Dom João I., tried, in restoring the cloister, to copy the already existing features and as usual betrayed the real date by his later details. A few of the old capitals still remain, and are of good romanesque form such as may be seen in any part of southern France or in Spain.[40] To the chapter-house, a plain oblong room with a panelled wood ceiling, there leads, from the east cloister walk, an unaltered archway, flanked as usual by two openings, one on either side. The doorway arch is plain, slightly horseshoe in shape, and is carried by short strong half-columns whose capitals are elaborately carved with animals and twisting branches, the animals, as is often the case,

FIG. 16.	**FIG. 17.**
DOOR OF CHAPTER HOUSE, N.S. DA OLIVEIRA. GUIMARÃES.	**CLOISTER. LEÇA DO BALIO.**

43 being set back to back at the angles so that one head does duty for each pair. Above is a large hollow hood-mould exactly similar to those which enclose the side

windows. The two lights of these windows are separated by short coupled shafts whose capitals, derived from the Corinthian or Composite, have stiff leaves covering the change from the round to the square, and between them broad tendrils which end in very carefully cut volutes at the angles. The heads themselves are markedly horseshoe in shape, which at first sight suggests some Moorish influence, but in everything else the details are so thoroughly Western, and by 1109 such a long time, over a hundred years, had passed since the Moors had been permanently expelled from that part of the country, that it were better to see in these horseshoes an unskilled attempt at stilting, rather than the work of some one familiar with Eastern forms. (Fig. 16.) 44

CHAPTER II
THE EARLY BUILDINGS IN THE SOUTH

IN 1057 Fernando, king of Castile, Leon and Galicia crossed the Douro, took Lamego, where the lower part of the tower is all that is left of the romanesque cathedral, and is indeed the only romanesque tower in the country. Vizeu fell soon after, and seven years later he advanced his borders to the Mondego by the capture of Coimbra. The Mondego, the only large river whose source and mouth are both in Portugal, long remained the limit of the Christian dominion, and nearly a hundred years were to pass before any further advance was made. In 1147 Affonso Henriques, who had but lately assumed the title of king, convinced at last that he was wasting his strength in trying to seize part of his cousin's dominions of Galicia, determined to turn south and extend his new kingdom in that direction. Accordingly in March of that year he secretly led his army against Santarem, one of the strongest of the Moorish cities standing high above the Tagus on an isolated hill. The vezir, Abu-Zakariah, was surprised before he could provision the town, so that the garrison were able to offer but a feeble resistance, and the Christians entered after the attack had lasted only a few days. Before starting the king had vowed that if successful he would found a monastery in token of his gratitude, and though its vast domestic buildings are now but barracks and court-houses, the great Cistercian abbey of Alcobaça still stands to show how well his vow was fulfilled.

Although Santarem was taken in 1147, the first stone of Alcobaça was not laid till 1153, and the building was carried out very slowly and in a style, imported directly from France, quite foreign to any previous work in Portugal. It were better, therefore, before coming to this, the largest church and the richest foundation in the whole country, to have done 45 with the other churches which though contemporary with Alcobaça are not the work of French but of native workmen, or at least of such as had not gone further than to Galicia for their models.

Sé, Lisbon.

The same year that saw the fall of Santarem saw also the more important capture of Lisbon. Taken by the Moors in 714, it had long been their capital, and although thrice captured by the Christians had always been recovered. In this enterprise Affonso Henriques was helped by a body of Crusaders, mostly English, who sailing from Dartmouth were persuaded by the bishop of Oporto to begin their Holy War in Portugal, and when Lisbon fell, one of them, Gilbert of Hastings, was rewarded by being made its first bishop. Of the cathedral, begun three years later, in 1150, little but the plan of the nave and transept has survived. Much injured by an earthquake in 1344, the whole choir was rebuilt on a French model by Affonso IV. only to be again destroyed in 1755. The original plan must have been very like that of Braga, an aisleless transept, a nave and aisles of six bays, and two square towers beyond with a porch between. The two towers are now very plain with large belfry windows near the top, but there are traces here and there of old built-up round-headed openings which show that the walls at least are really old. The outer arch of the porch has been rebuilt since the earthquake, but the original door remains inside, with a carved hood-mould, rich abacus, and four orders of mouldings enriched with small balls in their hollows. The eight plain shafts stand on unusually high pedestals and have rather long capitals, some carved with flat acanthus leaves and some with small figures of men and animals.

Like that of the cathedral of Coimbra, which was being built about the same time, the inside is clearly founded on the great cathedral of Santiago, itself a copy of S. Sernin at

Toulouse, and quite uninfluenced by the French design of Alcobaça. The piers are square with a half-shaft on each face, the arches are round, and the aisles covered with plain unribbed fourpart vaulting, while the main aisle is roofed with a round barrel. Instead of the large open gallery, which at Santiago allows the quadrant vault supporting the central barrel to be seen, there is here a low blind arcade of small round arches. Unfortunately, when restored after the disaster of 1755 the whole inside was plastered, all the capitals both of the main 46

PLAN OF CATHEDRAL, LISBON

piers and of the gallery were converted into a semblance of gilt Corinthian capitals, and large skylights were cut through the vault. Only the inside of the low octagonal lantern remains to show that the church must have been at least as interesting, if not more so, than the Sé Velha or old cathedral at Coimbra. If the nave has suffered such a transformation the fourteenth-century 47 choir has been even worse treated. The whole upper part, which once was as high as the top of the lantern, fell and was re-roofed in a most miserable manner, having only the ambulatory and its chapels uninjured. But these, the cloister and a rather fine chapel to the north-west of the nave, had better be left for another chapter.[41]

Sé Velha, Coimbra.

PLAN OF CATHEDRAL, COIMBRA

Smaller but much better preserved than Lisbon Cathedral is the Sé Velha or old cathedral of Coimbra. According to the local tradition, the cathedral is but a mosque turned into a church after the Christian conquest, and it may well be that in the time of Dom Sesnando, the first governor of Coimbra—a Moor who, becoming a Christian, was made count of Coimbra by King Fernando, and whose tomb, broken open by the French, may still be seen outside the north wall of the church—the chief mosque of the town was used as the cathedral. But although an Arab inscription[42] is built into the outer wall of the nave, there can be no doubt that the present building is as Christian in plan and design as any church can be. If the nave of the cathedral of Lisbon is like Santiago in construction, the nave here is, on a reduced scale, undoubtedly a copy of Santiago not only constructively but also in its general details. The piers are shorter but of the same plan, the great triforium gallery looks towards the nave, as at Santiago and at Toulouse, by a double opening whose arches spring from single shafts at the sides to rest on double shafts in the centre, both being enclosed under one larger arch, while the barrel vault and the supporting vaults of the gallery are exactly similar. Now Santiago was practically finished in 1128, and there still exists a book called the *Livro Preto* in which is given a list of the gifts made by Dom Miguel, who ruled the see of Coimbra from 1162 to 1176, towards the building and 48 adorning of the church. Nothing is said as to when the church was begun, but we are told that Dom Miguel gave 124 morabitinos to Master Bernardo[43] who had directed the building for ten years; the presents too of bread and wine made to his successor Soeiro are also mentioned, so that it seems probable that the church may have been begun soon after Dom Miguel became bishop, and that it was finished some time before the end of his episcopate.

Though the nave is like that of Santiago, the transepts and choir are much simpler. There the transept is long and has an aisle on each side; here it is short and aisleless. There the choir is deep with a surrounding aisle and radiating chapels, here it is a simple apse flanked by two smaller apses. Indeed throughout the whole of the Peninsula the French east end was seldom used except in churches of a distinctly foreign origin, such as Santiago, Leon or Toledo in Spain, or Alcobaça in Portugal, and so it is natural here to find Bernardo rejecting the elaboration and difficult construction of his model, and returning to the simpler plan which had already been so often used in the north. (Fig. 18.)

Inside the piers are square with four half-shafts, one of which runs up in front to carry the barrel vault, which is about sixty feet high. All the capitals are well carved, and a moulded string which runs along under the gallery is curiously returned against the vaulting shafts as if it had once been carried round them and had afterwards been cut off. Almost the only light in the nave comes from small openings in the galleries, the aisle windows being nearly all blocked up by later altars, and from a large window at the west end. The transept on the other hand is very light, with several windows at either end, and eight in the square lantern, so that the effect is extremely good of the dark nave followed by the brilliant transept and ending in a great carved and gilt reredos. This reredos, reaching up to the blue-and-gold apse vault, was given to the cathedral in 1508 by Bishop D. Jorge d'Almeida, and was the work of 'Master 49 Vlimer a Framengo,' that is, a Fleming, and of his partner, João D'ipri, or of Ypres, two of the many foreigners who at that time worked for King D. Manoel. There are several picturesque tombs in the church, especially two in the north-east corner of the transept, whose recesses still retain their original tile decoration. Later tiles still cover the aisle walls and altar recesses, but beautiful examples of the Mozárabe or Moorish style which once covered the piers of the nave, as well as the wooden choir gallery with its finely panelled under side, have been swept away by a recent well-meaning if mistaken restoration. The outside of the church is more unusual than the inside. The two remaining original apses are much hidden by the sacristy, built probably by Bishop Jorge de Castello Branco in 1593, but in their details they are greatly like those of the church of San Isidoro at Leon, and being like it built of fine limestone, are much more delicately ornamented than are those of any of the granite churches further north. The side aisles are but little lower than the central aisle or than the transepts, and are all crowned with battlements very like those on the castle of Guimarães. The buttresses are only shallow strips, which in the transepts are united by round arches, but in the aisles end among the battlements in a larger merlon. The west front is the most striking and original part of the whole church. Below, at the sides, a perfectly plain window lights the aisles, some feet above it runs a string course, on which stands a small two-light window for the gallery, flanked by larger blind arches, and then many feet of blank walling ending in battlements. Between these two aisle ends there projects about ten feet a large doorway or porch. This doorway is of considerable size; some of its eight shafts are curiously twisted and carved, its capitals are very refined and elaborate, and its arches well moulded with, as at Lisbon, small bosses in the hollows. The abacus is plain, and the broad pilasters which carry the outermost order are beautifully carved on the broader face with a small running pattern of leaves. The same 'black book' which tells of the bishop's gifts to the church, tells how a certain Master Robert came four times from Lisbon to perfect the work of the door, and how each time he received seven morabitinos, besides ten for his expenses, as well as bread, wine and meat for his four apprentices and food for his four asses. It is not often that the name of a man who worked on 50 a mediæval church has been so preserved, and it is worth noticing that the west door at Lisbon has on it exactly the same ball ornament as that with which Master Robert and his four helpers enriched the archway here. Above the door runs an arched corbel table on which stands the one large window which the church possesses. This window,|44| which is much more like a door than a window, is deeply recessed within four orders of mouldings, resting on shafts and capitals, four on each side, all very like the door below. Above, the whole projection is carried up higher than the battlements in an oblong embattled belfry, having two arched openings in front and one at the side, added in 1837 to take the place of a detached belfry which once stood to the south of the church, and to hold some bells brought from Thomar after that rich convent had been suppressed. (Fig. 19.)

Of the two other doorways, that at the end of the north transept, which has a simple archway on either side, and is surmounted by an arcade of five arches, has been altered in the early sixteenth century with good details of the first French renaissance, while the larger doorway in the third bay of the nave has at the same time been rebuilt as a beautiful three-storied porch, reaching right up to the battlements. To the south lie the cloisters, added about the end of the thirteenth century, but now very much mutilated. They are of the usual Portuguese type of vaulted cloister, a large arch, here pointed, enclosing two round arches below with a circular opening above.

The central lantern—the only romanesque example surviving except that of Lisbon Cathedral—is square, and not as there octagonal. It has two round-headed windows on each side whose sills are but little above the level of the flat roof—for, like almost all vaulted churches in Portugal, the roofs are flat and paved—and is now crowned by a picturesque dome covered with many-coloured tiles.

Somewhat older than the cathedral, but not unlike it, was the church of São Christovão now destroyed, while São Thiago still has a west door whose shafts are even more elaborately carved and twisted than are those at the Sé Velha.[45]

There is more than one building, such as the Templar

FIG. 18.   **FIG. 19.**
COIMBRA.   **COIMBRA.**
SÉ VELHA.   **WEST FRONT OF SÉ VELHA.**

[51] church at Thomar, older than the cathedral of Evora, and indeed older than the Sé Velha at Coimbra; but Evora, except that its arches are pointed instead of round, is so clearly derived directly from the Sé at Lisbon that it must be mentioned next in order.

Sé, Evora.

Although the great province of Alemtejo, which reaches from the south bank of the Tagus to within about twenty-five or thirty miles of the Southern Sea, had more than once been entered by the victorious Portuguese king Affonso Henriques, it was not till after his death in 1185, indeed not till the beginning of the thirteenth century, that it could be called a part of Portugal. As early as 1139 Affonso Henriques had met and defeated five kings at Ourique not far from Beja, a victory which was long supposed to have secured his country's independence, and which was therefore believed to have been much greater and more important than was really the case.[46] Evora, the Roman capital of the district, did not fall into the hands of the Christians till 1166, when it is said to have been taken by stratagem by Giraldo Sem Pavor, or 'the Fearless,' an outlaw who by this capture regained the favour of the king. But soon the Moors returned, first in 1174 when they won back the whole of the province, and again in 1184 when Dom Sancho, Affonso's son, utterly defeated and killed their leader, Yusuf. Yusuf's son, Yakub, returned to meet defeat in 1188 and 1190 when he was repulsed from Thomar, but when he led a third army across the Straits in 1192 he found that the Crusaders who had formerly helped Dom Sancho had sailed on to Palestine, and with his huge army was able to drive the Christians back beyond the Tagus and compel the king to come to terms, nor did the Christian borders advance again for several years. It is said that the cathedral begun in 1185 or 1186[47] was dedicated in 1204, so it must have been still incomplete when Yakub's successful invasion took place, and [52] only finished after the Christians had again recovered the town, though it is difficult to see how the church can have been dedicated in that year as the town remained in Moorish power till after Dom Sancho's death in 1211. Except the Sé Velha at Coimbra, Evora is the best-preserved of all the older Portuguese cathedrals, and must always have been one of the largest. The plan is evidently founded on those of the cathedrals of Lisbon and Braga; a nave of eight bays 155 feet long by 75 wide, leads to an aisleless transept 125 by 30, with lantern at the crossing, to the east of which were five chapels. Unfortunately in 1718 the Capella Mor or main chancel was pulled down as being too small for the dignity of an archiepiscopal see, and a new one of many-coloured marbles built in its stead, measuring 75 feet by 30.[48]

PLAN OF SÉ, EVORA

[53]

To the west are two large square towers; to the south a cloister added in 1376; and at the end of the north transept a chapel built at the end of the fifteenth century and entered by a large archway well carved with rich early renaissance ornament. If there is no advance from the romanesque plan of older churches, there is none in construction. All the arches are pointed, but that is the only direction in which any change has been made. The piers are all cross-shaped with a large half-shaft on each of the four main faces and a smaller round shaft in each angle. The capitals have square moulded abaci, and are rather rudely carved with budlike curled leaves; the pointed arches of the arcade are well moulded, and above them runs a continuous triforium gallery like that in the nave at Lisbon, but with small pointed arches. The main vault is a pointed barrel with bold ribs; it is held up by a half-barrel over the aisles, which have groined vaults with very large transverse arches. The galleries over the aisles are lit by small pointed windows of two lights with a cusped circle between, but except in the lantern which has similar windows, in the transept ends and the west front, these are the only original openings which survive. (Fig. 20.) Both transepts have large rose windows, the northern filled with tracery, like that, common in Champagne, radiating towards and not from the centre. The southern is more interesting. The whole, well moulded, is enclosed in a curious square framing. In the centre a doubly cusped circle is surrounded by twelve radiating openings, whose trefoiled heads abut against twelve other broad trefoils, which are rather curiously run into the mouldings of the containing circle. Over the west porch is a curious eight-light window. There are four equal two-light openings below; on the two in the centre rests a large plain circle, and the space between it and the enclosing arch is very clumsily filled by a rib which, springing from the apex of either light, runs concentrically with the enclosing arch till it meets the larger circle. The whole building is surmounted by brick battlements, everything else being of granite, resting on a good trefoil corbel table, and, as the roofs are perfectly flat, there are no gables.

The two western towers are very picturesque. The northern, without buttresses, has its several windows arranged without any regard to symmetry, and finishes in a round spire covered with green and white glazed tiles. In the 54 southern plain buttresses run up to the belfry stage which has round-headed openings, and above it is a low octagonal spire set diagonally and surrounded by eight pinnacles.

The most unusual feature of the whole cathedral is the fine octagonal lantern at the crossing. Each face has a two-light window, pointed outside, with a round-headed arch within, leaving a passage between the two walls. At each angle are plain buttresses, weathered back a few feet below the corbel table, above which stand eight octagonal pinnacles each with eight smaller pinnacles surrounding a conical stone spire. The whole lantern is covered by a steep stone roof which, passing imperceptibly from the octagonal to the round, is covered, as are all the other pinnacles, with scales carved in imitation of tiles. Inside the well-moulded vaulting ribs do not rise higher than the windows, leaving therefore a large space between the vault and the outer stone capping. (Fig. 21.)

Lanterns, especially octagonal lanterns, are particularly common in Spain, and at Salamanca and its neighbourhood were very early developed and attained to a remarkable degree of perfection before the end of the twelfth century. It is strange, therefore, that they should be so rare in Portugal where there seem now to be only three: one, square, at Coimbra, an octagonal at Lisbon, and one here, where however there is nothing of the internal dome which is so striking at Salamanca. Probably this lantern was one of the enrichments added to the church by Bishop Durando who died in 1283, for the capitals of the west door look considerably later.

This door is built entirely of white marble with shafts which look, as do those of the south transept door, almost like Cipollino, taken perhaps from some Roman building. It has well-moulded arches and abaci; capitals richly carved with realistic foliage, and on each side six of the apostles, all very like each other, large-headed, long-bearded, and long-haired, with rather good drapery but bodies and legs which look far too short. St. Peter alone, with short curly hair and beard, has any individuality, but is even less prepossessing than his companions. They are, however, among the earliest specimens of large figure sculpture which survive, and by their want of grace make it easier to understand why Dom Manoel employed so many foreign artists in the early years of the sixteenth century.

FIG. 20.
EVORA.SÉ.
INTERIOR.

FIG. 21.
EVORA.SÉ.
FROM CLOISTERS.
SHEWING CENTRAL LANTERN.

55 The large cloister to the south must once have been one of the best in the country. Here the main arches alone survive, having lost whatever subsidiary arches or tracery they may once have contained, but higher up under the corbel table are large open circles, not as everywhere else enclosed under the large arch, but quite independent of it. Many of these circles are still filled with thin slabs of granite all pierced with most beautiful patterns, some quite Gothic, but the majority almost Moorish in design, not unlike the slabs

in the circles over the cloister arcades at Alcobaça, but though this is probably only a coincidence, still more like those at Tarragona in Cataluña. (Fig. 22.)

Templar Church, Thomar.

Like the cathedral at Evora, some of the arches in the Templar Church at Thomar are pointed, yet like it again, it is entirely romanesque both in construction and in detail.

The Knights Templars were already established in Portugal in 1126. With their headquarters at Soure, a little to the south of Coimbra, they had been foremost in helping Affonso Henriques in his attacks on the Moors, and when Santarem was taken in 1147 they were given the ecclesiastical superiority of the town. This led to a quarrel with Dom Gilberto, the English bishop of Lisbon, which was settled in 1150, when Dom Gualdim Paes, the most famous member the order ever produced in Portugal, was chosen to be Grand Master. He at once gave up all Santarem to the bishop, except the church of São Thiago, and received instead the territory of Cêras some forty or fifty miles to the north-east. There on the banks of the river Nabão, on a site famous for the martyrdom under Roman rule of Sant' Iria or Irene, Dom Gualdim built a church, and began a castle which was soon abandoned for a far stronger position on a steep hill some few hundred yards to the west across the river. This second castle, begun in 1160, still survives in part but in a very ruinous condition; the walls and the keep alike have lost their battlements and their original openings, though a little further west, and once forming part of the fortified enclosure, the church, begun in 1162, still remains as a high tower-like bastion crowned with battlements. Dom Gualdim had the laudable habit of carving inscriptions telling of any striking event, so that we may still read, not only how the castle was founded, but how 'In the year of the Era of Cæsar, 1228 (that is 1190 A.D., on the 3rd of July), came the King of Morocco, leading four hundred thousand horsemen 56 and five hundred thousand foot and besieged this castle for six days, destroying everything he found outside the walls. God delivered from his hands the castle, the aforesaid Master and his brethren. The same king returned to his country with innumerable loss of men and of animals.'[49] Doubtless the size of Yakub the Almohade leader's army is here much exaggerated, but that he was forced to retire from Thomar, and by pestilence from Santarem is certain, and though he made a more successful invasion two years later the Moors never again gained a footing to the north of the Tagus.

Dom Gualdim's church, since then enlarged by the addition of a nave to the west, was originally a polygon of sixteen sides with a circular barrel-vaulted aisle surrounding a small octagon, which with its two stories of slightly pointed arches contains the high altar.[50] (Fig. 23.)

The round-headed windows come up high, and till it was so richly adorned by Dom Manoel during his grand mastership of the Order of Christ more than three hundred years later, the church must have been extremely simple. Outside the most noticeable feature is the picturesque grouping of the bell-towers and gable, added probably in the seventeenth century, which now rise on the eastern side of the polygon, and which, seen above the orange and medlar trees of a garden reaching eastwards towards the castle, forms one of the most pleasing views in the whole country.

São João de Alporão, Santarem.

If Evora and the Templar church at Thomar show one form of transition, where the arches are pointed, but the construction and detail is romanseque, São João de Alporão at Santarem shows another, where the construction is Gothic but the arches are still all round.

FIG. 22.
EVORA.SÉ.
CLOISTER.

FIG. 23.
THOMAR.
TEMPLARS' CHURCH.

57 This church is said to stand on the site of a mosque and to have been at first called Al Koran, since corrupted into Alporão, but the present building can hardly have been begun till the early years of the thirteenth century. The church consists of an aisleless nave with good groined vaulting and a five-sided apsidal chancel. The round-arched west door stands under a pointed gable, but seems to have lost by decay and consequent restoration whatever ornament its rather flat mouldings may once have had. Above is a good wheel

window, with a cusped circle in the centre, surrounded by eight radiating two-arched lights separated by eight radiating columns. The two arches of each light spring from a detached capital which seems to have lost its shaft, but as there is no trace of bases for these missing shafts on the central circle they probably never existed. All the other nave windows are mere slits; and above them runs a rich corbel table of slightly stilted arches with their edges covered with ball ornament resting on projecting corbels. In the apse the five windows are tall and narrow with square heads, and the corbel table of a form common in Portugal but rare elsewhere, where each corbel is something like the bows of a boat.[51]

The inside, now turned into a museum, is much more interesting. The chancel is entered, under a circular cusped window, by a wide round arch, whose outer moulding is curiously carried by shafts with capitals set across the angle as if to carry a vaulting rib; in the chancel itself the walls are double, the outer having the plain square-headed windows seen outside, and the inner very elegant two-light round-headed openings resting on very thin and delicate shafts, with a doubly cusped circle above. The vault, whose wall arches are stilted and slightly pointed, has strong well-moulded ribs springing from the well-wrought capitals of tall angle shafts. It will be seen that this is a very great advance on any older vaulting, since previously, except in the French Church at Alcobaça, groined vaults had only been attempted over square spaces. The finest of the many objects preserved in the museum is the tomb of Dom Duarte de Menezes, who was killed in Africa in 1464 and buried in the church of São Francisco, whence, São Francisco having become a cavalry stable, it was brought here not many years ago. (Fig. 24.)

Such are, except for the church at Idanha a Velha and that 58 of Castro de Avelans near Braganza, nearly all the early buildings in the country. Castro de Avelans is interesting and unique as having on the outside brick arcades, like those on the many Mozarabic churches at Toledo, a form of decoration not found elsewhere in Portugal. The church of Alcobaça is

PLAN OF ALCOBAÇA

of course, in part, a good deal older than are some of those mentioned above; but the whole, the romanesque choir as well as the early pointed nave, is so unlike anything that has come before or anything that has come after, that it seemed better to take it by itself without regard to strict chronological order.

FIG. 24.	FIG. 25.
SANTAREMAPSE, SÃO JOÃO DE ALPORÃO.	TRANSEPTALCOBAÇA.
Alcobaça.	

59 The first stone was laid in 1158, but the church was barely finished when King Sancho I. died in 1211 and was not dedicated till 1220, while the monastic buildings were not ready till 1223, when the monks migrated from Sta. Maria a Velha, their temporary home. The abbey was immensely wealthy: it had complete jurisdiction over fourteen villages whose inhabitants were in fact its serfs: it or its abbot was visitor to all Benedictine abbeys in the country and was, for over three hundred years, till the reign of Cardinal King Henry, the superior of the great military Order of Christ. It early became one of the first centres of learning in Portugal, having begun to teach in 1269. It helped Dom Diniz to found the University of Lisbon, now finally settled at Coimbra, with presents of books and of money, and it only acknowledged the king in so far as to give him a pair of boots or shoes when he chanced to come to Alcobaça. All these possessions and privileges of the monks were confirmed by Dom João IV. (1640-56) after the supremacy of the Spaniards had come to an end, and were still theirs when Beckford paid them his memorable visit near the end of the eighteenth century and was so splendidly entertained with feastings and even with plays and operas performed by some of the younger brothers. Much harm was of course done by the French invasion, and at last in 1834 the brothers were turned out, their house made into barracks, and their church and cloister left to fall into decay—a decay from which they are only being slowly rescued at the present time.

The first abbot, Ranulph, was sent by St. Bernard of Clairvaux himself at the king's special request, and he must have brought with him the plan of the abbey or at least of the church. Nearly all Cistercian churches, which have not been altered, are of two types which resemble each other in being very simple, having no towers and very little ornament of any kind. In the simpler of these forms, the one which prevailed in England, the transept is aisleless, with five or more chapels, usually square, to the east, of which the largest, in the centre, contains the main altar. Such are Fontenay near Monbart and Furness in Lancashire, and even Melrose, though there the church has been rebuilt more or less on the old plan but with a wealth of detail and size of window quite foreign to the original rule. In the other, a more complex type, the transept may have a western aisle, and instead of a plain square 60 chancel there is an apse with surrounding aisle and beyond it a series of four-sided chapels. Pontigny, famous for the shelter it gave to Thomas-à-Becket, and begun in 1114, is of this type, and so was Clairvaux itself, begun in 1115 and rebuilt in the eighteenth century. Now this is the type followed by Alcobaça, and it is worthy of notice that, as far as the plan of choir and transept goes, Alcobaça and Clairvaux are practically identical. Pontigny has a choir of three bays between the transept and the apse and seven encircling chapels; Clairvaux had, and Alcobaça still has, a choir of but one bay and nine instead of seven chapels. Both had long naves, Clairvaux of eleven and Alcobaça of thirteen bays, but at the west end there is a change, due probably to the length of time which passed before it was reached, for there is no trace of the large porch or narthex found in most early Cistercian churches.

The church is by far the largest in Portugal. It is altogether about 365 feet long, the nave alone being about 250 feet by 75, while the transept measures about 155 feet from north to south. Except in the choir all the aisles are of the same height, about 68 feet.

The east end is naturally the oldest part and most closely resembled its French original; the eight round columns of the apse have good plain capitals like those found in so many early Cistercian churches, even in Italy;[52] the round-headed clerestory windows are high and narrow, and there are well-developed flying buttresses. Unfortunately all else has been changed: in the apse itself everything up to the clerestory level has been hidden by two rows of classic columns and a huge reredos, and all the choir chapels have been filled with rococo woodwork and gilding, the work of an Englishman, William Elsden, who was employed to beautify the church in 1770.[53] Why except for the choir aisle, and the chapels in choir and transept, the whole church should be of the same height, it is difficult to say, for such a method of building was unknown in France and equally unknown in Spain or Portugal. Possibly by the time the nave was reached the Frenchmen who had planned the church were dead, and the native workmen, being quite unused to such a method of construction, for all the older vaulted churches have their central barrel upheld 61 by the half-barrel vault of the galleries, could think of no other way of supporting the groining of the main aisle. They had of course the flying buttresses of the choir apse to guide them, but there the points of support come so much closer together, and the weight to be upheld is consequently so much less than could be the case in the nave, that they may well have thought that to copy them was too dangerous an experiment as well as being too foreign to their traditional manner of construction.[54] Whatever may be the reason, the west aisle of the transept and the side aisles of the nave rise to the full height of the building. Their arches are naturally very much stilted, and with the main vault rest on piers of quite unusual size and strength. The transverse arches are so large as almost to hide the diagonal ribs and to give the impression that the nave has, after all, a pointed barrel vault. The piers are throughout cross-shaped with a half-shaft on each cardinal face: at the crossing there is also a shaft in the angle, but elsewhere this shaft is replaced by a kind of corbel capital[55] at the very top which carries the diagonal ribs—another proof, as is the size of the transverse arches, that such a ribbed vault was still a half-understood novelty. The most peculiar point about nave piers is the way in which not only the front vaulting shafts but even that portion of the piers to which they are attached is, except in the two western bays, cut off at varying heights from the ground. In the six eastern bays, where the corbels are all at the same level, this was done to leave room for the monks' stalls,[56] but it is difficult to see why, in the case of the following five piers, against which, as at Clairvaux, stood the stalls of the lay brothers, the level of the corbels should vary so much. Now all stalls are gone and the church is very bare and desolate, with nothing but the horrible reredos to detract from that severity and sternness which was what St. Bernard wished to see in all churches of the Order. (Fig. 25.)

The small chapel to the west of the south transept is the only part of the church, except the later sixteenth-century [62] sacristy, where there is any richness of detail, and there it is confined to the tombs of some of the earlier kings and queens, and especially to those of D. Pedro and the unfortunate Inez de Castro which belongs of course to a much later date.

The windows which are high up the aisle walls are large, round-headed, and perfectly plain. At the transept ends are large round windows filled with plain uncusped circles, and there is another over the west door filled with a rococo attempt at Gothic tracery, which agrees well with the two domed western towers whose details are not even good rococo. Between these towers still opens the huge west door, a very plainly moulded pointed arch of seven orders, resting on the simple capitals of sixteen shafts: a form of door which became very common throughout the fourteenth century. The great cloister was rebuilt later in the time of Dom Diniz, leaving only the chapter-house entrance, which seems even older than the nave. As usual there is one door in the centre, with a large two-light opening on each side: all the arches are round and well moulded, and the capitals simply carved with stiff foliage showing a gradual transition from the earlier romanesque. In the monastery itself, now a barrack, there are still a few vaulted passages which must belong to the original building, but nearly all else has been rebuilt, the main cloister in the fourteenth and sixteenth centuries and the greater part of the domestic buildings in the eighteenth, so that except for the cloister and sacristy, which will be spoken of later on, there is little worthy of attention.[57]

Now none of these buildings may show any very great originality or differ to any marked degree from contemporary buildings in Spain or even in the south of France, yet to a great extent they fixed a type which in many ways was followed down to the end of the Gothic period. The plan of Braga, Pombeiro, Evora or Coimbra is reproduced with but little change at Guarda, and if the western towers be omitted, at Batalha, some two hundred years later, and the flat paved roofs of Evora occur again at Batalha and at Guarda. The barrel-vaulted nave also long survived, being found as late as the beginning of the fourteenth century in the church of [63] Santa Clara at Coimbra, and even about seventy years later in the church of the Knights of São Thiago at Palmella.

The battlements also of the castle at Guimarães are found not only at Coimbra, but as late as 1336 in the church of Leça do Balio near Oporto, and, modified in shape by the renaissance even in the sixteenth-century churches of Villa do Conde and of Azurara.

Although the distinctively French features of Alcobaça seem to have had but little influence on the further development of building in Portugal, a few peculiarities are found there which are repeated again. For example, the unusually large transverse arches of the nave occur at Batalha, and the large plain western door is clearly related to such later doors as those at Leça do Balio or of São Francisco at Oporto. Again the vaulting of the apse in São João de Alporão is arranged very much in the way which was almost universal during the fourteenth and fifteenth centuries in the chancels and side chapels of many a church, such as Santa Maria do Olival at Thomar, or the Graça at Santarem itself, and the curious boat-like corbels of São João are found more than once, as in the choir of the old church, formerly the cathedral of Silves, far south in the Algarve. The large round windows at Evora do not seem to be related to the window at São João, but to be of some independent origin; probably, like the similar windows at Leça and at Oporto, they too belong to the thirteenth or fourteenth centuries. [64]

CHAPTER III
THE THIRTEENTH AND FOURTEENTH CENTURIES DOWN TO THE BATTLE OF ALJUBARROTA

IN Portugal the twelfth century is marked by a very considerable activity in building, but the thirteenth, which in France and England saw Gothic architecture rise to a height of perfection both in construction and in ornament which was never afterwards excelled, when more great churches and cathedrals were built than almost ever before or since, seems here to have been the least productive period in the whole history of the country. In the thirteenth century, indeed, Portugal reached its widest European limits, but the energies,

31

alike of the kings and of the people, seem to have been expended rather in consolidating their conquests and in cultivating and inhabiting the large regions of land left waste by the long-continued struggle. Although Dom Sancho's kingdom only extended from the Minho to the Tagus, in the early years of the thirteenth century the rich provinces of Beira, and still more of Estremadura, were very thinly peopled: the inhabitants lived only in walled towns, and their one occupation was fighting, and plunder almost their only way of gaining a living. It is natural then that so few buildings should remain which date from the reigns of Dom Sancho's successors, Affonso II. (1211-1223), Sancho II. (1223-1248), and Affonso III. (1248-1279): the necessary churches and castles had been built at once after the conquest, and the people had neither the leisure nor the means to replace them by larger and more refined structures as was being done elsewhere. Of course some churches described in the last chapter may be actually of that period though belonging artistically and constructionally to an earlier time, as for instance a large part of the cathedral of Evora or the church of São João at Santarem.

São Francisco, Guimarães.

The Franciscans had been introduced into Portugal by Dona Sancha, the daughter of Dom Sancho I., and houses 65 were built for them by Dona Urraca, the wife of Dom Affonso II., at Lisbon and at Guimarães. Their church at Guimarães has been very much altered at different times, mostly in the eighteenth century, but the west door may very well belong to Dona Urraca's building. It has a drip-mould covered with closely set balls, and four orders of mouldings of which the second is a broad chamfer with a row of flat four-leaved flowers; the abacus is well moulded, but the capitals, which are somewhat bell-shaped, have the bell covered with rude animals or foliage which are still very romanesque in design. The entrance to the chapter-house is probably not much later in date: from the south walk of the simple but picturesque renaissance cloister a plain pointed doorway leads into the chapter-house, with, on either side, an opening of about equal size and shape. In these openings there stand three pairs of round coupled shafts with plain bases, rudely carved capitals and large square overhanging abaci, from which spring two pointed arches moulded only on the under side: resting on these, but connected with them or with the enclosing arch by no moulding or fillet, is a small circle, moulded like the arches only on one side and containing a small quatrefoil.[58] This is one of the earliest attempts at window tracery in the country, for the west window at Evora seems later, but like it, it shows that tracery was not really understood in the country, and that the Portuguese builders were not yet able so to unite the different parts as to make such a window one complete and beautiful whole. Indeed so unsuccessful are their attempts throughout that whenever, as at Batalha, a better result is seen, it may be put down to foreign influence. Much better as a rule are the round windows, mostly of the fourteenth century, but they are all very like one another, and are probably mostly derived from the same source, perhaps from one of the transept windows at Evora, or from the now empty circle over the west door at Lisbon.

São Francisco, Santarem.

Much more refined than this granite church at Guimarães has been São Francisco at Santarem, now unfortunately degraded into being the stable of a cavalry barracks. There the best-preserved and most interesting part is the west door, which does not lead directly into the church but into a low 66 porch or narthex. The narthex itself has central and side aisles, all of the same height, is two bays in length and is covered by a fine strong vault resting on short clustered piers.[59] The doorway itself, which is not acutely pointed, stands under a gable which reaches up to the plain battlemented parapet of the flat narthex roof. There are four shafts on each side with a ring-moulding rather less than half-way up, which at once distinguishes them from any romanesque predecessors; the capitals are round with a projecting moulding half-way up and another one at the top with a curious projection or claw to unite the round cap and the square moulded abacus. Of the different orders of the arch, all well moulded, the outer has a hood with billet-mould; the second a well-developed chevron or zigzag; and the innermost a series of small horseshoes, which like the chevron stretch across the hollow so as to hold in the large roll at the angle.[60] (Fig. 26.)

Santa Maria dos Olivaes, Thomar.

In a previous chapter the building of a church at Thomar by Dom Gualdim Paes, Grand Master of the Templars, has been mentioned. Of this church and the castle built at the same time, both of which stood on the east or flat bank of the river Nabão, nothing now remains except perhaps the lower part of the detached bell-tower. This church, Santa Maria dos Olivaes, was the Matriz or mother church of all those held, first by the Templars and later by their successors, the Order of Christ, not only in Portugal but even in Africa, Brazil, and in India. Of so high a dignity it is scarcely worthy, being but a very simple building neither large nor richly ornamented. A nave and aisles of five bays, three polygonal apses to the east and later square chapels beyond the aisles, make up the whole building. The roofs are all of panelled wood of the sixteenth century except in the three vaulted apses, of which the central is entered by an arch, which, rising no higher than the aisle arches, leaves room for a large window under the roof. All the arches of the aisle arcade spring from the simple moulded capitals of piers whose section is that of four half-octagons placed together.

FIG. 26.   **FIG. 27.**
SANTAREM   **SÉ SILVES.**
W. DOOR, SÃO FRANCISCO.

67 In the clerestory are windows of one small light, in the aisles of two larger lights, and in the apses single lancets. The great simplicity of the building notwithstanding it can scarcely be as old as the thirteenth century: the curious way in which the two lancet lights of the aisle windows are enclosed under one larger trefoiled arch recalls the similar windows in the church at Leça do Balio near Oporto begun in 1336, though there the elliptical head of the enclosing arch is much less satisfactory than the trefoiled head here used. The only part of the church which can possibly have been built in the thirteenth century is the central part of the west front. The pointed door below stands under a projecting gable like that at São Francisco Santarem, except that there is a five-foiled circle above the arch containing a pentalpha, put there perhaps to keep out witches. The door itself has three large shafts on each side with good but much-decayed capitals of foliage, and a moulded jamb next the door. The arch itself is terribly decayed, but one of its orders still has the remains of a series of large cusps, arranged like the horseshoe cusps at Santarem but much larger. Above the door gable is a circular window of almost disproportionate size. It has twelve trefoil-headed lights radiating from a small circle, and curiously crossing a larger circle some distance from the smaller. Unfortunately the spaces between the trefoils and the outer mouldings have been filled up with plaster and the lights themselves subdivided with meaningless wood tracery to hold the horrible blue-and-red glass now so popular in Portugal. Though Santa Maria dos Olivaes cannot be nearly as old as has usually been believed, it is one of the earliest churches built on the plan derived perhaps first from Braga Cathedral or from the Franciscan and Dominican churches in Galicia, of a wooden roofed basilica with or without transept, and with three or more apses to the east; a form which to the end of the Gothic period was the most common and which is found even in cathedrals as at Silves or at Funchal in Madeira.

Dom Sancho II., whose reign had begun with brilliant attacks on the Moors, had, because of his connection with Dona Mencia de Haro, the widow of a Castilian nobleman, and his consequent inactivity, become extremely unpopular, so was supplanted in 1246 by his brother Dom Affonso III. The first care of the new king was to carry on the conquest 68

Silves.
of the Algarve, which his brother had given up when he fell under the evil influence of Dona Mencia, and by about 1260 he had overrun the whole country. At first Alfonso X., the Wise, king of Castile and Leon, was much displeased at this extension of Portuguese power, but on Dom Affonso agreeing to marry his daughter Beatriz de Guzman, the Spanish king allowed his son-in-law to retain his conquests and to assume the title of King of the Algarve, a title which his descendants still bear. The countess of Boulogne, Affonso's first wife, was indeed still alive, but that seems to have troubled neither Dona Beatriz nor her father. At Silves or Chelb, for so the Moorish capital had been called, a bishopric was soon founded, but the cathedral,[61] though many of its details seem to proclaim an early origin,

was probably not begun till the early, and certainly not finished till near the later, years of the fourteenth century. It is a church of the same type as Santa Maria at Thomar but with a transept. The west door, a smaller edition of that at Alcobaça, leads to a nave and aisles of four bays, with plain octagonal columns, whose bases exactly resemble the capitals reversed—an octagon brought to a square by a curved chamfer. The nave has a wooden roof, transepts a pointed barrel vault, and the crossing and chancel with its side chapels a ribbed vault. Though some of the capitals at the east end look almost romanesque, the really late date is shown by the cusped fringing of the chancel arch, a feature very common at Batalha, which was begun at the end of the fourteenth century, and by the window tracery, where in the two-light windows the head is filled by a flat pierced slab. Outside, the chancel has good buttresses at the angles, and is crowned by that curious boat-like corbel table seen at Santarem and by a row of pyramidal battlements. The church is only about 150 feet long, but with its two picturesque and dilapidated towers, and the wonderful deep purple of its sandstone walls rising above the whitewashed houses and palms of the older Silves and backed by the Moorish citadel, it makes a most picturesque and even striking centre to the town, which, standing high above the 69 river, preserves the memory of its Moslem builders in its remarkable and many-towered city walls.[62] (Fig. 27.)

Beja.

King Diniz the Labourer, so called for his energy in settling and reclaiming the land and in fixing the moving sands along the west coast by plantations of pine-trees, and the son of Dom Affonso and Dona Beatriz, was a more active builder than any of his immediate predecessors. Of the many castles built by him the best preserved is that of Beja, the second town of Alemtejo and the Pax Julia of Roman times. The keep, built about 1310, is a great square tower over a hundred feet high. Some distance from the top it becomes octagonal, with the square fortified by corbelled balconies projecting far out over the corners. Inside are several stories of square halls finely vaulted with massive octagonal vaults; below, the windows are little more than slits, but on one floor there are larger two-light pointed openings.[63]

Leiria.

Far finer and larger has been the castle of Leiria, some fifty miles south of Coimbra: it or the keep was begun by Dom Diniz in 1324.[64] The rock on which it stands, in steepness and in height recalls that of Edinburgh Castle, but without the long slope of the old town leading nearly to the summit: towering high above Leiria it is further defended on the only accessible quarter by the river Lis which runs round two sides not far from the bottom of the steep descent. Unfortunately all is ruined, only enough remaining to show that on the steepest edge of the rock there stood a palace with large pointed windows looking out over the town to the green wooded hills beyond. On the highest part stands what is left of the keep, and a little lower the castle-church whose bell-tower, built over the gate, served to defend the only access to the inner fortification. This church, built about the same time, with a now roofless nave which was never vaulted, is entered by a door on the south, and has a polygonal vaulted 70 apse. The mouldings of the door as well as the apse vault and its tall two-light windows show a greater delicacy and refinement than is seen in almost any earlier building, and some of the carving has once been of great beauty, especially of the boss at the centre of the apse.[65]

But besides those two castles there is another building of this period which had a greater and more lasting effect on the work of this fourteenth century. In England the arrival of the Cistercians and the new style introduced or rather developed by them seems almost more than anything else to have determined the direction of the change from what is usually, perhaps wrongly,[66] called Norman to Early English, but in Portugal the great foundation of Alcobaça was apparently powerless to have any such marked effect except in the one case of cloisters. Now with the exception of the anomalous and much later Claustro Real at Batalha, all cloisters in Portugal, before the renaissance, follow two types: one, which is clearly only a modification of the continuous romanesque arcades resting on coupled shafts, has usually a wooden roof, and consists of a row of coupled shafts bearing pointed arches, and sometimes interrupted at intervals by square piers; this form of cloister is found at Santo

Thyrso near Guimarães, at São Domingos in Guimarães itself, and in the Cemetery cloister built by Prince Henry the Navigator at Thomar in the fifteenth century.

Cloister, Cellas.

The most remarkable of all the cloisters of the first type is that of the nunnery of Cellas near Coimbra. Founded in 1210 by Dona Sancha, daughter of Sancho I., the nunnery is now a blind asylum. The cloister, with round arches and coupled columns, seems thoroughly romanesque in character, as are also the capitals. It is only on looking closer that the real date is seen, for the figures on the capitals, which are carved with scenes such as the beheading of St. John the Baptist, are all dressed in the fashion that prevailed under Dom Diniz—about 1300—while the foliage on others, though still romanesque in arrangement, is much later in detail. More than half of the arcades were rebuilt in the seventeenth century, but enough remains to make the cloister of Cellas 71 one of the most striking examples of the survival of old forms and methods of building which in less remote countries had been given up more than a hundred years before.

The church, though small, is not without interest. It has a round nave of Dom Manoel's time with a nuns' choir to the west and a chancel to the east, and is entered by a picturesque door of the later sixteenth century.

Cloister, Coimbra.
Cloister, Alcobaça.

More interesting is the second type which was commonly used when a cloister with a vault was wanted; and of it there are still examples to be seen at the Sé Velha Coimbra, at Alcobaça, Lisbon Cathedral, Evora, and Oporto. None of these five examples are exactly alike, but they resemble each other sufficiently to make it probable that they are all, ultimately at least, derived from one common source, and there can be no doubt that that source was Cistercian. In France what was perhaps its very first beginnings may be seen in the Cistercian abbey of Fontenay near Monbart, where in each bay there are two round arches enclosed under one larger round arch. This was further developed at Fontfroide near Narbonne, where an arcade of four small round arches under a large pointed arch carries a thin wall pierced by a large round circle. Of the different Portuguese examples the oldest may very well be that at Coimbra which differs only from Fontfroide in having an arcade of two arches in each bay instead of four, but even though it may be a little older than the large cloister of Alcobaça, it must have been due to Cistercian influence. The great Claustro do Silencio at Alcobaça was, as an inscription tells, begun in the year 1310,[67] when on April 13th the first stone was laid by the abbot in the presence of the master builder Domingo Domingues.[68] In this case each bay has an arcade of two or three pointed arches resting on coupled columns with strong buttresses between each bay, but the enclosing arch is not pointed as at Coimbra or Fontfroide but segmental and springs from square jambs at the level of the top of the buttresses, and the circles have been all filled with pierced 72 slabs, some of which have ordinary quatrefoils and some much more intricate patterns, though in no case do they show the Moorish influence which is so noticeable at Evora. On the north side projects the lavatory, an apsidal building with two stories of windows and with what in France would be regarded as details of the thirteenth century and not, as is really the case, of the fourteenth. A few bays on the west walk seem rather later than the rest, as the arches of the arcade are trefoil-headed, while the upper part of a small projection on the south side which now contains a stair, as well as the upper cloister to which it leads, were added by João de Castilho for Cardinal Prince Henry, son of Dom Manoel, and commendator of the abbey in 1518. (Fig. 28.)

Cloister, Lisbon.

In the cloister at Lisbon which seems to be of about the same date, and which, owing to the nature of the site, runs round the back of the choir, there is no outer containing arch, and in some bays there are two large circles instead of one, but in every other respect, except that some of the round openings are adorned with a ring of dog-tooth moulding, the details are very similar, the capitals and bases being all of good thirteenth-century French form.[69] (Fig. 29.)

Cloister, Oporto.

If the cloister at Evora, which was built in 1376 and has already been described, is the one which departs furthest from the original type, retaining only the round opening, that of the cathedral of Oporto, built in 1385, comes nearer to Fontfroide than any of the others. Here each bay is designed exactly like the French example except that the small arches are pointed, that the large openings are chamfered instead of moulded, and that there are buttresses between each bay. The capitals which are rather tall are carved with rather shallow leaves, but the most noticeable features are the huge square moulded abaci which are so large as to be more like those of the romanesque cloisters at Moissac or of Sta. Maria del Sar at Santiago than any fourteenth-century work.

Sta. Clara, Coimbra.

The most important church of the time of Dom Diniz is, or rather was, that of the convent of Poor Clares founded at Coimbra by his wife St. Isabel. Although a good king, Diniz had not been a good husband, and the queen's sorrows had been still further increased by the rebellion of

FIG 28.	FIG. 29.
ALCOBAÇA.	LISBON
CLOISTER OF DOM DINIZ, OR DO SILENCIO.	CATHEDRAL CLOISTER.

73 her son, afterwards Affonso IV., a rebellion to which Isabel was able to put an end by interposing between her husband and her son. When St. Isabel died in 1327, two years after her husband, the church was not yet quite finished, but it must have been so soon after. Unfortunately the annual floods of the Mondego and the sands which they bring down led to the abandonment of the church in the seventeenth century, and have so buried it that the floor of the barn—for that is the use to which it is now put—is almost level with the springing of the aisle arches, but enough is left to show what the church was like, and were not its date well assured no one would believe it to be later than the end of the twelfth century. The chancel, which was aisleless and lower than the rest of the church, is gone, but the nave and its aisles are still in a tolerable state of preservation, though outside all the detail has been destroyed except one round window on the south side filled in with white marble tracery of a distinctly Italian type, and the corbel table of the boat-keel shape. The inside is most unusual for a church of the fourteenth century. The central aisle has a pointed barrel vault springing from a little above the aisle arches, while the aisles themselves have an ordinary cross vault. All the capitals too look early, and the buttresses broad and rather shallow. (Fig. 30.)

Leça do Balio.

A few miles north of Oporto on the banks of the clear stream of the Leça a monastery for men and women had been founded in 986. In the course of the next hundred years it had several times fallen into decay and been restored, till about the year 1115 when it was handed over to the Knights Hospitaller of St. John of Jerusalem and so became their headquarters in Portugal. The church had been rebuilt by Abbot Guntino some years before the transfer took place, and had in time become ruinous, so that in 1336 it was rebuilt by Dom Frei Estevão Vasques Pimentel, the head of the Order. This church still stands but little altered since the fourteenth century, and though not a large or splendid building it is the most complete and unaltered example of that thoroughly national plan and style which, developed in the previous century, was seen at Thomar and will be seen again in many later examples. The church consists of a nave and aisles of four bays, transepts higher than the side but lower than the centre aisle of the nave, three vaulted apses to the east, and at 74 the south-west corner a square tower. Like many Portuguese buildings Sta. Maria de Leça do Balio looks at first sight a good deal earlier than is really the case. The west and the south doors, which are almost exactly alike, except that the south door is surmounted by a gable, have three shafts on each side with early-looking capitals and plain moulded archivolts, and within these, jambs moulded at the angles bearing an inner order whose flat face is carved with a series of circles enclosing four and five-leaved flowers. Above the west door runs a projecting gallery whose parapet, like all the other parapets of the church, is defended by a close-set row of pointed battlements. Above the gallery is a large rose-window in which twelve spokes radiate from a cusped circle in the middle to the circumference, where the

36

lights so formed are further enriched by cusped semicircles. The aisle and clerestory windows show an unusual attempt to include two lancets into one window by carrying on the outer framing of the window till it meets above the mullion in a kind of pendant arch.[70]

The square tower is exceedingly plain, without string course or buttress to mitigate its severity. Half-way up on the west side is a small window with a battlemented balcony in front projecting out on three great corbels; higher up are plain belfry windows. At the top, square balconies or bartizans project diagonally from the corners; the whole, though there are but three pyramidal battlements on each side, being even more strongly fortified than the rest of the church. Now in the fourteenth century such fortification of a church can hardly have been necessary, and they were probably built rather to show that the church belonged to a military order than with any idea of defence. The inside is less interesting, the pointed arches are rather thin and the capitals poor, the only thing much worthy of notice being the font, belonging to the time of change from Gothic to Renaissance, and given in 1512.[71]

Chancel, Sé, Lisbon.

Of the other buildings of the time of Dom Affonso IV. who succeeded his father Diniz in 1328 the most important

FIG. 30.
COIMBRA
STA. CLARA.

[75] has been the choir of the cathedral at Lisbon; the church had been much injured by an earthquake in 1344 and the whole east end was at once rebuilt on the French plan, otherwise unexampled in Portugal except by the twelfth-century choir at Alcobaça. Unfortunately the later and more terrible earthquake of 1755 so ruined the whole building that of Dom Affonso's work only the surrounding aisle and its chapels remain. The only point which calls for notice is that the chapels are considerably lower than the aisle so as to admit of a window between the chapel arch and the aisle vault. All the chapels have good vaulting and simple two-light windows, and capitals well carved with naturalistic foliage. In one chapel, that of SS. Cosmo and Damião, screened off by a very good early wrought-iron grill, are the tombs of Lopo Fernandes Pacheco and of his second wife Maria Rodrigues. Dona Maria, lying on a stone sarcophagus, which stands on four short columns, and whose sides are adorned with four shields with the arms of her father, Ruy di Villa Lobos, has her head protected by a carved canopy and holds up in her hands an open book which, from her position, she could scarcely hope to read.[72]

Royal tombs, Alcobaça. (Fig. 31.)

Far more interesting both historically and artistically than these memorials at Lisbon are the royal tombs in the small chapel opening off the south transepts of the abbey church at Alcobaça. This vaulted chapel, two bays deep and three wide, was probably built about the same time as the cloister, and has good clustered piers and well-carved capitals. On the floor stand three large royal tombs and two smaller for royal children, and in deep recesses in the north and south walls, four others. Only the three larger standing clear of the walls call for notice; and of these one is that of Dona Beatriz, the wife of Dom Affonso III., who died in 1279, the same lady who married Dom Affonso while his wife the countess of Boulogne was still alive. Her tomb, which stands high above the ground on square columns with circular ringed shafts at the corners, was clearly not made for Dona Beatriz herself, but for some one else at least a hundred years before. It is of a white marble, sadly mutilated at one corner [76] by French treasure-seekers, and has on each side a romanesque arcade with an apostle, in quite archaic style, seated under each arch; at the ends are large groups of seated figures, and on the sloping lid Dona Beatriz herself, in very shallow relief, evidently carved out of the old roof-shaped cover, which not being very thick did not admit of any deep cutting. Far richer, indeed more elaborate than almost any other fourteenth-century tombs, are those of Dom Pedro I. who died in 1367, and of Inez de Castro who was murdered in 1355. When only sixteen years old Dom Pedro, to strengthen his father Affonso the Fourth's alliance with Castile, had been married to Dona Costança, daughter of the duke of Penafiel. In her train there came as a lady-in-waiting Dona Inez de Castro, the daughter of the high chamberlain of Castile, and with her Dom Pedro soon fell in love. As long as his wife, who was the mother of King Fernando, lived no one thought much of his connection with Dona Inez, or of that with Dona Thereza Lourenço, whose son afterwards became the great liberator, King João I., but after Dona Costança's death it was soon seen that he loved Dona Inez more than any one had imagined, and he was believed even to have married her. This, and his refusal to accept any of the royal princesses chosen by his father, so enraged Dom Affonso that he determined to have Dona Inez killed, and this was done by three knights on 7th January 1355 in the Quinta das Lagrimas—that is, the Garden of Tears—near Coimbra. Dom Pedro, who was away hunting in the south, would have rebelled against his father, but was persuaded by the queen to submit after he had devastated all the province of Minho. Two years later Dom Affonso died, and after Dom Pedro had caught and tortured to death two of the murderers—the third escaped to Castile—he in 1361 had Dona Inez's body removed from its grave, dressed in the royal robes and crowned, and swearing that he had really married her, he compelled all the court to pay her homage and to kiss her hand: then the body was placed on a bier and carried by night to the place prepared for it at Alcobaça, some seventy miles away. When six years later, in 1367, he came to die himself he left directions that they should be buried with their feet towards one another, that at the resurrection the first thing he should see should be Dona Inez rising from her tomb. Unfortunately the French soldiers in 1810 broke open both tombs, 77 smashing away much fine carved work and scattering their bones.[73] The two tombs are much alike in design and differ only in detail; both rest on four lions; the sides, above a narrow border of sunk quatrefoils, are divided by tiny buttresses rising from behind the gables of small niches into six parts, each of which has an arch under a gable whose tympanum is filled with the most minute tracery. Each of these arches is cusped and foliated differently according to the nature of the figure subject it contains. Behind the tops of the gables and pinnacles of the buttresses runs a small arcade with beautiful little figures only a few inches high: above this a still more delicate arcade runs round the whole tomb, interrupted at regular intervals by shields, charged on Dom Pedro's tomb with the arms of Portugal and on that of Dona Inez with the same and with those of the Castros alternately. At the foot of Dom Pedro's is represented the Crucifixion, and facing it on that of Dona Inez the Last Judgment. Nothing can exceed the delicacy and beauty of the figure sculpture, the drapery is all good, and the smallest heads and hands are worked with a care not to be surpassed in any country. (Fig. 32.)

On the top of one lies King Pedro with his head to the north, on the other Dona Inez with hers to the south; both are life size and are as well wrought as are the smaller details below. Both have on each side three angels who seem to be just about to lift them from where they lie or to have just laid them down. These angels, especially those near Dom Pedro's head, are perhaps the finest parts of either tomb, with their beautiful drapery, their well-modelled wings, and above all with the outstretching of their arms towards the king and Dona Inez. There seems to be no record as to who worked or designed these tombs, but there can be little or no doubt that he was a Frenchman, the whole feeling, alike of the architectural detail and the figures themselves, is absolutely French; there had been no previous figure sculpture in the country in any way good enough to lead up to the skill in design and in execution here shown, nor, with regard to the mere archi 78 tectural detail, had Gothic tracery and ornament yet been sufficiently developed for a native workman to have invented the elaborate cuspings, mouldings, and other enrichments which make both tombs so pre-eminent above all that came before them.[74] These tombs, as indeed the whole church, as well as the neighbouring convent of Batalha, are constructed of a wonderfully fine limestone, which seems to be practically the same as Caen Stone, and which, soft and easy to cut when first quarried, grows harder with exposure and in time, when not in a too shady or damp position, where it gets black, takes on a most beautiful rich yellow colour.

These tombs, beautiful as they are, do not seem to have any very direct influence on the work of the next century: it is true that a distinct advance was made in modelling the effigies of those who lay below, but apart from that the decoration of these high tombs is in no case even remotely related to that of the later monuments at Batalha; nor, except that the national method of church planning was more firmly established than ever, and that some occasional features such as the cuspings on the arch-mould of the door of São Francisco Santarem, which are copied on an archaistic door at Batalha, are found in later work, is there much to point to the great advance that was soon to be made alike in detail and in construction.

CHAPTER IV
BATALHA AND THE DELIVERANCE OF PORTUGAL

TOWARDS the end of the fourteenth century came the most important and critical years that Portugal had yet known. Dom Pedro, dying after a reign of only ten years, was succeeded by his only legitimate son, Fernando, in 1367. Unfortunately the new king at his sister's wedding saw and fell in love with the wife of a northern nobleman, and soon openly married this Dona Leonor Telles de Menezes, though he was himself already betrothed to a Castilian princess, and though her own husband was still alive. At the first court or Beja Manos held by Dona Leonor at Leça near Oporto, all the Portuguese nobility except Dom Diniz, the king's half-brother and a son of Inez de Castro, acknowledged her as queen. But soon the evil influence she exercised over the king and the stories of her cruelty made her extremely unpopular and even hated by the whole nation. The memory of the vengeance she took on her own sister, Dona Maria Telles, is preserved by an interesting old house in Coimbra which has indeed been rebuilt since, in the early sixteenth century, but is still called the House of the Telles. To the dislike Queen Leonor felt for the sons of Inez de Castro, owing to Dom Diniz's refusal to kiss her hand, was added the hatred she had borne her sister, who was married to Dom João, another son of Dona Inez, ever since this sister Dona Maria had warned her to have nothing to do with the king; she was also jealous because Dona Maria had had a son while her own two eldest children had died. So plotting to be rid of them both, she at last persuaded Dom João that his wife was not faithful to him, and sent him full of anger to that house at Coimbra where Dona Maria was living and where, without even giving his wife time to speak, he stabbed her to death. Soon after Dona Leonor came in and laughed at him 80 for having believed her lies so as to kill his own wife. Failing to kill the queen, Dom João fled to Castile.

When Dom Fernando himself died in 1383 he left his widow as regent of the kingdom on behalf of their only daughter, Dona Brites, whom they had married to Don Juan I. of Castile. It was of course bad enough for the nation to find itself under the regency of such a woman, but to be absorbed by Castile and Leon was more than could be endured. So a great Cortes was held at Coimbra, and Dom João, grand master of the Order of Aviz, and the son of Dom Pedro and Dona Thereza Lourenço, was elected king. The new king at once led his people against the invaders, and after twice defeating them met them for the final struggle at Aljubarrota, near Alcobaça, on 14th August 1385. The battle raged all day till at last the Castilian king fled with all his army, leaving his tent with its rich furniture and all his baggage. Before the enemy had been driven from the little town of Aljubarrota, the wife of the village baker made herself famous by killing nine Spaniards with her wooden baking shovel—a shovel which may still be seen on the town arms. When all was over Dom João dedicated the spoil he had taken in the Castilian king's tent to Our Lady of the Olive Tree at Guimarães where may still be seen, with many other treasures, a large silver-gilt triptych of the Nativity and one of the silver angels from off the royal altar.[75] Besides this, he had promised if victorious to rebuild the church at Guimarães and to found where the victory had been won a monastery as a thankoffering for his success.

Batalha.

This vow was fulfilled two years later in 1387 by building the great convent of Sta. Maria da Victoria or Batalha, that is Battle, at a place then called Pinhal[76] in a narrow valley some nine or ten miles north of Aljubarrota and seven south of Leiria. Meanwhile John of

Gaunt had landed in Galicia with a large army to try and win Castile and Leon, which he claimed for his wife Constance, elder daughter of Pedro the Cruel; marching through Galicia he met Dom João at Oporto in February 1387, and then the Treaty of Windsor, which had been signed the year before and which 81 had declared the closest union of friendship and alliance to exist between England and Portugal, was further strengthened by the marriage of King João to Philippa, the daughter of John of Gaunt and of his first wife, Blanche of Lancaster. Soon after, the peace of the Peninsula was assured by the marriage of Catherine, the only child of John of Gaunt and of Constance of Castile, to Enrique, Prince of the Asturias and heir to the throne of Castile.

PLAN OF BATALHA

But it is time now to turn from the history of the foundation of Batalha to the buildings themselves, and surely no more puzzling building than the church is to be found anywhere. The plan, indeed, of the church, omitting the Capella do Fundador and the great Capellas Imperfeitas, presents no difficulty as it is only a repetition of the already well-known and national arrangement of nave with aisles, an aisleless transept, with in this case five apsidal chapels to the east. Now in all this there is nothing the least unusual or different from what might be expected, except perhaps that the nave, of eight bays, is rather longer than in any 82 previous example. But the church was built to commemorate a great national deliverance, and by a king who had just won immense booty from his defeated enemy, and so was naturally built on a great and imposing scale.[77]

The first architect, Affonso Domingues, perhaps a grandson of the Domingo Domingues who built the cloister at Alcobaça, is said to have been born at Lisbon and so, as might have been expected, his plan shows no trace at all of foreign influence. And yet even this ordinary plan has been compared by a German writer to that of the nave and transepts of Canterbury Cathedral, a most unlikely model to be followed, as Chillenden, who there carried out the transformation of Lanfranc's nave, did not become prior till 1390, three years after Batalha had been begun.[78] But though it is easy enough to show that the plan is not English but quite national and Portuguese, it is not so easy to say what the building itself is. Affonso Domingues died in 1402, and was succeeded by a man whose name is spelt in a great variety of ways, Ouguet, Huguet, or Huet, and to whom most of the building apart from the plan must have been due. His name sounds more French than anything else, but the building is not at all French except in a few details. Altogether it is not at all easy to say whence those peculiarities of tracery and detail which make Batalha so strange and unusual a building were derived, except that there had been in Portugal nothing to lead up to such tracery or to such elaboration of detail, or to the constructive skill needed to build the high groined vaults of the nave or the enormous span required to cover the chapter-house. Perhaps it may be better to describe the church first outside and then in, and then see if it is possible to discover from the details themselves whence they can have come.

The five eastern apses, of which the largest in the centre is also twice as high as the other four, are probably the oldest part of the building, but all, except the two outer apses and the upper part of the central, have been concealed by the Pateo 83 built by Dom Manoel to unite the church with the Capellas Imperfeitas, or unfinished chapels, beyond. Here there is nothing very unusual: the smaller chapels all end in three-sided apses, at whose angles are buttresses, remarkable only for the great number of string courses, five in all, which divide them horizontally; these buttresses are finished by two offsets just below a plain corbel table which is now crowned by an elaborately pierced and cusped parapet which may well have been added later. Each side of the apse has one tall narrow single-light window which, filled at some later date from top to bottom with elaborate stone tracery, has two thin shafts at each side and a rather bluntly-pointed head. The central apse has been much the same but with five sides, and two stories of similar windows one above the other. So far there is nothing unexpected or what could not easily have been developed from already existing buildings, such as the church at Thomar or the Franciscan and Dominican churches no further away than Pontevedra in Galicia.

Coming to the south transept, there is a large doorway below under a crocketed gable flanked by a tall pinnacle on either side. This door with its thirteenth-century mouldings is one of the most curious and unexpected features of the whole building. Excepting that the capitals are well carved with leaves, it is a close copy of the west door of São Francisco at Santarem. Here the horseshoe cuspings are on the out-most of the five orders of mouldings, and the chevron on the fourth, while there is also a series of pointed cusps on the second. Only the innermost betrays its really late origin by the curious crossing and interpenetrating of the mouldings of its large trefoiled head. All this is thoroughly Portuguese and clearly derived from what had gone before; but the same cannot be said for the crockets or for the pinnacles with their square and gabled spirelets. These crockets are of the common vine-leaf shape such as was used in England and also in France early in the fourteenth century, while the two-storied pinnacles with shallow traceried panels on each face, and still more the square spirelets with rather large crockets and a large bunchy finial, are not at all French, but a not bad imitation of contemporary English work. On the gable above the door are two square panels, each containing a coat-of-arms set in a cusped quatrefoil, while the vine-leaves which fill in the 84 surface between the quatrefoils and the outer mouldings of the square, as also those on the crowns which surmount the coats, are also quite English. The elaborate many-sided canopies above are not so much so in form though they might well have been evolved from English detail. Above the gable comes another English feature, a very large three-light window running up to the very vault; at the top the mullions of each light are carried up so as to intersect, with cusped circles filling in each space, while the whole window to the top is filled with a veil of small reticulated tracery. Above the top of the large window there is a band of reticulated panelling whose shafts run down till they reach the crocketed hood-mould of the window: and above this an elaborately pierced and foliated parapet between the square pinnacles of the angle buttresses, which like these of the apses are remarkable for the extraordinary number (ten) of offsets and string courses.

The next five bays of the nave as well as the whole north side (which has no buttresses) above the cloister are all practically alike; the buttresses, pinnacles and parapet are just the same as those of the transept: the windows tall, standing pretty high above the ground, are all of three lights with tracery evidently founded on that of the large transept window, but set very far back in the wall with as many as three shafts on each side, and with each light now filled in with horrid wood or plaster work. The clerestory windows, also of three lights with somewhat similar tracery, are separated by narrow buttresses bearing square pinnacles, between which runs on a pointed corbel table the usual pierced parapet, and by strong flying buttresses, which at least in the western bays are doubly cusped, and are, between the arch and the straight part, pierced with a large foliated circle and other tracery. The last three bays on the south side are taken up by the Founder's Chapel (Capella do Fundador), in which are buried King João, Queen Philippa, and four of their sons. This chapel, which must have been begun a good deal later than the church, as the church was finished in 1415 when the queen died and was temporarily buried before the high altar, while the chapel was not yet ready when Dom João made his will in 1426, though it was so in 1434 when he and the queen were there buried, is an exact square of about 80 feet externally, within which an octagon of about 38 feet in diameter rises above the flat roof of the square, rather higher than to 85 the top of the aisles. Each exposed side of the square is divided into three bays, one wider in the centre with one narrower on each side. The buttresses, pinnacles and corbel table are much the same as before, but the parapet is much more elaborate and more like French flamboyant. Of the windows the smaller are of four lights with very elaborate and unusual flowing tracery in their heads; small parts of which, such as the tracery at the top of the smaller lights, is curiously English, while the whole is neither English nor French nor belonging to any other national school. The same may be said of the larger eight-light window in the central bay, but that there the tracery is even more elaborate and extravagant. The octagon above has buttresses with ordinary pinnacles at each corner, a parapet like that below, and flying buttresses, all pierced, cusped and crocketed like those at the west front. On each face is a tall two-light window with flowing tracery packed in rather tightly at the top.

As for the west front itself, which has actually been compared to that of York Minster, the ends of the aisles are much like the sides, with similar buttresses, pinnacles and parapet, but with the windows not set back quite so far. On each side of the large central door are square buttresses, running up to above the level of the aisle roof in six stories, the four upper of which are panelled with what looks like English decorated tracery, and ending in large square crocketed and gabled pinnacles. The door itself between these buttresses is another strange mixture. In general design and in size it is entirely French: on either side six large statues stand on corbels and under elaborate many-sided canopies, while on the arches themselves is the usual French arrangement of different canopied figures: the tympanum is upheld by a richly cusped segmental arch, and has on it a curiously archaistic carving of Our Lord under a canopy surrounded by the four Evangelists. Above, the crocketed drip-mould is carried up in an ogee leaving room for the coronation of the Virgin over the apex of the arch. So far all might be French, but on examining the detail, a great deal of it is found to be not French but English: the half octagonal corbels with their panelled and traceried sides, and still more the strips of panelling on the jambs with their arched heads, are quite English and might be found in almost any early perpendicular reredos or tomb, nor are the larger canopies quite French. (Fig. 33.) 86

Above the finial of the ogee runs a corbel table supporting a pierced and crested parapet, a little different in design from the rest.

Above this parapeted gallery is a large window lighting the upper part of the nave, a window which for extravagance and exuberance of tracery exceeds all others here or elsewhere. The lower part is evidently founded on the larger windows of the Capella do Fundador. Like them it has two larger pointed lights under a big ogee which reaches to the apex of a pointed arch spanning the whole window, the space between this ogee and the enclosing arch being filled in with more or less ordinary flowing tracery. These two main lights are again much subdivided: at the top is a circle with spiral tracery; below it an arch enclosing an ogee exactly similar to the larger one above, springing from two sub-lights which are again subdivided in exactly the same manner, into circle, sub-arch, ogee and two small lights, so that the whole lower part of the window is really built up from the one motive repeated three times. The space between the large arch and the window head is taken up by a large circle completely filled with minute spiral tracery and two vesicae also filled in with smaller vesicae and circles. Now such a window could not have been designed in England, in France, or anywhere else; not only is it ill arranged, but it is entirely covered from top to bottom with tracery, which shows that an attempt was being made to adapt forms suitable in a northern climate to the brilliant summer sun of Portugal, a sun which a native builder would rather try to keep out than to let in. Above the window is a band of reticulated tracery like that below, and the front is finished with a straight line of parapet pierced and foliated like that below, joining the picturesque clusters of corner pinnacles. The only other part of the church which calls for notice is the bell-tower which stands at the north end of a very thick wall separating the sacristy from the cloister; it is now an octagon springing strangely from the square below, with a rich parapet, inside which stands a tall spire; this spire, which has a sort of coronet rather more than half-way up, consists of eight massive crocketed ribs ending in a huge finial, and with the space between filled in with very fine pierced work.[79] From such of the original detail which has

FIG. 33.
BATALHA
WEST FRONT OF CHURCH.
FROM A PHOTOGRAPH BY E. BIEL & CO., OPORTO.

87 survived the beautiful alterations of Dom Manoel, the details of the cloister must have been very like those of the church. The refectory to the west of the cloister is a plain room roofed with a pointed barrel-vault; but the chapter-house is constructively the most remarkable part of the whole convent. It is a great room over sixty feet square, opening off the east cloister walk by a large pointed door with a two-light window each side. This great space is covered by an immense vault, upheld by no central shaft; arches are thrown across the corners bringing the square to an octagon, and though not very high, it is one of the

boldest Gothic vaults ever attempted; there is nowhere else a room of such a size vaulted without supporting piers, and probably none where the buttresses outside, with their small projection, look so unequal to the work they have to do, yet this vault has successfully withstood more than one earthquake.

The inside of the church is in singular contrast to the floridness of the outside. The clustered piers are exceptionally large and tall; there is no triforium, and the side windows are set so far back as to be scarcely seen. The capitals have elaborate Gothic foliage, but are so square as to look at a distance almost romanesque. In front of each pier triple vaulting shafts run up, but instead of the side shafts carrying the diagonal ribs as they should have done, all three carry bold transverse arches, leaving the vaulting ribs to spring as best they can. Each bay has horizontal ridge ribs, though their effect is lost by the too great strength of the transverse arches. The chancel, a little lower than the nave and transepts, is entered by an acutely pointed and richly cusped arch, and has a regular Welsh groined vault, with a well-developed ridge rib. Unfortunately almost all the church furniture was destroyed during the French retreat, and of the stained glass only that in the windows of the main apse survives, save in the three-light window of the chapter-house, a window which can be exactly dated as it displays the arms of Portugal and Castile quartered. This could only have been done during the life of Dom Manoel's first wife, Isabel, eldest daughter and heir of Ferdinand and Isabella. Dom Manoel married her in 1497, and she died in 1498 leaving a son who, had he lived, would have inherited the whole Peninsula and so saved Spain from the fatal connection with the Netherlands inherited by Charles V. from his own father. (Fig. 34.) 88

The most elaborate part of the interior is not unnaturally the Capella do Fundador. though even there, the four beautiful carved and painted altars and retables on the east side, and the elaborate carved presses on the west, have all vanished from their places, burned for firewood by the invaders in 1810. In the centre under the lantern, lie King João who died in 1433, and on the right Queen Philippa of Lancaster who died seventeen years before. The high tomb itself is a plain square block of stone from which on each side there project four lions: at the head are the royal arms surrounded by the Garter, and on the sides long inscriptions in honour of the king and queen. The figures of the king and queen lie side by side with very elaborate canopies at their heads. King João is in armour, holding a sword in his left hand and with his other clasping the queen's right hand. The figures are not nearly so well carved as are those of Dom Pedro and Inez de Castro at Alcobaça, nor is the tomb nearly as elaborate. On the south wall are the recessed tombs of four of their younger sons. The eldest, Dom Duarte, intended to be buried in the great unfinished chapel at the east, but still lies with his wife before the high altar. Each recess has a pointed arch richly moulded, and with broad bands of very unusual leaves, while above it rises a tall ogee canopy, crocketed and ending in a large finial. The space between arch and canopy and the sills of the windows is covered with reticulated panelling like that on the west front, and the tombs are divided by tall pinnacles. The four sons here buried are, beginning at the west: first, Dom Pedro, duke of Coimbra; next him Dom Henrique, duke of Vizeu and master of the Order of Christ, famous as Prince Henry the Navigator; then Dom João, Constable of Portugal; and last, Dom Fernando, master of the Order of Aviz, who died an unhappy captive in Morocco. During the reign of his brother Dom Duarte he had taken part in an expedition to that country, and being taken prisoner was offered his freedom if the Portuguese would give up Ceuta, captured by King João in the year in which Queen Philippa died. These terms he indignantly refused and died after some years of misery. On the front of each tomb is a large panel on which are two or three shields—one on that of Dom Henrique being surrounded with the Garter—while all the surface is covered with beautifully carved foliage. Dom Henrique alone has an

FIG. 34.
CHURCH,
BATALHA.
INTERIOR.

FIG. 35.
BATALHA
CAPELLA DO FUNDADOR AND TOMB OF DOM JOÃO I AND DONA FILIPPA.

43

[89] effigy, the others having only covers raised and panelled, while the back of the Constable's monument has on it scenes from the Passion.

The eight piers of the lantern are made up of a great number of shafts with a moulded angle between each. The capitals are covered with two tiers of conventional vine-leaves and have octagonal, not as in the church square abaci, while the arches are highly stilted and are enriched with most elaborate cusping, each cusp ending in a square vine-leaf. (Fig. 35.)

Such then are the main features of the church, the design of which, according to most writers, was brought straight from England by the English queen, an opinion which no one who knows English contemporary buildings can hold for a moment.

First, to take the entirely native features. The plan is only an elaboration of that of many already existing churches. The south transept door is a copy of a door at Santarem. The heavy transverse arches and the curious way the diagonal vaulting ribs are left to take care of themselves have been seen no further away than at Alcobaça; the flat-paved terraced roofs, whose origin the Visconde di Condeixa in his monograph on the convent, sought even as far off as in Cyprus, existed already at Evora and elsewhere.

Secondly, from France might have come the general design of the west door, and the great height of the nave, though the proportion between the aisle arcade and the clerestory, and the entire absence of any kind of triforium, is not at all French.

Thirdly, several details, as has been seen, appear to be more English than anything else, but they are none of them very important; the ridge ribs in the nave, the Welsh groining of the chancel vault, the general look of the pinnacles, a few pieces of stone panelling on buttresses or door, a small part of a few of the windows, the moulding of the chapter-house door, the leaves on the capitals of the Capella do Fundador, and the shape of the vine-leaves at the ends of the cuspings of the arches. From a distance the appearance of the church is certainly more English than anything else, but that is due chiefly to the flat roof—a thoroughly Portuguese feature—and to the upstanding pinnacles, which suggest a long perpendicular building such as one of the college chapels at Oxford.

Lastly, if the open-work spire is a real copy of that [90] destroyed in 1755, and if there ever was another like it on the Capella do Fundador,[80] they suggest German influence, although the earliest Spanish examples of such German work were not begun at Burgos till 1442, by which time the church here must have been nearly if not quite finished.

It is then not difficult to assign a great many details, with perhaps a certain amount of truth, to the influence of several foreign countries, yet as a whole the church is unlike any building existing in any of these countries or even in Spain, and it remains as difficult, or indeed as impossible, to discover whence these characteristics came. So far there had been scarcely any development of window tracery to lead up to the elaborate and curious examples which are found here; still less had any such constructive skill been shown in former buildings as to make so great a vault as that of the chapter-house at all likely, for such a vault is to be found perhaps nowhere else.

Probably the plan of the church, and perhaps the eastern chapel and lower part of the transept, are the work of Affonso Domingues, and all the peculiarities, the strange windows, the cusped arches, the English-looking pinnacles, as well as all the constructive skill, are due to Huguet his successor, who may perhaps have travelled in France and England, and had come back to Portugal with increased knowledge of how to build, but with a rather confused idea of the ornamental detail he had seen abroad.

When Dom João died in 1433 his eldest son, Dom Duarte or Edward, determined to build for himself a more splendid tomb-house than his father's, and so was begun the great octagon to the east.

Unfortunately Dom Duarte's reign was short; he died in 1438, partly it is said of distress at the ill success of his expedition to Morocco and at the captivity there of his youngest brother, so that he had no time to finish his chapel, and his son Affonso V., the African, was too much engaged in campaigning against the Moors to be able to give either money or attention to his father's work; and it was still quite unfinished when Dom Manoel came to the throne in 1495, and though he did much towards carrying on the work it was 91 unfinished when he died in 1521 and so remains to the present day. It is in designing this chapel that Huguet showed his greatest originality and constructive daring: a few feet behind the central apse he planned a great octagon about seventy-two feet in diameter, surrounded by seven apsidal chapels, one on each side except that next the church, while between these chapels are small low chambers where were to be the tombs themselves. There is nothing to show how this chapel was to be united to the church, as the great doorway and vaulted hall were added by Dom Manoel some seventy years later. When Dom Duarte died in 1438, or when Huguet himself died not long after, [81] the work had only been carried out as far as the tops of the surrounding chapels, and so remained all through his son's and his grandson's reigns, although in his will the king had specially asked that the building should be carried on. In all this original part of the Capellas Imperfeitas there is little that differs from Huguet's work in the church. The buttresses and corbel table are very similar (the pinnacles and parapets have been added since 1834), and the apses quite like those of the church. (Fig. 36.)

The tracery of the chief windows too is not unlike that of the lantern windows of the founder's chapel except that there is a well-marked transome half-way up—a feature which has been attributed to English influence—while the single windows of the tomb chambers are completely filled with geometric tracery. Inside, the capitals of the chapel arches as well as their rich cuspings are very like those of the founder's chapel; the capitals having octagonal abaci and stiff vine-leaves, and the trefoiled cusps ending in square vine-leaves, while the arch mouldings are, as in King João's chapel, more English than French in section. There is nothing now to show how the great central octagon was to be roofed—for the eight great piers which now rise high above the chapel were not built till the time of Dom Manoel—but it seems likely that the vault was meant to be low, and not to rise much above the chapel roofs, finishing, as everywhere else in the church, in a flat, paved terrace. 92

The only important addition made during the reigns of Dom Affonso V. and of Dom João II. was that of a second cloister, north of the Claustro Real, and still called the Cloister of Affonso. This cloister is as plain and wanting in ornament as everything else about the monastery is rich and elaborate, and it was probably built under the direction of Fernão d'Evora, who succeeded his uncle Martim Vasques as master of the works before 1448, and held that position for nearly thirty years. Unlike the great cloister, whose large openings must, from the first, have been meant for tracery, the cloister of Affonso V. is so very plain and simple, that if its date were not known it would readily be attributed to a period older even than the foundation of the monastery. On each side are seven square bays separated by perfectly plain buttresses, each bay consisting of two very plain pointed arches resting on the moulded capitals of coupled shafts. Except for the buttresses and the vault the cloister differs in no marked way from those at Guimarães and elsewhere whose continuous pointed arcades show so little advance from the usual romanesque manner of cloister-building. Above is a second story of later date, in which the tiled roof rests on short columns placed rather far apart, and with no regard to the spacing of the bays below. Round this are the kitchens and various domestic offices of the convent, and behind it lay another cloister, now utterly gone, having been burned by the French in 1810. Such are the church and monastery of Batalha as planned by Dom João and added to by his son and grandson, and though it is not possible to say whence Huguet drew his inspiration, it remains, with all the peculiarities of tracery and detail which make it seem strange and ungrammatical—if one may so speak— to eyes accustomed to northern Gothic, one of the most remarkable examples of original planning and daring construction to be found anywhere. Of the later additions which give character to the cloister and to the Capellas Imperfeitas nothing can be said till the time of Dom Manoel is reached.

FIG. 36.
BATALHA
CAPELLAS IMPERFEITAS.
FROM A PHOTOGRAPH BY E. BIEL & CO., OPORTO.
CHAPTER V
THE EARLIER FIFTEENTH CENTURY

Guimarães.

[93] BESIDES building Batalha, King João dedicated the spoils he had taken at Aljubarrota to the church of Nossa Senhora da Oliviera at Guimarães, which he rebuilt from the designs of Juan Garcia of Toledo. The most important of these spoils is the silver-gilt reredos taken in the Spanish king's travelling chapel. It is in the shape of a triptych about four feet high. In the centre is represented the Virgin with the Infant Christ on a bed, with Joseph seated and leaning wearily on his staff at the foot, the figures being about fourteen inches high; above two angels swing censers, and the heads of an ox and an ass appear feeding from a manger. All the background is richly diapered, and above are four cusped arches, separated by angels under canopies, while above the arches to the top there rises a rich mass of tabernacle work, with the window-like spaces filled in with red or green enamel. At the top are two half-angels holding the arms of Portugal, added when the reredos was dedicated to Our Lady by Dom João. The two leaves, each about twenty inches wide, are divided into two equal stories, each of which has two cusped and canopied arches enclosing, those on the left above, the Annunciation, and below the Presentation, and those on the right, the Angel appearing to the Shepherds above, and the Wise Men below. All the tabernacle work is most beautifully wrought in silver, but the figures are less good, that of the Virgin Mary being distinctly too large.[82] (Fig. 37.)

Of the other things taken from the defeated king's tent, only one silver angel now remains of the twelve which were sent to Guimarães. [94]

Of the church rebuilt in commemoration of this great victory, only the west front has escaped a terrible transformation carried out not so long ago, and which has made it impossible to see what the inside was once like. If the builder was a Spaniard, as his name, Juan Garcia de Toledo, seems to imply, there is nothing Spanish about his design. The door is like many another door of about the same period, with simple mouldings ornamented with small bosses, but the deeply recessed window above is most unusual. The tracery is gone, but the framing of the window remains, and is far more like that of a French door than of a window. On either jamb are two stories of three canopied niches, containing figures, while the arches are covered with small figures under canopies; all is rather rude, but the whole is most picturesque and original.

To the left rises the tower, standing forward from the church front: it is of three stories, with cable moulding at the corners, a picturesque cornice and battlements at the top; a bell gable in front, and a low octagonal spire. On the ground floor are two large windows defended by simple but good iron grilles, and in the upper part are large belfry windows. This is not the original tower, for that was pulled down in 1515, when the present one was built in its stead by Pedro Esteves Cogominho. Though of so late a date it is quite uninfluenced, not only by those numerous buildings of Dom Manoel's time, which are noted for their fantastic detail, but by the early renaissance which had already begun to show itself here and there, and it is one of the most picturesque church towers in the country.

A few feet to the west of the church there is a small open shrine or chapel, a square vault resting on four pointed arches which are well moulded, enriched with dog-tooth and surmounted by gables. This chapel was built soon after 1342 to commemorate the miracle to which the church owes its name. Early in the fourteenth century there grew at São Torquato, a few miles off, an olive-tree which provided the oil for that saint's lamp. It was transported to Guimarães to fulfil a like office there for the altar of Our Lady. It naturally died, and so remained for many years till 1342, when one Pedro Esteves placed on it a cross which his brother had bought in Normandy. This was the 8th of September, and three days after the dead olive-tree broke into leaf, a miracle

FIG. 37.
CAPELLA OF D. JUAN OF CASTILLE.
TAKEN AT THE BATTLE OF ALJUBARROTA BY JOÃO I,
1385, AND
NOW IN THE TREASURY OF N.S. DA OLIVEIRA
GUIMARÃES.

FIG. 38.
GUARDA
N. SIDE OF
CATHEDRAL.

greatly to the advantage and wealth of the church and of the town. From that day the church was called Our Lady of the Olive Tree.

Guarda.

Far more interesting than this church, because much better preserved and because it is clearly derived, in part at least, from Batalha, is the cathedral of Guarda, begun by João I. Guarda is a small town, not far from the Spanish border, built on a hill rising high above the bleak surrounding tableland to a height of nearly four thousand feet, and was founded by Dom Sancho I. in 1197 to guard his frontier against the Spaniards and the Moors. Begun by João I. the plan and general design of the whole church must belong to the beginning of the fifteenth century, though the finishing of the nave, and the insertion of larger transept windows, were carried out under Dom Manoel, and though the great reredos is of the time of Dom João III. Yet the few chapels between the nave buttresses are almost the only real additions made to the church. Though of but moderate dimensions, it is one of the largest of Portuguese cathedrals, being 175 feet long by 70 feet wide and 110 feet across the transepts. It is also unique among the aisled and vaulted churches in copying Batalha by having a well-developed clerestory and flying buttresses.

CATHEDRAL. GUARDA.

The plan consists of a nave and aisles of five bays, a transept projecting one bay beyond the aisles, and three apses to the east. At the crossing the vault is slightly raised so as to admit of four small round windows opening above the flat roofs of the central aisle and transepts. The only peculiarity about the plan lies in the two western towers, which near the ground are squares set diagonally to the front of the church and higher up change to octagons, and so rise a few feet 96 above the flat roof. About the end of the fifteenth century two small chapels were added to the north of the nave, and later still the spaces between the buttresses were filled in with shallow altar recesses.

The likeness to Batalha is best seen in the Capella Mor. As the apse has only three instead of five sides, the windows are rather wider, and there are none below, but otherwise the resemblance is as great as may be, when the model is of fine limestone and the copy of granite. The buttresses have offset string courses, and square crocketed pinnacles just as at Batalha; there has even been an attempt to copy the parapet, though only the trefoil corbel table is really like the model, for the parapet itself is solid with a cresting of rather clumsy fleurs-de-lis. These pinnacles and this crested parapet are found everywhere all round the church, though the pinnacles on the aisle walls from which the plain flying buttresses spring are quite different, being of a Manoelino design. Again the north transept door has evidently been inspired by the richness of Batalha. Here the door itself is plain, but well moulded, with above it an elaborately crocketed ogee drip-mould, which ends in a large finial; above this rises to a considerable height some arcaded panelling, ending at the top in a straight band of quatrefoil, and interrupted by a steep gable. (Fig. 38.)

No other part of the outside calls for much notice except the boat-keel corbels of the smaller apses, the straight gable-less ends to transept and nave which show that the roofs are flat and paved, and the western towers. These are of three stories. The lowest is square at the bottom and octagonal above, the change being effected by a curved offset at two corners, while at the third or western corner the curve has been cut down so as to leave room for an eighteenth-century window, lighting the small polygonal chapel inside, a chapel originally lit by two narrow round-headed windows on the diagonal sides. In the second story there are again windows on the same diagonal sides, but they have been built up: while on the third or highest division—where the octagon is complete on all sides—are four belfry windows. The whole is finished by a crested parapet. The west front between these towers is very plain. At the top a cresting, simpler than that elsewhere, below a round window without tracery, lower still two picturesque square rococo windows, and at the 97 bottom a rather elaborate Manoelino doorway, built not many years ago to replace one of the same date as the windows above.

Throughout the clerestory windows are not large. They are round-headed of two lights, with simple tracery, and deep splays both inside and out. The large transept windows with half octagonal heads under a large trefoil were inserted about the beginning of the sixteenth century.

Inside the resemblance to Batalha is less noticeable. The ribs of the chancel vault are well moulded, as are the arches of the lantern, but in the nave, which cannot have been finished till the end of the fifteenth century, the design is quite different. The piers are all a hollow square set diagonally with a large round shaft at each corner. In the aisle arches the hollows of the diagonal sides are carried round without capitals, with which the round shafts alone are provided; while the shaft in front runs up to a round Manoelino capital with octagonal abacus from which springs the vaulting at a level higher than the sills of the clerestory windows.[83] The most unusual part of the nave is the vaulting of all three aisles, where all the ribs, diagonal as well as transverse, are of exactly the same section and size as is the round shaft from which they spring, even the wall rib being of the same shape though a little smaller. At the crossing there are triple shafts on each side, those of the nave being twisted, which is another Manoelino feature. The nave then must be about a hundred years later than the eastern parts of the church, where the capitals are rather long and are carved with foliage and have square abaci, while those of the nave are all of the time of King João II. or of King Manoel. At about the same time some small and picturesque windows were inserted above the smaller apses on the east side of the transept, and rather later was built the chapel to the north-east of the nave, which is entered through a segmental arch whose jambs and head are well carved with early renaissance foliage and figures, and which contains the simple tomb of a bishop. The pulpits, organs, and stalls, both in the chancel and in the western choir gallery, are fantastic and late, but the great reredos which rises in three divisions to the springing of the vault is the largest and one of the finest in the country, but 98 belonging as it does to a totally different period and school must be left for another chapter.

Nossa Senhora do Vencimento do Monte do Carmo, Lisbon.

Much need not be said about the Carmo at Lisbon, another church of the same date, as it has been almost entirely wrecked by the earthquake of 1755. The victory of Aljubarrota was due perhaps even more to the grand Constable of Portugal, Dom Nuno Alvares Pereira, than to the king himself, and, like the king, the Constable commemorated the victory by founding a monastery, a great Carmelite house in Lisbon. The church of Nossa Senhora do Vencimento do Monte do Carmo stands high up above the central valley of Lisbon on the very verge of the steep hill. Begun in July 1389 the foundations twice gave way, and it was only after the Constable had dismissed his first master and called in three men of the same name, Affonso, Gonçalo, and Rodrigo Eannes, that a real beginning could be made, and it was not finished till 1423, when it was consecrated; at the same time the founder assumed the habit of a Carmelite and entered his own monastery to die eight years later, and to become an object of veneration to the whole people. In plan the church was almost exactly like that of Batalha, though with a shorter nave of only five bays.[84] To the east of the transept are still five apses—the best preserved part of the whole building—having windows and buttresses like those at Batalha. The only other part of the church which has escaped destruction is the west door, a large simple opening of six moulded arches springing from twelve shafts whose capitals are carved with foliage. From what is left it seems that the church was more like what Batalha was planned to be, rather than what it became under the direction of Huguet: but the downfall of the nave has been so complete that it is only possible to make out that there must have been a well-developed clerestory and a high vaulted central aisle. What makes this destruction all the more regrettable is the fact that the church was full of splendid tombs, especially that of the Holy Constable himself: a magnificent piece of carving in alabaster sent from Flanders by Dom João's daughter, Isabel, duchess of Flanders.[85]99

After this catastrophe an attempt was made to rebuild the church, but little was done, and it still remains a complete ruin, having been used since the suppression of all monasteries in 1834 as an Archæological Museum where many tombs and other architectural fragments may still be seen.

Villar de Frades.

48

Towards the end of King João's reign a man named João Vicente, noting the corruption into which the religious orders were falling, determined to do what he could by preaching and example to bring back a better state of things. He first began his work in Lisbon, but was driven from there by the bishop to find a refuge at Braga. There he so impressed the archbishop that he was given the decayed and ruined monastery of Villar de Frades in 1425. Soon he had gathered round him a considerable body of followers, to whom he gave a set of rules and who, after receiving the papal sanction, were known as the Canons Secular of St. John the Evangelist or, popularly, Loyos, because their first settlement in Lisbon was in a monastery formerly dedicated to St. Eloy. The church at Villar, which is of considerable size, was probably long of building, as the elliptical-headed west door with its naturalistic treelike posts has details which did not become common till at least the very end of the century. Inside the church consists of a nave of five bays, flanked with chapels but not aisles, transepts which are really only enlarged chapels, and a chancel like the nave but without chapels. The chief feature of the inside is the very elaborate vaulting, which with the number and intricacy of its ribs, is not at all unlike an English Perpendicular vault, and indeed would need but little change to develop into a fan vault. Here then there has been a considerable advance from the imperfect vaulting of the central aisle at Batalha, where the diagonal ribs had to be squeezed in wherever they could go, although there are at Villar no side aisles so that the construction of supporting buttresses was of course easier than at Batalha: and it is well worth noticing how from so imperfect a beginning as the nave at Batalha the Portuguese masters soon learned to build elaborate and even wide vaults, without, as a rule, covering them with innumerable and meaningless twisting ribs as was usually done in Spain. In the north-westernmost chapel stands the font, an elaborate work of the early renaissance; an octagonal bowl with twisted sides resting on a short twisted base. 100

Matriz, Alvito.

Not unlike the vaulting at Villar is that of the Matriz or mother church of Alvito, a small town in the Alemtejo, nor can it be very much later in date. Outside it is only remarkable for its west door, an interesting example of an attempt to use the details of the early French renaissance, without understanding how to do so—as in the pediment all the entablature except the architrave has been left out—and for the short twisted pinnacles which somehow give to it, as to many other buildings in the Alemtejo, so Oriental a look, and which are seen again at Belem. Inside, the aisles are divided from the nave by round chamfered arches springing from rather short octagonal piers, which have picturesque octagonal capitals and a moulded band half-way up. Only is the easternmost bay, opening to large transeptal chapels, pointed and moulded. The vaulting springs from corbels, and although the ribs are but simply chamfered they are well developed. Curiously, though the central is so much higher than the side aisles, there is no clerestory, nor any signs of there ever having been one, while the whole wall surface is entirely covered with those beautiful tiles which came to be so much used during the seventeenth century.

In the year 1415 her five sons had sailed straight from the deathbed of Queen Philippa to the coast of Morocco and had there captured the town of Ceuta, a town which remained in the hands of the Portuguese till after their ill-fated union with Spain; for in 1668 it was ceded to Spain in return for an acknowledgment of Portuguese independence, thus won after twenty-seven years' more or less continuous fighting. This was the first time any attempt had been made to carry the Portuguese arms across the Straits, and to attack their old enemies the Moors in their own land, where some hundred and seventy years later King João's descendant, Dom Sebastião, was to lose his life and his country's freedom.

Tomb in Graça, Santarem.

The first governor of Ceuta was Dom Pedro de Menezes, count of Viana. There he died in 1437, after having for twenty-two years bravely defended and governed the city— then, as is inscribed on his tomb, the only place in Africa possessed by Christians. This tomb, which was made at the command of his daughter Dona Leonor, stands in the church of the Graça at Santarem, a church which had been founded by his grandfather the count of Ourem in 1376 for canons regular of St. Augustine. Inside the church itself is not

49

very 101 remarkable,[86] having a nave and aisles with transepts and three vaulted chapels to the east, built very much in the same style as is the church at Leça do Balio, except that it has a fine west front, to be mentioned later, that the roof of the nave was knocked down by the Devil in 1548 in anger at the extreme piety of Frey Martinho de Santarem, one of the canons, and that many famous people, including Pedro Alvares Cabral, the discoverer of Brazil, are therein buried.

In general outline the tomb of the count of Viana is not unlike that of his master Dom João, but it is much more highly decorated. On eight crouching lions rests a large altar-tomb. It has a well-moulded and carved base and an elaborately carved cornice, rich with deeply undercut foliage, while on the top lie Pedro de Menezes and his wife Dona Beatriz Coutinho, with elaborately carved canopies at their heads, and pedestals covered with figures and foliage at their feet. Beneath the cornice on each of the longer sides is cut in Gothic letters a long inscription telling of Dom Pedro's life, and lower down and on all four sides there is in the middle a shield, now much damaged, with the Menezes arms. On each side of these shields are carved spreading branches, knotted round a circle in the centre in which is cut the word 'Aleo.' Once, when playing with King João at a game in which some kind of club or mallet was used, the news came that the Moors were collecting in great numbers to attack Ceuta. The king, turning to Dom Pedro, asked him what reinforcements he would need to withstand the attack; the governor answered: 'This "Aleo," or club, will be enough,' and in fact, returning at once to his command, he was able without further help to drive back the enemy. So this word has been carved on his tomb to recall how well he did his duty.[87] (Fig. 39.)

Tomb in São João de Alporão.

Not far from the Graça church is that of São João de Alporão, of which something has already been said, and in it now stands the tomb of another Menezes, who a generation later also died in Africa, fighting to save the life of his king, Dom Affonso V., grandson of King João. Notwithstanding the ill-success of the expedition of his father, Dom Duarte, to Tangier, Dom Affonso, after having got rid of his uncle the duke of Coimbra, who had governed the country during his 102 minority, and who fell in battle defending himself against the charge of treason, led several expeditions to Morocco, taking first Alcazar es Seghir or Alcacer Seguer, and later Tangier and Arzilla, thereby uselessly exhausting the strength of the people, and hindering the spread of maritime exploration which Dom Henrique had done so much to extend.

This Dom Duarte de Menezes, third count of Viana, was, as an inscription tells, first governor of Alcacer Seguer, which with five hundred soldiers he successfully defended against a hundred thousand Moors, dying at last in the mountains of Bonacofú in defence of his king in 1464.[88]

The monument was built by his widow, Dona Isabel de Castro, but so terribly had Dom Duarte been cut to pieces by the Moors, that only one finger could be found to be buried there.[89] Though much more elaborate, the tomb is not altogether unlike those of the royal princes at Batalha. The count lies, armed, with a sword drawn in his right hand, on an altar-tomb on whose front, between richly traceried panels, are carved an inscription above, upheld by small figures, and below, in the middle a flaming cresset, probably a memorial of his watchfulness in Africa, and on each side a shield.

Surmounting the altar-tomb is a deeply moulded ogee arch subdivided into two hanging arches which spring from a pendant in the middle, while the space between these sub-arches and the ogee above is filled with a canopied carving of the Crucifixion. At about the level of the pendant the open space is crossed by a cusped segmental arch supporting elaborate flowing tracery. The outer sides of the ogee, which ends in a large finial, are enriched with large vine-leaf crockets. On either side of the arch is a square pier, moulded at the angles, and with each face covered with elaborate tracery. Each pier, which ends in a square crocketed and gabled half-way

FIG. 39.

SANTAREM

CHURCH OF THE GRAÇA.TOMB OF D.

FIG. 40.

SANTAREM

TOMB OF DOM DUARTE DE

103 up a small figure standing on an octagonal corbel under an elaborate canopy. The whole at the top is finished with a cornice running straight across from pier to pier, and crested with interlacing and cusped semicircles, while the flat field below the cornice and above the outer moulding of the great arch is covered with flaming cressets. (Fig. 40.)

This is perhaps one of the finest of the tombs of the fifteenth century, and like those at Alcobaça is made of that very fine limestone which is found in more than one place in Portugal.

At Abrantes.

Farther up the Tagus at Abrantes, in the church of Santa Maria do Castello, are some more tombs of the same date, more than one of which is an almost exact copy of the princes' tombs at Batalha, though there is one whose arch is fringed with curious reversed cusping, almost Moorish in appearance.

Cloister at Thomar.

Before turning to the many churches built towards the end of the fifteenth century, one of the cloisters of the great convent at Thomar must be mentioned. It is that called 'do Cemiterio,' and was built by Prince Henry the Navigator, duke of Vizeu, during his grandmastership of the Order of Christ about the year 1440. Unlike those at Alcobaça or at Lisbon, which were derived from a Cistercian plan, and were always intended to be vaulted, this small cloister followed the plan, handed down from romanesque times, where on each side there is a continuous arcade resting on coupled shafts. Such cloisters, differing only from the romanesque in having pointed arches and capitals carved with fourteenth-century foliage, may still be seen at Santo Thyrso and at São Domingos, Guimarães, in the north. Here at Thomar the only difference is that the arches are very much wider, there being but five on each side, and that the bell-shaped capitals are covered with finely carved conventional vine-leaves arranged in two rows round the bells. As in the older cloisters one long abacus unites the two capitals, but the arches are different, each being moulded as one deep arch instead of two similar arches set side by side. 104

CHAPTER VI
LATER GOTHIC

DURING the last ten or fifteen years of the fifteenth century there was great activity in building throughout almost the whole country, but it now becomes almost impossible to take the different buildings in chronological order, because at this time so many different schools began to struggle for supremacy. There was first the Gothic school which, though increasing in elaboration of detail, went on in some places almost uninfluenced by any breath of the renaissance, as for instance in the porch and chancel of Braga Cathedral, not built till about 1532. Elsewhere this Gothic was affected partly by Spanish and partly by Moorish influence, and gradually grew into that most curious and characteristic of styles, commonly called Manoelino, from Dom Manoel under whom Portugal reached the summit of its prosperity. In other places, again, Gothic forms and renaissance details came gradually to be used together, as at Belem.

To take then first those buildings in which Gothic detail was but little influenced by the approaching renaissance.

Graça, Santarem.

One of the earliest of these is the west front, added towards the end of the fifteenth century to that Augustinian church of the Graça at Santarem whose roof the Devil knocked down in 1548. Here the ends of the side aisles are, now at any rate, quite plain, but in the centre there is a very elaborate doorway with a large rose-window above. It is easy to see that this doorway has not been uninfluenced by Batalha. From well-moulded jambs, each of which has four shafts, there springs a large pointed arch, richly fringed with cusping on its inner side. Two of its many mouldings are enriched with smaller cuspings, and one, the outermost, with a line of wavy tracery, while the whole ends in a crocketed ogee. Above the arch is a strip of shallow panelling, enclosed, as is the 105 whole doorway, in a square moulded frame. May it not be that this square frame is due to the almost universal Moorish habit of setting an archway in a square frame, as may be seen at Cordoba and in the palace windows at Cintra? The rest of the gable is perfectly plain but for the round window, filled with elaborate spiral flowing tracery. Here, though the details are more French than national, there is a good example of the excellent result so often reached by later Portuguese—and Spanish—builders, who concentrated all their elaborate ornament on one part of the building while leaving the rest absolutely plain—often as here plastered and whitewashed.

São João Baptista, Thomar.

Not long after this front was built, Dom Manoel in 1494 began a new parish church at Thomar, that of São João Baptista. The plan of this church is that which has already become so familiar: a nave and aisles with wooden roof and vaulted chancel and chapels to the east, with here, the addition of a tower and spire to the north of the west front. The inside calls for little notice: the arches are pointed, and the capitals carved with not very good foliage, but the west front is far more interesting. As at the Graça it is plastered and whitewashed, but ends not in a gable but in a straight line of cresting like Batalha, though here there is no flat terrace behind, but a sloping tile roof. At the bottom is a large ogee doorway whose tympanum is pierced with tracery and whose mouldings are covered with most beautiful and deeply undercut foliage. The outside of the arch is crocketed, and ends in a tall finial thrust through the horizontal and crested moulding which, as at the Graça, sets the whole in a square frame. There are also doorways in the same style half-way along the north and south sides of the church. The only other openings on the west front are a plain untraceried circle above the door, and a simple ogee-headed window at the end of each aisle.

The tower, which is not whitewashed, rises as a plain unadorned square to a little above the aisle roof, then turns to an octagon with, at the top, a plain belfry window on each face. Above these runs a corbelled gallery within which springs an octagonal spire cut into three by two bands of ornament, and ending in a large armillary sphere, that emblem of all the discoveries made during his reign, which Dom Manoel put on to every building with which he had anything to do.

Inside the chapels are as usual overloaded with huge ⌐106⌐ reredoses of heavily carved and gilt wood, but the original pulpit still survives, a most beautiful example of the finest late Gothic carving. It consists of four sides of an octagon, and stands on ribs which curve outwards from a central shaft. Round the bottom runs a band of foliage most marvellously undercut, above this are panels separated the one from the other by slender pinnacles, and the whole ends in a cornice even more delicately carved than is the base. At the top of each panel is some intricate tabernacle work, below which there is on one the Cross of the Order of Christ, on another the royal arms, with a coronet above which stands out quite clear of the panel, and on a third there has been the armillary sphere, now unfortunately quite broken off. But even more interesting than this pulpit itself is the comparison between its details and those of the nave or Coro added about the same time to the Templar church on the hill behind. Here all is purely Gothic, there there is a mixture of Gothic and renaissance details, and towards the west front an exuberance of carving which cannot be called either Gothic or anything else, so strange and unusual is it.

Villa do Conde.

Another church of almost exactly the same date is that of São João Baptista, the Matriz of Villa do Conde. The plan shows a nave and aisles of five bays, large transeptal chapels, and an apsidal chancel projecting beyond the two square chapels by which it is flanked. As usual the nave and aisles have a wooden roof, only the chancel and chapels being vaulted. There is also a later tower at the west end of the north aisle, and a choir gallery across the west end of the church. Throughout the original windows are very narrow and round-headed, and there is in the north-western bay a pointed door, differing only from those of about a hundred years earlier in having twisted shafts. One curious feature is the parapet of the central aisle, which is like a row of small classical pedestals, each bearing a stumpy obelisk. By far the finest feature of the outside is the great west door. On each side are clusters of square pinnacles ending in square crocketed spirelets, and running up to a horizontal moulding which, as so often, gives the whole design a rectangular form. Within comes the doorway itself; a large trefoiled arch of many mouldings of which the outermost, richly crocketed, turns up as an ogee, to pierce the horizontal line above with its finial. Every moulding is filled with foliage, most elaborately and finely [107] cut, considering that it is worked in granite. Across the trefoil at its springing there runs a horizontal moulding resting on the flat elliptical arch of the door itself. On the tympanum is a figure of St. John under a very elaborate canopy with, on his right, a queer carving of a naked man, and on his left a dragon. The space between the arch and the top moulding is filled with intricate but shallow panelling, among which, between two armillary spheres, are set, on the right, a blank shield crowned—probably prepared for the royal arms—and on the left the town arms—a galley with all sails set. Lastly, as a cresting to the horizontal moulding, there is a row of urnlike objects, the only renaissance features about the whole door. (Fig. 41.)

Inside, all the piers are octagonal with a slender shaft at each angle; these shafts alone having small capitals, while their bases stand on, and interpenetrate with, the base of the whole pier. All the arches are round—as are those leading to the chancel and transept chapels—and are moulded exactly as are the piers. All the vaults have a network of well-moulded ribs.

The tower has been added some fifty years later and is [108] very picturesque. It is of four stories: of these the lowest has rusticated masonry; the second, on its western face, a square-headed window opening beneath a small curly and broken pediment on to a balcony with very fine balusters all upheld by three large corbels. The third story has only a clock, and the fourth two plain round-headed belfry windows on each face. The whole—above a shallow cornice which is no bigger than the mouldings dividing the different stories—ends in a low stone dome, with a bell gable in front, square below, and arched above, holding two bells.

Azurara.

Scarcely a mile away, across the river Ave, lies Azurara, which was made a separate parish in 1457 and whose church was built by Dom Manoel in 1498.

In plan it is almost exactly the same as Villa do Conde, except that there are no transept chapels nor any flanking the chancel. Outside almost the only difference lies in the parapet which is of the usual shape with regular merlons; and in the west door which is an interesting example of the change to the early renaissance. The door itself is round-headed, and has Gothic mouldings separated by a broad band covered with shallow renaissance carving. On each side are twisted shafts which run up some way above the door to a sort of horizontal entablature, whose frieze is well carved, and which is cut into by a curious ogee moulding springing from the door arch. Above this entablature the shafts are carried up square for some way, and end in Gothic pinnacles. Between them is a niche surmounted by a large half-Gothic canopy and united to the side shafts by a broken and twisted treelike moulding. What adds to the strangeness of this door is that the blank spaces are plastered and whitewashed, while all the rest of the church is of grey granite. Higher up there is a round window—heavily moulded—and the whole gable ends in a queer little round pediment set between two armillary spheres.

Inside the piers are eight-sided with octagonal bases and caps, and with a band of ornament half-way up the shaft. The arches are simply chamfered but are each crossed by three carved voussoirs.

The tower is exactly like that at Villa do Conde except that the bottom story is not rusticated, and that instead of a dome there is an octagonal spire covered with yellow and white tiles.

FIG. 41.
VILLA DO CONDE.
SÃO JOÃO BAPTISTA.

Caminha.

[109] As at Azurara, the parish church of Santa Maria dos Anjos at Caminha is in plan very like the Matriz at Villa do Conde. Caminha lies on the Portuguese side of the estuary of the Minho, close to its mouth, and the church was begun in 1488, but was not finished till

53

the next century, the tower indeed not being built till 1556. Like the others, the plan shows a nave and rather narrow aisles of five bays, and two square vaulted chapels with an apsidal chancel between to the east. Three large vaulted chapels and the tower have been added, opening from the north aisle. Probably the oldest part is the chancel with its flanking chapels, which are very much more elaborate than any portion of the churches already described. There are at the angles deep square buttresses which end in groups of square spire-capped pinnacles all elaborately crocketed, and not at all unlike those at Batalha. Between these, in the chancel are narrow round-headed windows, whose mouldings are enriched with large four-leaved flowers, and on all the walls from buttress to buttress there runs a rich projecting cornice crowned by a wonderfully pierced and crested parapet; also not unlike those at Batalha, but more wonderful in that it is made of granite instead of fine limestone. The rest of the outside is much plainer, except for the two doorways, and two tall buttresses at the west end. These two doorways—which are among the most interesting in the country—must be a good deal later than the rest of the church, indeed could not have been designed till after the work of that foreign school of renaissance carvers at Coimbra had become well known, and so really belong to a later chapter.

Inside the columns are round, with caps and bases partly round and partly eight-sided, the hollow octagons interpenetrating with the circular mouldings. The arches of the arcade are also round, though those of the chancel and eastern chapels are pointed. Attached to one of the piers is a small eight-sided pulpit, at whose angles are Gothic pinnacles, but whose sides and base are covered with cherubs' heads, vases, and foliage of early renaissance.

But the chief glory of the interior are the splendid tiles with which its walls are entirely covered, and still more the wonderful wooden roof, one of the finest examples of Moorish carpentry to be found anywhere, and which, like the doorways, can now only be merely mentioned.

The tower, added by Diogo Eannes in 1556, is quite 110 plain with one belfry opening in each face close to the top and just below the low parapet which, resting on corbels, ends in a row of curious half-classic battlements.[90]

Funchal.

This plan was not confined only to parish churches, for about 1514 we find it used by Dom Manoel at Funchal for the cathedral of the newly founded diocese of Madeira. The only difference of importance is that there is a well-developed transept entered by arches of the same height as that of the chancel. Here the piers are clustered, and with rather poorly carved capitals, the arches pointed and moulded, but rather thin. As in the other churches of this date, the round-headed clerestory windows come over the piers, not over the arches. The chancel, which is rather deeper than usual, is entered by a wide foliated arch, and like the apsidal chapels is vaulted. As at Caminha, the nave roof is of Moorish design, but of even greater interest are the reredos and the choir-stalls. This reredos is three divisions in height and five in width—each division, except the two lower in the centre where there is a niche for the image of the Virgin, containing a large picture.

The divisions are separated perpendicularly by a series of Gothic pinnacles, and horizontally by a band of Gothic tabernacle work at the bottom, and above by beautifully carved early renaissance friezes. The whole ends in a projecting canopy, divided into five bays, each bay enriched with vaulting ribs, and in front with very delicately carved hanging tracery. Above the horizontal cornice is a most elaborate cresting of interlacing trefoils and leaves having in the middle the royal arms with on each side an armillary sphere. Some of the detail of the cresting is not all unlike that of the great reredos in the Sé Velha at Coimbra, and like it has a Flemish look, so that it may have been made perhaps, if not by Master Vlimer, who finished his work at Coimbra in 1508, at any rate by one of his pupils. The stalls, which at the back are separated by Gothic pilasters and pinnacles, have also a continuous canopy, and a high and splendid cresting, which though Gothic in general appearance, is quite renaissance in detail.

Outside, the smaller eastern chapels have an elaborate cresting, and tall twisted pinnacles. The large plain tower 111 which rises east of the north transept has a top crowned with battlements, within which stands a square tile-covered spire.

Sé, Lamego.

Before going on to discuss the long-continued influence of the Moors, three buildings in which Gothic finally came to an end must be discussed. These are the west front of Lamego, the cathedral of Vizeu, and the porch and chancel of the Sé at Braga. Except for its romanesque tower and its west front the cathedral of Lamego has been entirely rebuilt; and of the west front only the lower part remains uninjured. This front is divided by rather elaborate buttresses into three nearly equal parts—for the side aisles are nearly as wide as the central. In each of these is a large pointed doorway, that in the centre being at once wider and considerably higher than those of the aisles. The central door has six moulded shafts on either side, all with elaborately carved capitals and with deeply undercut foliage in the hollows between, this foliage being carried round the whole arch between the mouldings. Above the top of the arch runs a band of flat, early renaissance carving with a rich Gothic cresting above.

The side-doors are exactly similar, except that they have fewer shafts, four instead of six, and that in the hollows between the mouldings the carving is early renaissance in character and is also flatter than in the central door. Above runs the same band of carving— but lower down—and a similar but simpler cresting.

Sé, Vizeu.

Unlike Lamego, while the cathedral of Vizeu has been but little altered within, scarcely any of the original work is to be seen outside. The present cathedral was built by Bishop Dom Diego Ortiz de Vilhegas about the year 1513, and his arms as well as those of Dom Manoel and of two of his sons are found on the vault. The church is not large, having a nave and aisles of four bays measuring about 105 feet by 62; square transept chapels, and a seventeenth-century chancel with flanking chapels. To the west are two towers, built between the years 1641 and 1671, and on the south a very fine renaissance cloister of two stories, the lower having been built, it is said, in 1524,[91] and the upper about 1730. A choir gallery too, with an elaborate Gothic vault below and a fine renaissance balustrade, crosses the whole west end and extends over the porch between the two western towers. But if the cathedral in its plan follows the ordinary type, in design and 112 in construction it is quite unique. Instead of there being a wooden roof as is usual in churches of this period, the whole is vaulted, and that too in a very unusual and original manner. Throughout the piers consist of twelve rounded shafts set together. Of these the five towards the central aisle are several feet higher than the other seven from which spring the aisle arches as well as the ribs of the aisle vault. Consequently the vault of the central aisle is considerably lower at the sides than it is in the middle, and in this ingenious way its thrust is counteracted by the vaults of the side aisles; and at the same time these side vaults are not highly stilted as they would of necessity have been, had the three aisles been of exactly the same height. All the ribs are of considerable projection and well moulded, and of all, except the diagonal ribs, the lowest moulding is twisted like a rope. This rope-moulding is repeated on all the ridge ribs, and in each it is tied in a knot half-way along, a knot which is so much admired that the whole vault is called 'a abobada dos nós' or vault of the knots.

The capitals are more curious than beautiful; the lower have clumsy, early-looking foliage and a large and curious abacus. First each capital has a square abacus of some depth, then comes a large flat circle, one for each three caps, and at the top a star-shaped moulding of hollow curves, the points projecting beyond the middle of the square abaci below. The higher capitals are better. They are carved with more elaborate foliage and gilt, and the abaci follow more exactly the line of the caps below and are carved and gilded in the same way. (Fig. 42.)

Perhaps, however, the chief interest of the cathedral is found in the sacristy, a fine large room opening from the north transept chapel. On its tiled walls there hang several large and some smaller paintings, of which the finest is that of St. Peter. Other pictures are found in the chapter-house, and a fine one of the crucifixion in the Jesus Chapel below it; but this is not the place to enter into the very difficult question of Portuguese painting, a question on which popular tradition throws only a misleading light by attributing everything to a more or less mythical painter, Grão Vasco, and on which all authorities differ, agreeing only in considering this St. Peter one of the finest paintings in the country.

FIG. 42.   **FIG. 43.**

SÉ, VIZEU.   BRAGA.

W. PORCH OF CATHEDRAL.

Sé, Braga.

Perhaps the chancel of the cathedral at Braga ought rather 113 to be left to a chapter dealing with what is usually called the Manoelino style—that strange last development of Gothic which is found only in Portugal—but it is in many respects so like the choir chapels of the church at Caminha, and has so little of the usual Manoelino peculiarities, that it were better to describe it now. Whatever may be thought of the chancel, there is no doubt about the large western porch, which is quite free of any Manoelino fantasies.

Both porch and chancel were built by Archbishop Dom Diego de Souza about the year 1530—a most remarkable date when the purely Gothic work here is compared with buildings further south, where Manoelino had already been succeeded by various forms of the classic renaissance. The porch stretches right across the west end of the church, and is of three bays. That in the centre, considerably wider than those at the side, is entered from the west by a round-headed arch, while the arches of the others are pointed. The bays are separated by buttresses of considerable projection, and all the arches, which have good late mouldings, are enriched with a fine feathering of cusps, which stands out well against the dark interior. Unfortunately the original parapet is gone, only the elaborate canopies of the niches, of which there are two to each bay, rise above the level of the flat paved roof. Inside there is a good vault with many well-moulded ribs, but the finest feature of it all is the wrought-iron railing which crosses each opening. This, almost the only piece of wrought-iron work worthy of notice in the whole country, is very like contemporary screens in Spain. It is made of upright bars, some larger, twisted from top to bottom, some smaller twisted at the top, and plain below, alternating with others plain above and twisted below. At the top runs a frieze of most elaborate hammered and pierced work—early renaissance in detail in the centre, Gothic in the side arches, above which comes in the centre a wonderful cresting. In the middle, over the gate which rises as high as the top of the cresting, is a large trefoil made of a flat hammered band intertwined with a similar band after the manner of a Manoelino doorway.[92] (Fig. 43.)

Of the chancel little has been left inside but the vault and the tombs of Dona Theresa (the first independent ruler of 114 Portugal) and of her husband Count Henry of Burgundy—very poor work of about the same date as the chancel. The outside, however, has been unaltered. Below it is square in plan, becoming at about twenty feet from the ground a half-octagon having the eastern a good deal wider than the diagonal sides. On the angles of the lower square stand tall clustered buttresses, rising independently of the wall as far as the projecting cornice, across which their highest pinnacles cut, and united to the chancel at about a third of the height, by small but elaborate flying buttresses. On the eastern face there is a simple pointed window, and there is nothing else to relieve the perfectly plain walls below except two string courses, and the elaborate side buttresses with their tall pinnacles and twisted shafts. But if the walling is plain the cornice is most elaborate. It is of great depth and of considerable projection, the hollows of the mouldings being filled with square flowers below and intricate carving above. On this stands a high parapet of traceried quatrefoils, bearing a horizontal moulding from which springs an elaborate cresting; all being almost exactly like the cornice and parapet at Caminha, but larger and richer, and like it, a marvellous example of carving in granite. At the angles are tall pinnacles, and the pinnacles of the corner buttresses are united to the parapet by a curious contorted moulding.

Conceiçao, Braga.

Opposite the east end of the cathedral there stands a small tower built in 1512 by Archdeacon João de Coimbra as a chapel. It is of two stories, with a vaulted chapel below and a belfrey above, lit by round-headed windows, only one of which retains its tracery. Just above the string which divides the two stories are statues[93] under canopies, one projecting

56

on a corbel from each corner, and one from the middle, while above a cornice, on which stand short pinnacles, six to each side, the tower ends in a low square tile roof. The chapel on the ground floor is entered by a porch, whose flat lintel rests on moulded piers at the angles and on two tall round columns in the centre, while its three openings are filled with plain iron screens, the upper part of which blossoms out into large iron flowers and leaves. Inside there is on the east wall a reredos of early renaissance date, and on the south a large 115 half-classical arch flanked by pilasters under which there is a life-size group of the Entombment made seemingly of terra cotta and painted.

So, rather later than in most other lands, and many years after the renaissance had made itself felt in other parts of the country, Gothic comes to an end, curiously enough not far from where the oldest Christian buildings are found. 116

CHAPTER VII
THE INFLUENCE OF THE MOORS

IT is now time to turn back for a century and a half and to speak of the traces left by the Moors of their long occupation of the country. Although they held what is now the northern half of Portugal for over a hundred years, and part of the south for about five hundred, there is hardly a single building anywhere of which we can be sure that it was built by them before the Christian re-conquest of the country. Perhaps almost the only exceptions are the fortifications at Cintra, known as the Castello dos Mouros, the city walls at Silves, and possibly the church at Mertola. In Spain very many of their buildings still exist, such as the small mosque, now the church of Christo de la Luz, and the city walls at Toledo, and of course the mosque at Cordoba and the Alcazar at Seville, not to speak of the Alhambra. Yet it must not be forgotten that, while Portugal reached its furthest limits by the capture of the Algarve under Affonso III. about the middle of the thirteenth century, in Spain the progress was slower. Toledo indeed fell in 1085, but Cordoba and Seville were only taken a few years before the capture of the Algarve, and Granada was able to hold out till 1492. Besides, in what is now Portugal there had been no great capital like Cordoba. And yet, though this is so, hardly a town or a village exists in which some slight trace of their art cannot be found, even if it be but a tile-lining to the walls of church or house. In such towns as Toledo, Moorish builders were employed not only in the many parish churches but even in the cathedral, and in Portugal we find Moors at Thomar even as late as the beginning of the sixteenth century, when such names as Omar, Mafamedi, Bugimaa, and Bebedim occur in the list of workmen.

It is chiefly in three directions that Moorish influence made itself felt, in actual design, in carpentry, and in tiling, 117 and of these the last two, and especially tiling, are the most general, and long survived the disappearance of Arab detail.

Cintra.

Some eighteen miles from Lisbon, several sharp granite peaks rise high above an undulating tableland. Two of these are encircled by the old Moorish fortification which climbs up and down over huge granite boulders, and on a projecting spur near their foot, and to the north, there stands the old palace of Cintra. As long as the Walis ruled at Lisbon, it was to Cintra that they came in summer for hunting and cool air, and some part at least of their palace seems to have survived till to-day.

Cintra was first taken by Alfonso VI. of Castile and Leon in 1093—to be soon lost and retaken by Count Henry of Burgundy sixteen years later, but was not permanently held by the Christians till Affonso Henriques expelled the Moors in 1147. The Palace of the Walis was soon granted by him to Gualdim Paes, the famous grand master of the Templars, and was held by his successors till it was given to Dom Diniz's queen, St. Isabel. She died in 1336, when the palace returned to the Order of Christ—which had meanwhile been formed out of the suppressed Order of the Temple—only to be granted to Dona Beatriz, the wife of D. AffonsoIV., in exchange for her possessions at Ega and at Torre de Murta. Dom João I. granted the palace in 1385 to Dom Henrique de Vilhena, but he soon sided with the Spaniards, for he was of Spanish birth, his possessions were confiscated and Cintra returned to the Crown. Some of the previous kings may have done something to the palace, but it was

57

King João who first made it one of the chief royal residences, and who built a very large part of it.

A few of the walls have been examined by taking off the plaster, and have been found to be built in the usual Arab manner, courses of rubble bonded at intervals with bands of thin bricks two or three courses deep. Such are the back wall of the entrance hall and a thick wall near the kitchen. Outside all the walls are plastered, all the older windows, of one or two lights, are enclosed in square frames—for the later windows of Dom Manoel's time are far more elaborate and fantastic—and most of the walls end in typical Moorish battlements. High above the dark tile roofs there tower the two strange kitchen chimneys, huge conical spires ending in round funnels, now all plastered, but once covered with a pattern of green and white tiles. 118

PLAN OF PAÇO, CINTRA

The whole is so extremely complicated that without a plan it would be almost useless to attempt a description. Speaking roughly, all that lies to the west of the Porte Cochère which leads from the entrance court through to the kitchen court and 119 stables beyond is, with certain alterations and additions, the work of Dom João, and all that lies to the east is the work of Dom Manoel, added during the first years of the sixteenth century. Entering through a pointed gateway, one finds oneself in a long and irregular courtyard, having on the right hand a long low building in which live the various lesser palace officials, and on the left, first a comparatively modern projecting building in which live the ladies-in-waiting, then somewhat further back the rooms of the controller of the palace and his office. From the front wall of this office, which itself juts out some feet into the courtyard, there runs eastwards a high balustraded terrace reaching as far as another slightly projecting wing, and approached by a great flight of steps at its western end. Not far beyond the east end of the terrace an inclined road leads to the Porte Cochère, and beyond it are the large additions made by Dom Manoel. (Fig. 44.)

On this terrace stands the main front of the palace. Below are four large pointed arches, and above five beautiful windows lighting the great Sala dos Cysnes or Swan Hall. Originally these four arches were open and led into a large vaulted hall; now they are all built up—perhaps by Dona Maria I. after the great earthquake—three having small two-light windows, and one a large door, the chief entrance to the palace. In the back wall of this hall may still be seen three windows which must have existed before it was built, for what is now their inner side was evidently at first their outer; and this wall is one of those found to be built in the Arab manner, so that clearly Dom João's hall was built in front of a part of the Walis' palace, a part which has quite disappeared except for this wall.

From the east end of this lower hall a straight stair, which looks as if it had once been an outside stair, leads up to a winding stair by which another hall is reached, whose floor lies at a level of about 26 feet above the terrace. [94] From this hall, which may be of later date than Dom João's time, a door leads down to the central pateo or courtyard, or else going up a few steps the way goes through a smaller square room, once an open verandah, through a wide doorway inserted by Dom Manoel into the great Swan Hall. This hall, the largest room in the palace, measuring about 80 feet long by 25 wide, is so called from the swans painted in the eight-sided panels of its wonderful roof. The story is that while the palace was still 120 building ambassadors came to the king from the duke of Burgundy asking for the hand of his daughter Isabel. Among other presents they brought some swans, which so pleased the young princess that she made them collars of red velvet and persuaded her father to build for them a long narrow tank in the central court just under the north windows of this hall. Here she used to feed them till she went away to Flanders, and from love of his daughter King João had the swans with their collars painted on the ceiling of the hall. The swans may still be seen, but not those painted for Dom João, for all the mouldings clearly show that the present ceiling was reconstructed some centuries later. The hall is lit by five windows looking south across the entrance court to the Moorish castle on the hill beyond, and by three looking over the swan tank into the central pateo.

58

These windows, and indeed all those in Dom João's part of the palace, are very like each other. They are nearly all of two lights—never of more—and are made of white marble. In every case there is a square-headed moulded frame enclosing the whole window, the outer mouldings of this frame resting on small semicircular corbels, and having Gothic bases. Inside this framework stand three slender shafts, with simple bases and carved capitals. These capitals are not at all unlike French capitals of the thirteenth century, but are really of a common Moorish pattern often found elsewhere, as in the Alhambra. On them, moulded at the ends, but not in front or behind, rest abaci, from which spring stilted arches. (Fig. 45.)

Each arch is delicately moulded and elaborately cusped, but, though in some cases—for the shape varies in almost every window—each individual cusp may have the look of a Gothic trefoil, the arrangement is not Gothic at all. There are far more than are ever found in a Gothic window, sometimes as many as eleven, and they usually begin at the bottom with a whole instead of a half cusp. From the centre of each abacus, cutting across the arch mouldings, another moulding runs up, which being returned across the top encloses the upper part of each light in a smaller square frame. It is this square frame which more than anything else gives these windows their Eastern look, and it has been shown how often, and indeed almost universally a square framing was put round doorways all through the last Gothic period.

FIG. 44.	FIG. 45.
PALACE, CINTRA.	PALACE, CINTRA.
ENTRANCE COURT.	WINDOW OF SALA DAS SEREIAS.

121 In only one instance are the shafts anything but plain, and that is in the central window overlooking the entrance court, where they are elaborately twisted, and where also they start at the level of the floor instead of standing on a low parapet.

In the room itself the walls up to a certain height are covered with tiles, diamonds of white and a beautiful olive green which are much later than Dom João's time. There is also near the west end of the north side a large fireplace projecting slightly from the wall; at either end stands a shaft with cap and base like those of the windows, bearing a long flat moulded lintel, while on the hearth there rest two very fine wrought-iron Gothic fire-dogs.

East of the fireplace a door having a wide flat ogee head leads into a small porch built in the corner of the pateo to protect the passage to the Sala das Pegas, the first of the rooms to the south of this pateo.

In the angle formed by the end wall of the Sala dos Cysnes and the side of the Sala das Pegas there is a small low room now called the Sala de Dom Sebastião or do Conselho. It is entered from the west end of the Swan Hall through a door, which was at first a window just like all the rest. This Hall of Dom Sebastião or of the Council is so called from the tradition that it was there that in 1578 that unhappy king held the council in which it was decided to invade Morocco, an expedition which cost the king his life and his country her independence. In reality the final solemn council was held in Lisbon, but some informal meeting may well have been held there. Now the room is low and rather dark, being lit only by two small windows opening above the roof of the controller's office. It is divided into two unequal parts by an arcade of three arches, the smaller part between the arches and the south wall being raised a step above the rest. When first built by Dom João this raised part formed a covered verandah, the rest being, till about the time of Maria I., open to the sky and forming a charming and cool retreat during the heat of summer. The floor is of tiles and marble, and all along the south wall runs a bench entirely covered with beautiful tiles. At the eastern end is a large seat, rather higher than the bench and provided with arms, doubtless for the king, and tiled like the rest.

Passing again from the Swan Hall the way leads through 122 the porch into the Sala das Pegas or of the magpies. The door from the porch to the room is one of the most beautiful parts of Dom João's work. It is framed as are the windows, and has shafts, capitals, abaci, and bases just like those already described; but the arch is different. It is beautifully moulded, but is—if one may so speak—made up of nine reversed cusps, whose convex sides form the arch: the inner square moulding too is enriched with ball ornament. Inside the walls are covered to half their height with exquisite tiles of Moorish pattern, blue, green and brown on a white ground.

On the north wall is a great white marble chimney-piece, once a present from Pope Leo X. to Dom Manoel and brought by the great Marques de Pombal from the ruined palace of Almeirim opposite Santarem. Two other doors, with simple pointed heads, lead one into the dining-room, and one into the Sala das Sereias. The Sala das Pegas, like the Swan Hall, is called after its ceiling, for on it are painted in 136 triangular compartments, 136 magpies, each holding in one foot a red rose and in its beak a scroll inscribed 'Por Bem.' Possibly this ceiling, which on each side slopes up to a flat parallelogram, is more like that painted for Dom João than is that of the Swan Hall, but even here some of the mouldings are clearly renaissance, and the painting has been touched up, but anyhow it was already called Camera das Pegas in the time of Dom Duarte; further, tradition tells that the magpies were painted there by Dom João's orders, and why. It seems that once during the hour of the midday siesta the king, wandering about his unfinished house, found in this room one of the maids of honour. Her he kissed, when another maid immediately went and told the queen, Philippa of Lancaster. She was angry, but Dom João only said 'Por bem,' meaning much what his queen's grandfather had meant when he said 'Honi soit qui mal y pense,' and to remind the maids of honour, whose waiting-room this was, that they must not tell tales, he had the magpies painted on the ceiling.

The two windows, one looking west and one into the pateo, are exactly like those already described.

From the Sala das Pegas one door leads up a few steps into the Sala das Sereias, and another to the dining-room. This Sala das Sereias, so called from the mermaids painted on | 123 | the ceiling, is a small room some eighteen feet square. It is lit by a two-light window opening towards the courtyard, a window just like those of the Sala das Pegas and of the Sala dos Cysnes. Some of its walls, especially that between it and the Sala das Pegas, are very thick and seem to be older than the time of Dom João. As usual, the walls are partly covered with beautiful tiles, mostly embossed with green vine-leaves, but round the door leading to the long narrow room, used as a servery, is an interlacing pattern of green and blue tiles, while the spandrils between this and the pointed doorhead are filled with a true Arabesque pattern, dark on a light ground, which is said to belong to the Palace of the Walis. There are altogether four doors, one leading to the servery, one to the Sala das Pegas, one to a spiral stair in the corner of the pateo, and one to the dining-room.

This dining-room projects somewhat to the west so as to leave space for a window looking south to the mountains, and one looking north across a small court, as well as one looking west. Of these, the two which look south and west are like each other, and like the other of Dom João's time except that the arches are not cusped; that the outer frame is omitted and that the abaci are moulded in front as well as at the ends; but the third window looking north is rather different. The framing has regular late Gothic bases, the capitals of the shafts are quite unlike the rest, having one large curly leaf at each angle, and the moulding running up the centre between the arches—which are not cusped—is plaited instead of being plain. Altogether it looks as if it were later than Dom João's time, for it is the only window where the capitals are not of the usual Arab form, and they are not at all like some in the castle of Sempre Noiva built about the beginning of the sixteenth century.

The wall-tiles of the dining-room are like those of the Sala das Sereias, but end in a splendid cresting. The ceiling is modern and uninteresting.

Next to the north comes the servery, a room without interest but for its window which looks west, and is like the two older dining-room windows.

Returning to the Sala das Sereias, a spiral stair leads down to the central pateo, which can also be reached from the porch in the south-west corner. All along the south side runs the tank made by Dom João for his daughter's swans, and on | 124 | three sides are beautiful white marble windows. At the east end of the north side three open arches lead to the bathroom. As is the case with the windows, the three arches are enclosed in a square frame. The capitals, however, are different, having an eight-sided bell on which rests a square block with a bud carved at each angle, and above an abacus, moulded all round. The arches are cusped like the windows, but are stilted and segmental. Inside is a recess framed in an arch of Dom Manoel's time, and from all over the tiled walls and the ceiling jets of water squirt out, so that the whole becomes a great shower-bath, delightful and cooling on a hot day but rather public. In the middle of the pateo there stands a curious column—not at all unlike the 'pelourinho'[95] of Cintra—which stands in a basin just before the entrance gate. This column is formed of three twisted shafts on whose capitals sit a group of boys holding three shields charged with the royal arms. All round the court is a dado of white and green tiles arranged in an Arab pattern.

In the north-west corner and reached by the same spiral stair, but at a higher level than the Sala das Sereias, is the Sala dos Arabes, so called because it is commonly believed to be a part of the original building. The walls may be so, but of the rest, nothing, but perhaps the shallow round fountain basin in the middle and the square of tiles which surrounds it, now so worn that little of their glazed surface is left. The walls half-way up are lined with tiles, squares and parallelograms, blue, white and green. The doors are framed in different tiles, and all are finished with an elaborate cresting. The most interesting thing in the room is the circular basin in the middle—a basin which gives it a truly Eastern look. Inside a round shallow hollow there stands a many-sided block of marble about six inches high. The sides are concave as in a small section of a Doric column, and within it is hollowed into a beautiful cup, shaped somewhat like a flower of many petals. In the middle there now is a strange object of gilt metal through which the water once poured. On a short stem stands a carefully modelled dish on which rest first leaves, like long acanthus leaves, then between them birds on whose backs sit small figures of boys. Between the boys and above the leaves are more figures exactly like seated Indian gods, and the whole ends in a cone. It is so completely Indian in 125 appearance that there can be little doubt but that it is really of Indian origin, and perhaps it is not too much to see in it part of the spoils brought to Dom Manoel by Vasco da Gama after he had in 1498 made his way round Africa to Calicut and back.

Returning to the Sala das Sereias and passing through the servery and another room an open court is reached called the Pateo de Diana, from a fountain over which Diana presides, and on to which one of the dining-room windows looks. A beautifully tiled stair— these tiles are embossed like those of the dining-room, but besides vine-leaves some have on them bunches of grapes—goes down from the Court of Diana to the Court of the Lion, the Pateo do Leão, where a lion spouts into a long tank. But the chief beauty of these two courts is a small window which overlooks them. This window is only of one light, and like the dining-room window near it its framing has Gothic bases. The capitals are smaller than in the other windows, and the framing partly covers the outer moulding of the window arch, making it look like a segment of a circle. But the cusps are the most curious part. They form four more or less trefoiled spaces with wavy outlines, and two of them—not the remaining one at the top—end in large well-carved vine-leaves, very like those at the ends of the cusps on the arches in the Capella do Fundador at Batalha. To add to the charm of the window, the space between the top of the arch and the framing is filled in with those beautiful tiles embossed with vine-leaves.

Going up again to the Sala dos Arabes, a door in the northern wall leads to a passage running northwards to the chapel. About half-way along the passage another branches off to the right towards the great kitchen.

The chapel stands at the northern edge of the palace buildings, having beyond it a terrace called the Terreiro da Meca or of Mecca; partly from this name, and partly from the tiles which still cover the middle of the floor it is believed that the chapel stands exactly on the site of the Walis' private mosque, with perhaps the chancel added.

The middle of the nave—the chapel consists of a nave and chancel, two small transeptal recesses, and two galleries one above the other at the west end—is paved with tiles once glazed and of varying colours, but now nearly all worn down till the natural red shows through. The pattern has been 126 elaborate; a broad border of diagonal checks surrounding a narrow oblong in which the checks are crossed by darker lines so as to form octagons, and between the outer border and the octagons a band of lighter ground down which in the middle runs a coloured line having on each side cones of the common Arab pattern exactly like the palace battlements.

Now the walls are bare and white, but were once covered with frescoes of the fifteenth century; the reredos is a clumsy addition of the eighteenth century.

The cornice and the long pilasters at the entrance to the chancel seem to have been added at the same time, but the windows and ceiling are still those of Dom João's time. The windows—there are now three, a fourth in the chancel having been turned into a royal pew—are of two or three lights, have commonplace tracery, and are only interesting as being one of the few wholly Gothic features in the palace.

Far more interesting is the ceiling, which is entirely Arab in construction and in design. In the nave it is an irregular polygon in section, and in the chancel is nearly a semicircle, having nine equal sides. The whole of the boarded surface is entirely covered with an intricate design formed of strips of wood crossing each other in every direction so as to form stars, triangles, octagons, and figures of every conceivable shape. The whole still retains its original colouring. At the centres of the main figures are gilt bosses—the one over the high altar being a shield with the royal arms—the wooden strips are black with a white groove down the centre of each, and the ground is either dark red or light blue. (Fig. 46.)

The whole is of great interest not only for its own sake, but because it is the only ceiling in the palace which has remained unchanged since the end of the fourteenth century, and because it is, as it were, the parent of the splendid roofs in the Sala dos Cysnes and of the still more wonderful one in the Sala dos Escudos.

The kitchen lies at the back of the chapel and at right angles to it. It is a building about 58 feet long by 25 wide, and is divided into two equal parts by a large arch. Each of these two parts is covered by a huge conical chimney so that the inside is more like the nave of St. Ours at Loches than anything else, while outside these chimneys rise high above all the rest of the palace. It is lit by small two-light Gothic windows, and has lately been lined with white tiles.

FIG. 46.
PALACE CHAPEL ROOF.
CINTRA.

[127] Now the chimneys serve only as ventilators, as ordinary iron ranges have been put in. There seems to be nothing in the country at all like these chimneys—for the kitchen at Alcobaça, although it has a stream running through it, is but a poor affair compared with this one, nor is its chimney in any way remarkable outside.[96]

The rest of the palace towards the west, between the west end of the chapel and the great square tower in which is the Sala dos Escudos, was probably also built about the time of Dom João I., but except for a few windows there is little of interest left which belongs to his time.

The great tower of the Sala dos Escudos was built by Dom Manoel on the top of an older building then called the Casa da Meca, in which Affonso V. was born in 1432—the year before his grandfather Dom João died—and where he himself died forty-nine years later. In another room on a higher floor—where his feet, as he walked up and down day after day, have quite worn away the tiles—Affonso VI. was imprisoned. Affonso had by his wildness proved himself quite unable to govern, and had also made himself hated by his queen, a French princess. She fell in love with his brother, so Affonso was deposed, divorced, and banished to the Azores. After some years it was found that he was there trying to form a party, so he was brought to Cintra and imprisoned in this room from 1674 till his death in 1683. These worn-out tiles are worthy of notice for their own sake since tiles with Moorish patterns, as are these here and those in the chapel, are very seldom used for flooring, and they are probably among the oldest in the palace.

Castles, Guimarães and Barcellos.

Such was the palace from the time of João I. to that of Dom Manoel, a building thoroughly Eastern in plan as in detail, and absolutely unlike such contemporary buildings as the palaces of the dukes of Braganza at Guimarães or at Barcellos, or the castle at Villa da Feira between Oporto and Aveiro. The Braganza palaces are both in ruins, but their details are all such as might be found almost anywhere in Christian Europe. Large pointed doors, traceried windows and tall chimneys—these last round and of brick—differ only from similar features found elsewhere, as one dialect may differ from another, whereas Cintra is, as it were, built in a 128

Villa da Feira.

totally different language. The castle at Villa da Feira is even more unlike anything at Cintra. A huge keep of granite, the square turrets projecting slightly from the corners give it the look of a Norman castle, for the curious spires of brick now on those turrets were added later, perhaps under Dom Manoel. Inside there is now but one vast hall with pointed barrel roof, for all the wooden floors are gone, leaving only the beam holes in the walls, the Gothic fireplaces, and the small windows to show where they once were.

It is then no wonder that Cintra has been called the Alhambra of Portugal, and it is curious that the same names are found given to different parts of the two buildings. The Alhambra has a Mirador de Lindaraxa, Cintra a Jardim de Lindaraya; the Alhambra a Torre de las dos Hermanas, Cintra a Sala das Irmãs or of the Sisters—the part under the Sala dos Escudos where Affonso V. was born; while both at the Alhambra and here there is a garden called de las or das Damas. 129

CHAPTER VIII
OTHER MOORISH BUILDINGS

THE old palace at Cintra is perhaps the only complete building to the north of the Tagus designed and carried out by Moorish workmen scarcely, if at all, influenced by what the conquering Christians were doing round them. Further south in the province of Alemtejo Moorish buildings are more common, and there are many in which, though the design and plan as well as most of the detail may be Western, yet there is something, the whitewashed walls, the round conical pinnacles, or the flat roofs which give them an Eastern look.

And this is natural. Alemtejo was conquered after the country north of the Tagus had been for some time Christian, and no large immigration of Christians ever came to take the place of the Moors, so that those few who remained continued for long in their own Eastern ways of building and of agriculture.

It is especially in and about the town of Evora that this is seen, and that too although the cathedral built at the end of the twelfth century is, except for a few unimportant details, a Western building.

Alvito.

But more completely Eastern than any one building at Evora is the castle at Alvito, a small town some thirty or forty miles to the south-west. The town stands at the end of a long low hill and looks south over an endless plain across to Beja, one of the most extensive and, in its way, beautiful views in the country.

At one end of the town on the slope of the hill stands the castle, and not far off in one of the streets is the town hall whose tower is too characteristic of the Alemtejo not to be noticed. The building is whitewashed and perfectly plain, with ordinary square windows. An outside stair leads to the 130 upper story, and behind it rises the tower. It, like the building, is absolutely plain with semicircular openings near the top irregularly divided by a square pier. Close above these openings is a simple cornice on which stand rather high and narrow battlements; within them rises a short eight-sided spire, and at each corner a short round turret capped by a conical roof. The whole from top to bottom is plastered and whitewashed, and it is this glaring whiteness more than anything else which gives to the whole so Eastern a look.

As to the castle, Haupt in his most interesting book, *Die Baukunst der Renaissance in Portugal*, says that, though he had never seen it, yet from descriptions of its plan he had come to the conclusion that it was the castle which, according to Vasari, was built by Andrea da Sansovino for Dom João II. Now it is well known that Sansovino was for nine years in Portugal and did much work there, but none of it can now be found except perhaps a beautiful Italian door in the palace at Cintra; Vasari also states that he did some work in the heavy and native style which the king liked. Is it possible that the castle of Alvito is one of his works in this native style?

Vasari says that Sansovino built for Dom João a beautiful palace with four towers, and that part of it was decorated by him with paintings, and it was because Haupt believed that this castle was built round an arcaded court—a regular Italian feature, but one quite unknown in Portugal—that he thought it must be Sansovino's lost palace.

As a matter of fact the court is not arcaded—there is only a row of rough plastered arches along one side; there are five and not four towers; there is no trace now of any fine painted decoration inside; and, in short, it is inconceivable that, even to please a king, an architect of the Italian renaissance could ever have designed such a building.

The plan of the castle is roughly square with a round tower at three of the corners, and at the fourth corner a much larger tower, rounded in front and projecting further from the walls. The main front is turned to the south-west, and on that side, as well as on the south-eastern, are the habitable parts of the castle. Farm buildings run along inside and outside the north-western, while the north-eastern side is bounded only by a high wall. 131

Half-way along the main front is the entrance gate, a plain pointed arch surmounted by two shields, that on the right charged with the royal arms, and that on the left with those of the Barão d'Alvito, to whose descendant, the Marques d'Alvito, the castle still belongs. There is also an inscription stating that the castle, begun in 1494 by the orders of Dom João II. and finished in the time of Dom Manoel, was built by Dom Diogo Lobo, Barão d'Alvito.[97]

In the court a stair, carried on arches, goes up to the third floor where are the chief rooms in the house. None of them, which open one from the other or from a passage leading to the chapel in the westernmost corner, are in any way remarkable except for their windows. The ceilings of the principal rooms are of wood and panelled, but are clearly of much later date than the building and are not to be compared with those at Cintra. Most of the original windows—for those on the main front have been replaced by plain square openings—are even more Eastern than those at Cintra. They are nearly all of two lights—there is one of a single light in the passage—but are without the square framing. Each window has three very slender white marble shafts, with capitals and with abaci moulded on each side. On some of the capitals are carved twisted ropes, while others, as in a window in the large southern tower, are like those at Cintra. As the shafts stand a little way back from the face of the wall the arches are of two orders, of which only the inner comes down to the central shaft. (Fig. 47.)

These arches, all horseshoe in shape, are built of red brick with very wide mortar joints, and each brick, in both orders, is beautifully moulded or cut at the ends so as to form a series of small trefoiled cusps, each arch having as many as twenty-seven or more. The whole building is plastered and washed yellow, so that the contrast between the bare walls and the elaborate red arches and white shafts is singularly pleasing. All the outer walls are fortified, but the space between each embrasure is far longer than usual; the four corner towers rise a good deal above the rest of the buildings, but in none, except the southern, are there windows above the main roof. It has one, shaped like the rest, but now all plastered and framed 132 in an ogee moulding. Half-way along the north-west wall, outside it, stands the keep, which curiously is not Arab at all. It is a large square tower of no great height, absolutely plain, and built of unplastered stone or marble. It has scarcely any windows, and walls of great thickness which, like those of the smaller round towers, have a slight batter. It seems to be older than the rest, and now its chief ornament is a large fig-tree growing near the top on the south side.[98]

Evora.

Of all the towns in the Alemtejo Evora is the one where Eastern influence is most strongly marked. Indeed the Roman temple and the cathedral are perhaps the only old buildings which seem to be distinctly Western, and even the cathedral has some trace of the East in its two western spires, one round and tiled, and the other eight-sided and plastered. For long Evora was one of the chief towns of the kingdom, and was one of those oftenest visited by the kings. Their palace stood close to the church of São Francisco, and must once have been a beautiful building.

Paços Reaes.

Unfortunately most of it has disappeared, and what is left, a large hall partly of the time of Dom Manoel, has been so horribly restored in order to turn it into a museum as to have lost all character.

A porch still stands at the south end, but scraped and pointed out of all beauty. It has in front four square stone piers bearing large horseshoe brick arches, and these arches are moulded and cusped exactly like those at Alvito.

Morgado de Cordovis.

There are no other examples of Moorish brickwork in the town, but there is more than one marble window resembling those at Alvito in shape. Of these the most charming are found in the garden of a house belonging to a 'morgado' or entailed estate called Cordovis. These windows form two sides of a small square summer-house; their shafts have capitals like those of the dining-room windows at Cintra, and the horseshoe arches are, as usual, cusped. A new feature, showing how the pure Arab details were being gradually combined with Gothic, is an ogee moulding which, uniting the two arches, ends in a large Gothic finial; other mouldings run up the cornice at the angles, and the whole, crowned with battlements, ends in a short round whitewashed spire.

FIG. 47.
CASTLE, ALVITO.
COURTYARD.

FIG. 48.
EVORA
CHAPTER HOUSE DOOR OF SÃO JOÃO, EVANGELISTA.

Sempre Noiva.

Some miles from Evora among the mountains, Affonso of 133 Portugal, archbishop of Evora, built himself a small country house which he called Sempre Noiva, or 'Ever New,' about the beginning of the sixteenth century. It is now a ruin having lost all its woodwork, but the walls are still well preserved. The plan is simple; a rectangle with a chapel projecting from the eastern side, and a small wing from the west end of the south side. All the ground floor is vaulted, as is the chapel, but the main rooms on the first floor had wooden roofs, except the one next the chapel which forms the middle floor of a three-storied tower, which, rising above the rest of the building, has a battlemented flat roof reached by a spiral stair. This stair, like the round buttresses of the chapel, is capped by a high conical plastered roof. As usual the whole, except the windows and the angles, is plastered and has a sgraffito frieze running round under the cornice. There is a large porch on the north side covering a stair leading to the upper floor, where most of the windows are of two lights and very like those of the pavilion at Evora. Two like them have the ogee moulding, and at the sides a rounded moulding carried on corbels and finished above the window with a carved finial. The capitals are again carved with leaves, but the horseshoe arches have no cusps, and the mouldings, like the capitals, are entirely Gothic; the union between the two styles, Gothic and Arab, was already becoming closer.

Naturally Moorish details are more often found in secular than in religious buildings: yet there are churches where such details exist even if the general plan and design is Christian.

São João Evangelista, Evora.

Just to the north of the cathedral of Evora, Rodrigo Affonso de Mello, count of Olivença, in 1485 founded a monastery for the Loyos, or Canons Secular of St. John the Evangelist. The church itself is in no way notable; the large west door opening under a flat arched porch is one of these with plain moulded arches and simple shafts which are so common over all the country, and is only interesting for its late date. At the left side is a small monument to the founder's memory; on a corbel stands a short column bearing an inscribed slab, and above the slab is a shield under a carved curtain. Inside are some tombs—two of them being Flemish brasses—and great tile pictures covering the walls. These give the life of São Lorenzo Giustiniani, patriarch of Venice, and canon of San Giorgio in Alga, where the founder of the 134 Loyos had been kindly received and whence

65

he drew the rules of his order, and are interesting as being signed and dated 'Antonius ab oliva fecit 1711.'

The cloisters are also Gothic with vine-covered capitals, but the entrance to the chapter-house and refectory is quite different. In general design it is like the windows at Sempre Noiva, two horseshoe arches springing from the capitals of thin marble shafts and an ogee moulding above. The three shafts are twisted, the capitals are very strange; they are round with several mouldings, some fluted, some carved with leaves, some like pieces of rope: the moulded abaci also have four curious corbels on two sides. The capitals are carried across the jambs and the outer moulding, which is of granite, as is the whole except the three shafts and their caps, and between the shafts and this moulding there is a broad band of carved foliage. The ogee and the side finials or pinnacles, which are of the same section as the outer moulding from which they spring, are made of a bundle of small rolls held together by a broad twisted ribbon. Lastly, between the arches and the ogee there is a flat marble disk on which is carved a curious representation of a stockaded enclosure, supposed to be memorial of the gallant attack made by Affonso de Mello on Azila in Morocco.[99] The whole is a very curious piece of work, the capitals and bases being, with the exception of some details at Thomar and at Batalha, the most strange of the details of that period, though, were the small corbels left out, they would differ but little from other Manoelino capitals, while the bases may be only an attempt of a Moorish workman to copy the interpenetration of late Gothic. (Fig. 48.)

São Francisco, Evora.

Not much need be said here of the church of São Francisco or of the chapel of São Braz, both begun at about the same time. São Francisco was long in building, for it was begun by Affonso V. in 1460 and not finished till 1501. It is a large church close to the ruins of the palace at Evora, and has a wide nave without aisles, six chapels on each side, larger transept chapels, and a chancel narrower than the nave. It is, like most of Evora, built of granite, has a pointed barrel vault cut into by small groins at the sides and scarcely any windows, for the outer walls of the side chapels are carried up so as to leave a narrow space between them and the nave wall. This was probably done to support the main vault, but the result is 135 that almost the only window is a large one over the west porch. It is this porch that most strongly shows the hand of Moorish workmen. It is five bays long and one deep, and most of the five arches in front, separated by Gothic buttresses and springing from late Gothic capitals, are horseshoe in shape. The white marble doorway has two arches springing from a thin central shaft, which like the arches and the two heavy mouldings, which forming the outer part of the jambs are curved over them, is made of a number of small rounds partly straight and partly twisted. At the corners of the church are large round spiral pinnacles with a continuous row of battlements between; these battlements interspersed with round pinnacles are even set all along the ridge of the vault. The reredos and the stalls made by Olivel of Ghent in 1508 are gone; so are Francisco Henriques' stained windows, but there are still some good tiles, and in a large square opening looking into the chancel there is a shaft with a beautiful early renaissance capital.

São Braz, Evora.

São Braz stands outside the town near the railway station. It was built as a pilgrimage chapel soon after 1482, when the saint had been invoked to stay a terrible plague. It is not large, has an aisleless nave of four bays, a large porch with three wide pointed arches at the west, and a sort of domed chancel. Most of the details are indeed Gothic, but there is little detail, and the whole is entirely Eastern in aspect. It is all plastered, the buttresses are great rounded projections capped with conical plastered roofs; there are battlements on the west gable and on the three sides of the porch, which also has great round conical-topped buttresses or turrets at the angles.

Inside there are still fine tiles, but the sgraffito frieze has nearly disappeared from the outer cornice.

There is also an interesting church somewhat in the same style as São Braz, but with aisles and brick flying buttresses at Vianna d'Alemtejo near Alvito. 136

CHAPTER IX

MOORISH CARPENTRY

IF it was only in the south that Moorish masons built in stone or brick, their carpenters had a much wider range. The wooden ceilings of as late as the middle of the seventeenth century may show no Eastern detail, yet in the method of their construction they are all ultimately descended from Moorish models. Such ceilings are found all over the country, but curiously enough the finest examples of truly Eastern work are found in the far north at Caminha and in the island of Madeira at Funchal.

Aguas Santas.

The old romanesque church at Aguas Santas near Oporto has a roof, simple and unadorned, the tie-beams of which are coupled in the Moorish manner. The two beams about a foot apart are joined in the centre by four short pieces of wood set diagonally so as to form a kind of knot. This is very common in Moorish roofs, and may be seen at Seville and elsewhere. The rest of the roof is boarded inside, boards being also fastened to the underside of the collar beams.

Azurara.

At Azurara the ties are single, but the whole is boarded as at Aguas Santas, and this is also the case at Villa do Conde and elsewhere.

In the palace chapel at Cintra, already described, the boarding is covered with a pattern of interlacing strips, but later on panelling was used, usually with simple mouldings. Such is the roof in the nave of the church of Nossa Senhora do Olival at Thomar, probably of the seventeenth century, and in many houses, as for instance in the largest hall in the castle at Alvito. From such simple panelled ceilings the splendid elaboration of those in the palace at Cintra was derived.

Caminha.

The roofs at Caminha and at Funchal are rather different. At Caminha the roof is divided into bays of such a size that 137 each of the three divisions, the two sloping sides and the flat centre under the collar ties, is cut into squares. In the sloping sides these squares are divided from each other by a strip of boarding covering the space occupied by three rafters. On this boarding are two bands of ornament separated by a carved chain, while one band, with the chain, is returned round the top and bottom of the square. Between each strip of boarding are six exposed rafters, and these are united alternately by small knots in the middle and at the ends, and by larger and more elaborate knots at the ends. In the flat centre under the collar ties each square is again surrounded by the band of ornament and by the chains, but here band and chain are also carried across the corners, leaving a large octagon in the centre with four triangles in the angles. Each octagon has a plain border about a foot wide, and within it a plain moulding surrounding an eight-sided hollow space. All these spaces are of some depth; each has in the centre a pendant, and in each the opening is fringed with tracery or foliation. In some are elaborate Gothic cuspings, in others long carved leaves curved at the ends; and in one which happens to come exactly over an iron tie-rod—for the rods are placed quite irregularly—the pendant is much longer and is joined to the tie by a small iron bar. At the sides the roof starts from a cornice of some depth whose mouldings and ornamentation are more classic than Gothic. (Fig. 49.)

In the side aisles the cornice is similar, but of greater projection, and the rafters are joined to each other in much the same way, but more simply.

Funchal.

At Funchal the roof is on a larger scale: there is no division into squares, but the rafters are knotted together with much greater elaboration, and the flat part is like the chapel roof at Cintra, entirely covered with interlacing strips forming an intricate pattern round hollow octagons.

Sala dos Cysnes, Cintra.

The simple boarding of the earlier roofs may well have led to the two wonderful ceilings at Cintra, those in the Sala dos Cysnes, and in the Sala dos Brazões or dos Escudos, but the idea of the many octagons in the Sala dos Cysnes may have come from some such roof as that at Caminha, when the octagons are so important a feature of the design. In that hall swans may have first been painted for Dom João, but the roof has clearly been remade since then, possibly under Dom Manoel. The gilt ornament on the mouldings 138 seem even later, but may of course have been added afterwards, though it is not very unlike some of the carving on the roof at Caminha, an undoubted work of Dom Manoel's time.

This great roof in the Swan Hall has a deep and projecting classical cornice; it is divided into three equal parts, two sloping and one flat, with the slopes returned at the ends. The whole is made up of twenty-three large octagons and of four other rather distorted ones in the corners, all surrounded with elaborate mouldings, carved and gilt like the cornice. From the square or three-sided spaces left between the octagons there project from among acanthus leaves richly carved and gilt pendants.

In each of the twenty-seven octagons there is painted on a flat-boarded ground a large swan, each wearing on its neck the red velvet and gold collar made by Dona Isabel for the real swans in the tank outside. These paintings, which are very well done, certainly seem to belong to the seventeenth century, for the trees and water are not at all like the work of an artist of Dom Manoel's time. (Fig. 50.)

Sala dos Escudos, Cintra.

Even more remarkable is the roof of the Sala dos Brazões or dos Escudos—that is 'of the shields'—also built by Dom Manoel, and also retouched at the same time as that in the Sala dos Cysnes. This other hall is a large room over forty feet square. The cornice begins about twelve feet from the ground, the walls being covered with hunting scenes on blue and white tiles of about the end of the seventeenth century. The cornice, about three feet deep and of considerable projection, is, like all the mouldings, painted blue and enriched with elaborate gilt carving. On the frieze is the following inscription in large gilt letters:

Pois		com		esforços		leais
Serviços			foram			ganhadas
Com	estas		e		outras	tais

Devem de ser comservadas.[100]

The inscription is interrupted by brackets, round which the cornice is returned, and on which rest round arches thrown across the four corners, bringing the whole to an equal-sided octagon.

FIG. 49.	**FIG. 50.**
CAMINHA.	**PALACE, CINTRA.**
ROOF OF MATRIZ.	**SALA DOS CYSNES.**

139

CINTRA.
PORTUGAL.
OLD PALACE.
SALA DOS BRAZÕES.

These triangular spaces are roofed with elaborate wooden vaults, with carved and gilt ribs leaving spaces painted blue and covered with gilt ornament. Above the cornice the panelling rises perpendicularly for about eleven feet; there being on each cardinal side eight panels, in two rows of four, one above the other, and over each arch four more—forty-eight panels in all. Above this begins an octagonal dome with elaborately carved and gilt mouldings, like those round the panels, in each angle and round the large octagon which comes in the middle of each side. The next stage is similar, but set at a different angle, and with smaller 140 and unequal-sided octagons, while the dome ends in one large flat eight-sided panel forty-five feet above the floor. All the space between the mouldings and the octagons is filled with most elaborate gilt carving on a blue ground. Nor does the decoration stop here, for the whole is a veritable Heralds' College for all the noblest families of Portugal in the early years of the sixteenth century. The large flat panel at the top is filled with the royal arms carved and painted, with a crown above and rich gilt mantling all round. In the eight panels below are the arms of Dom Manoel's eight children, and in the eight large octagons lower down are painted large stags with scrolls between their horns; lastly, in each of the forty-eight panels at the bottom, and of the six spaces which occur under each of the vaults in the four corners; in each of these seventy-two panels or spaces there is painted a

68

stag. Every stag has round its neck a shield charged with the arms of a noble family, between its horns a crest, and behind it a scroll on which is written the name of the family.[101]

The whole of this is of wood, and for beauty and originality of design, as well as for richness of colour, cannot be surpassed anywhere. In any northern country the seven small windows would not let in enough light, and the whole dome would be in darkness, but the sky and air of Portugal are clear enough for every detail to be seen, and for the gold on every moulding and piece of carving to gleam brightly from the blue background.

None of the ceilings of later date are in any way to be compared in beauty or richness with those of these two halls, for in all others the mouldings are shallower and the panels flatter.

Coimbra Misericordia.

In Coimbra there are two, both good examples of a simpler form of such ceilings. They are, one in the Misericordia—the headquarters of a corporation which owns and looks after all the hospitals, asylums and orphanages in the town—and one in the great hall of the University. The Misericordia, built by bishop Affonso de Castello Branco about the end of the sixteenth century, has a good cloister of the later renaissance, and opening off it two rooms of considerable size with panelled 141 ceilings, of which only one has its original painting. A cornice of some size, with brackets projecting from the frieze to carry the upper mouldings, goes round the room, and is carried across the corners so that at the ends of the room the ceiling has one longer and two quite short sides. The lower sloping part of the ceiling all round is divided into square panels with three-sided panels next the squares on the short canted sides; the upper slope is divided in exactly the same way so that the flat centre-piece consists of three squares set diagonally and of four triangles. All the panels are painted with a variety of emblems, but the colours are dark and the ceiling now looks rather dingy.

Sala dos Capellos University.

The great hall of the University built by the rector, Manoel de Saldanha, in 1655 is a very much larger and finer room. A raised seat runs round the whole room, the lower part of the walls are covered with tiles, and the upper with red silk brocade on which hang portraits of all the kings of Portugal, many doubtless as authentic as the early kings of Scotland at Holyrood. Here only the upper part of the cornice is carried across the corners, and the three sides at either end are equal, each being two panels wide.

As in the Misericordia the section of the roof is five-sided, each two panels wide. All the panels are square except at the half-octagonal ends where they diminish in breadth towards the top: they are separated by a large cable moulding and are painted alternately red and blue with an elaborate design in darker colour on each. (Fig. 51.)

The effect is surprisingly good, for each panel with its beautiful design of curling and twisting acanthus, of birds, of mermaids and of vases has almost the look of beautiful old brocade, for the blues and reds have grown soft with age.

Santa Clara, Villa do Conde.

Before finally leaving wood ceilings it were better to speak of another form or style which was sometimes used for their decoration although they are even freer from Moorish detail than are those at Coimbra, though probably like them ultimately derived from the same source. One of the finest of these ceilings is found in the upper Nuns' Choir in the church of Santa Clara at Villa do Conde. The church consists of a short nave with transepts and chancel all roofed with panelled wooden ceilings, painted grey as is often the case, and in no way remarkable. The church was founded in 1318, but the ceilings and stalls of both Nuns' Choirs, which, 142

Convent, Aveiro.

one above the other take up much the greater part of the nave, cannot be earlier than the first half of the seventeenth century. Like the other ceilings it is polygonal in section, but unlike all Moorish ones is not returned round the ends. Above a finely carved cornice with elaborate frieze, the whole ceiling is divided into deeply set panels, large and small squares with narrow rectangles between: all alike covered with elaborate carving, as are also the mouldings and the flat surfaces of the dividing bands. Here the wood is left in its natural colour, but in the nave of the church of a large convent at Aveiro, where the general design of the ceiling is almost the same, pictures are painted in the larger panels, and all the rest is heavily gilt, making the whole most gorgeous.

As time went on wooden roofs became less common, stone barrel vaults taking their place, but where they were used they were designed with a mass of meaningless ornament, lavished over the whole surface, which was usually gilt. One of the most remarkable examples of such a roof is found in the chancel of that same church at Aveiro. It is semicircular in shape and is all covered with greater and smaller carved and gilt circles, from the smallest of which in the middle large pendants hang down.

These circles are so arranged as to make the roof almost like that of Henry VII. Chapel, though the two really only resemble each other in their extreme richness and elaboration. This same extravagance of gilding and of carving also overtook altar and reredos. Now almost every church is full of huge masses of gilt wood, in which hardly one square inch has been left uncarved; sometimes, if there is nothing else, and the whole church—walls and ceiling alike—is a mass of gilding and painting, the effect is not bad, but sometimes the contrast is terrible between the plain grey walls of some old and simple building and the exuberance behind the high altar.

FIG. 51.
COIMBRA.
HALL OF UNIVERSITY.

143

CHAPTER X
EARLY MANOELINO

AFFONSO V., the African, had died and been succeeded by his son João II. in 1487. João tried, not without success, to play the part of Louis XI. of France and by a judicious choice of victims (he had the duke of Braganza, the richest noble in the country, arrested by a Cortes at Evora and executed, and he murdered his cousin the duke of Vizeu with his own hand) he destroyed the power of the feudal nobility. Enriched by the confiscation of his victims' possessions, the king was enabled to do without the help of the Cortes, and so to establish himself as a despotic ruler. Yet he governed for the benefit of the people at large, and reversing the policy of his father Affonso directed the energies of his people towards maritime commerce and exploration instead of wasting them in quarrelling with Castile or in attempting the conquest of Morocco. It was he who, following the example of his grand-uncle Prince Henry, sent out ship after ship to find a way to India round the continent of Africa. Much had already been done, for in 1471 Fernando Po had reached the mouth of the Niger, and all the coast southward from Morocco was well known and visited annually, for slaves used to cultivate the vast estates in the Alemtejo; but it was not till 1484 that Diogo Cão, sent out by the king, discovered the mouth of the Congo, or till 1486 that Bartholomeu Diaz doubled the Cabo Tormentoso, an ill-omened name which Dom João changed to Good Hope.

Dom João II. did not live to greet Vasco da Gama on his return from India, for he died in 1495, but he had already done so much that Dom Manoel had only to reap the reward of his predecessor's labours. The one great mistake he made was that in 1493 he dismissed Columbus as a dreamer, and so left the glory of the discovery of America to Ferdinand 144 and Isabella. Besides doing so much for the trade of his country, Dom João did what he could to promote literature and art. Andrea da Sansovino worked for him for nine years from 1491 to 1499, and although scarcely anything done by him can now be found, he here too set an example to Dom Manoel, who summoned so many foreign artists to the country and who sent so many of his own people to study in Italy and in Flanders.

Four years before Dom João died, his only son Affonso, riding down from Almerim to the Tagus to meet his father, who had been bathing, fell from his horse and was killed. In 1495 he himself died, and was succeeded by his cousin, Manoel the Fortunate. Dom Manoel indeed deserved the name of 'Venturoso.' He succeeded his cousin just in time to see Vasco da Gama start on his great voyage which ended in 1497 at Calicut. Three years later Pedro Alvares Cabral landed in Brazil, and before the king died, Gôa—the great Portuguese capital of the East—had become the centre of a vast trade with India, Ormuz[102] in the Persian

Gulf of trade with Persia, while all the spices[103] of the East flowed into Lisbon and even Pekin[104] had been reached.

From all these lands, from Africa, from Brazil, and from the East, endless wealth poured into Lisbon, nearly all of it into the royal treasury, so that Dom Manoel became the richest sovereign of his time.

In some other ways he was less happy. To please the Catholic Kings, for he wished to marry their daughter Isabel, widow of the young Prince Affonso, he expelled the Jews and many Moors from the country. As they went they cursed him and his house, and Miguel, the only child born to him and Queen Isabel, and heir not only to Portugal but to all the Spains, died when a baby. Isabel had died at her son's birth, and Manoel, still anxious that the whole peninsula should be united under his descendants, married her sister Maria. His wish was realised—but not as he had hoped—for his daughter Isabel married her cousin Charles V. and so was the mother of Philip II., who, when Cardinal King Henry died in 1580, was strong enough to usurp the throne of Portugal.

Being so immensely rich, Dom Manoel was able to cover 145 the whole land with buildings. Damião de Goes, who died in 1570, gives a list of sixty-two works paid for by him. These include cathedrals, monasteries, churches, palaces, town walls, fortifications, bridges, arsenals, and the draining of marshes, and this long list does not take in nearly all that Dom Manoel is known to have built.

Nearly all these churches and palaces were built or added to in that peculiar style now called Manoelino. Some have seen in Manoelino only a development of the latest phase of Spanish Gothic, but that is not likely, for in Spain that latest phase lasted for but a short time, and the two were really almost contemporaneous.

Manoelino does not always show the same characteristics. Sometimes it is exuberant Gothic mixed with something else, something peculiar, and this phase seems to have grown out of a union of late Gothic and Moorish. Sometimes it is frankly naturalistic, and this seems to have been developed out of the first; and sometimes Gothic and renaissance are used together. In this phase, the composition is still always Gothic, though the details may be renaissance. At times, of course, all phases are found together, but those which most distinctly deserve the name, Manoelino, are the first and second.

The shape of the arches, whether of window or of door, is one of the most characteristic features of Manoelino. After it had been well established they were rarely pointed. Some are round, some trefoils; some have a long line of wavy curves, others a line of sharp angles and curves together.[105] In others, like the door to the Sala das Pegas at Cintra, and so probably derived from Moorish sources, the arch is made of three or more convex curves, and in others again the arch is half of a straight-sided polygon, while in many of the more elaborate all or many of these may be used together to make one complicated whole of interlacing mouldings and hanging cusps.

The capitals too are different from any that have come before. Some are round, but they are more commonly eight-sided, or have at least an eight-sided abacus, often with the sides hollow forming a star. If ornamented with leaves, the leaves do not grow out of the bell but are laid round it like a 146 wreath. But leaf carving is not common; usually the caps are merely moulded, one or two of the mouldings being often like a rope; or branches may be set round them sometimes bound together with a broad ribbon like a bent faggot. The bases too are usually octagonal with an ogee section.

Another feature common to all phases is the use of round mouldings, either one by itself—often forming a kind of twisting broken hood-mould—or of several together, when they usually form a spiral. Such a round moulding has already been seen forming an ogee over the windows at Sempre Noiva and over the chapter-house door at São João Evangelista, Evora, and there are at Evora two windows side by side, in one of which this round moulding forms a simple ogee, while in the other it forms a series of reversed curves after the true Manoelino manner.

House of Resende, Evora.

They are in the house of Garcia de Resende, a man of many accomplishments whose services were much valued both by Dom João and by Dom Manoel. He seems too to have

71

been an architect of some distinction, if, as is said, he designed the Torre de São Vicente at Belem.

This second window in his house is one of the best examples of the complete union between Gothic and Moorish. It has three shafts, one (in the centre) with a Moorish capital, and two whose caps are bound round with a piece of rope. The semicircular arches consist of one round moulding with round cusps. A hollow mould runs down the two jambs and over the two arches, turning up as an ogee at the top. Beyond this hollow are two tall round shafts ending in large crocketed finials, while tied to them with carved cords is a curious hood-mould, forming three reversed cusps ending in large finials, one in the centre and one over each of the arches, and at the two ends curling across the hollow like a cut-off branch.

Here then we have an example not only of the use of the round moulding, but also of naturalistic treatment which was afterwards sometimes carried to excess.

Probably this window may be rather later in date than at least the foundation of the churches of Nossa Senhora do Popolo at Caldas da Rainha or of the Jesus Convent at Setubal; but it is in itself so good an example of the change from the simple ogee to the round broken moulding and of the use of naturalistic features, that it has been taken first.

Caldas da Rainha.

In 1485 Queen Leonor, wife of Dom João II., began a 147 hospital for poor bathers at the place now called after her, Caldas da Rainha, or Queen's hot baths. Beside the hospital was built a small church, now a good deal altered, with simple round-headed windows, and a curious cresting. Attached to it is a tower, interesting as being the only Manoelino church tower now existing. The lower part is square and plain, but the upper is very curious. On one side are two belfry windows, with depressed trefoil heads—that is the top of the trefoil has a double curve, exactly like the end of a clover leaf. On the outer side of each window is a twisted shaft with another between them, and from the top of these shafts grow round branches forming an arch over each window, and twining up above them in interlacing curves. The window on the east side has a very fantastic head of broken curves and straight lines. A short way above the windows the square is changed to an octagon by curved offsets. There are clock faces under small gables on each cardinal side, and at the top of it all rises a short eight-sided spire.

Probably this was the last part of the church to be built, and so would not be finished till about the year 1502, when the whole was dedicated.

Jesus, Setubal.

More interesting than this is the Jesus College at Setubal. Founded by Justa Rodrigues, Dom Manoel's nurse, in 1487 or 1488 and designed by one Boutaca or Boitaca,[106] it was probably finished sooner than the church at Caldas, and is the best example in the country of a late Gothic church modified by the addition of certain Manoelino details. Unfortunately it was a good deal injured by the great earthquake in 1755, when it lost all pinnacles and parapets. The church consists of a nave and aisles of three and a half bays and of a square chancel. Inside, the side aisles are vaulted with a half barrel and the central with a simple vault having large plain chamfered ribs. The columns, trefoils in section, are twisted, and have simple moulded caps. The chancel which is higher than the nave is entered by a large pointed arch, which like its jambs has one of its mouldings twisted. The chancel vault has many ribs, most of which are also twisted. All the piers and jambs as well as the windows are built of Arrabida marble, a red breccia found in the mountains to the 148 west of Setubal; the rest is all whitewashed except the arches and vaulting ribs which are painted in imitation of the marble piers.

Outside, the main door, also of Arrabida marble, is large and pointed, with many mouldings and two empty niches on each side. It has little trace of Manoelino except in the bent curves of the upturned drip-mould, and in the broken lines of the two smaller doors which open under the plain tympanum. The nave window is of two lights with simple tracery, but in the chancel, which was ready by 1495, the window shows more Manoelino tendencies. It is of three lights, with flowing tracery at the head, and with small cusped and crocketed arches thrown across each light at varying levels. There are niches on the jambs, and the outer moulding is carried round the window head in broken curves, after the manner of Resende's house at Evora. Though the chancel is square inside, the corners outside are cut off by a very broad chamfer, and a very curious ogee curve unites the two.

The cloisters to the north are more usual. The arches are round or slightly pointed, and like the short round columns with their moulded eight-sided caps and sides, are of Arrabida marble. Half-way along each walk two of the columns are set more closely together, and between them is a small round arch, with below it a Manoelino trefoil; there is too in the north-west corner a lavatory with a good flat vault.

Beja, Conceição.

At Beja the church of the Conceição, founded by Dom Manoel's father, has been very much pulled about, but the cornice and parapet with Gothic details, rope mouldings, and twisted pinnacles still show that it also was built when the new Manoelino style was first coming into use.

Castle.

In the ruins of the Castle there is a very picturesque window where two horseshoe arches are set so close together that the arches meet in such a way that the cusps at their meeting form a pendant, while another window in the Rua dos Mercadores, though very like the one in Resende's house in Evora, is more naturalistic. The outer shafts of the jambs are carved like tree trunks, and the hood moulding like a thick branch is bent and interlaced with other branches.

Paço, Cintra.

The additions made to the palace at Cintra by Dom Manoel are a complete treasury of Manoelino detail in its earlier phases. 149

The works were already begun in 1508, and in January of the previous year André Gonsalves, who was in charge, bought two notebooks for 240 reis in which to set down expenses, as well as paper for his office and four bottles of ink. From these books we learn what wages the different workmen received. Pero de Carnide, the head mason, got 50 reis or about twopence-halfpenny a day, and his helper only 35 reis. The chief carpenter, Johan Cordeiro, had 60 reis a day, and so had Gonçalo Gomes, the head painter. All the workmen are recorded from Pero de Torres, who was paid 3500 reis, about 14 shillings, for each of the windows he carved and set up, down to the man who got 35 reis a day for digging holes for planting orange-trees and for clearing out the place where the rabbits were kept. André Gonsalves also speaks of a Boitaca, master mason. He was doubtless the Boitaca or Boutaca of the Jesus Church at Setubal and afterwards at Belem, though none of his work at Setubal in any way resembles anything he may have done here.

The carriage entry which runs under the palace between Dom Manoel's addition and the earlier part of the palace, has in it some very characteristic capitals, two which support the entrance arch, while one belongs to the central column of an arcade which forms a sort of aisle on the west side. They are all round, though one belongs to an octagonal shaft. They have no abacus proper, but instead two branches are bent round, bound together by a wide ribbon. Below these branches are several short pieces of rope turned in just above the neck-mould, and between them carved balls, something like two artichokes stuck together face to face.

On the east side of the entry a large doorway leads into the newer part of the palace, in which are now the queen-dowager's private rooms. This doorhead is most typical of the style. In the centre two flat convex curves meet at an obtuse angle. At the end of about two feet on either side of the centre the moulding forming these curves is bent sharply down for a few inches to a point, and is then united to the jambs by a curve rather longer than a semicircle. Outside the round moulding forming these curves and bends is a hollow following the same lines and filled with branch-work, curved, twisted, and intertwined. Outside the hollow are shafts, resting on octagonal and interpenetrating bases. 150

These shafts are half-octagon in section with hollow—not as usual rounded—sides, ornamented with four-leafed flowers, and are twisted. Their capitals are formed by three carved wreaths, from which the shafts rise to curious half-Gothic pinnacles; they are also curved over to form a hood-mould. Above the central curves this moulding is broken and turned up to end in most curious cone-shaped horns, while from the middle there grows a large and elaborate finial.

In the front of the new part overlooking the entrance court there are six windows, three in each floor. They are all, except for a slight variation in detail, exactly alike, and are evidently derived from the Moorish windows in the other parts of the palace. Like them each has two round-headed lights, and a framing standing on corbelled-out bases at the sides. The capitals are various, most are mere wreaths of foliage, but one belonging to the centre shaft of the middle window on the lower floor has twisted round it two branches out of which grow the cusps. While at the sides there is no distinct abacus, in the centre it is always square and moulded. The cusps end in knobs like thistle-heads, and are themselves rather branchlike. In the hollow between the shafts and the framing there are sometimes square or round flowers, sometimes twisting branches. Branches too form the framing of all, they are intertwined up the sides, and form above the arches a straight-topped mass of interlacing twigs, out of which grow three large finials.

Originally the three windows of the upper floor belonged to a large hall whose ceiling was like that of the Sala dos Cysnes. Unfortunately the ceiling was destroyed, and the hall cut up into small rooms some time ago. (Fig. 52.)

Inside are several Manoelino doorways. One at the end of a passage has a half-octagonal head, with curved sides. Beyond a hollow moulding enriched with square flowers are thick twisted shafts, which are carried up to form a hood-mould following the curves of the opening below, and having at each angle a large radiating finial.

Besides these additions Dom Manoel made not a few changes in the older part of the palace. The main door leading into the Sala dos Cysnes is of his time, as is too a window in the upper passage leading to the chapel gallery. Though the walls of the Sala das Duas Irmãs are probably older, he altered it inside and built the two rows of columns 151 and arches which support the floor of the Sala dos Brazões above. The arches are round and unmoulded. The thin columns are also round, but the bases are eight-sided; so are the capitals, but with a round abacus of boughs and twisted ribbons. The great hall above is also Dom Manoel's work, though the ceiling may probably have been retouched since. His also are the two-light windows, with slender shafts and heads more or less trefoil in shape, but with many small convex curves in the middle. The lower part of the outer cornice too is interesting, and made of brick plastered. At the bottom is a large rope moulding, then three courses of tilelike bricks set diagonally. Above them is a broad frieze divided into squares by a round moulding; there are two rows of these squares, and in each is an opening with a triangular head like a pigeon-hole, which has given rise to the belief that it was added by the Marquez de Pombal after the great earthquake. Pombal means 'dovecot,' and so it is supposed that the marquis added a pigeon-house wherever he could. He may have built the upper part of the cornice, which might belong to the eighteenth century, but the lower part is certainly older.

The white marble door leading to the Sala dos Brazões from the upper passage is part of Dom Manoel's work. It has a flat ogee head with round projections which give it a roughly trefoil shape, and is framed in rope mouldings of great size, which end above in three curious finials.

Gollegã.

There are not very many churches built entirely in this style, though to many a door or a window may have been added or even a nave, as was done to the church of the Order of Christ at Thomar and perhaps to the cathedral of Guarda. Santa Cruz at Coimbra is entirely Manoelino, but is too large and too full of the work of the foreigners who brought in the most beautiful features of the French renaissance to be spoken of now. Another is the church at Gollegã, not far from the Tagus and about half-way between Santarem and Thomar. It is a small church, with nave and aisles of five bays and a square chancel. The piers consist of four half-round shafts round a square. In front the capitals are round next the neck moulding and square next the moulded abacus, while at the sides they become eight-sided. The arches are of two orders and only chamfered. The bases are curious, as each part belonging to a different member of the pier begins at 152 a different level. That of the shaft at the side begins highest, and of the shaft in front lowest, and both becoming eight-sided, envelop the base of the square centre. These eight-sided bases interpenetrate with the mouldings of a lower round base, and all stand on a large splayed octagon, formed from a square by curious ogee curves at the corners. The nave is roofed in wood, but the chancel is vaulted, having ribs enriched like the chancel arch with cable moulding. The west front has a plain tower at the end of the south aisle, buttresses with Gothic pinnacles, a large door below and a round window above. The doorhead is a depressed trefoil, or quatrefoil, as the central leaf is of two curves. Between the inner and outer round moulding is as usual a hollow filled with branches. The outer moulding, on its upper side, throws out the most fantastic curves and cusps, which with their finials nearly encircle two little round windows, and then in wilder curves push up through the square framing at the top to a finial just below the window. At the sides two large twisted shafts standing on very elaborate bases end in twisted pinnacles. The round window is surrounded by large rope moulding, out of which grow two little arms, to support armillary spheres.

Sé, Elvas.

Dom Manoel also built the cathedral at Elvas, but it has been very much pulled about. Only the nave—in part at least—and an earlier west tower survive. Outside the buttresses are square below and three-cornered above; all the walls are battlemented; the aisle windows are tall and round-headed. On the north side a good trefoil-headed door leads to the interior, where the arches are round, the piers clustered with cable-moulded capitals and starry eight-sided abaci. There is a good vault springing from corbels, but the clerestory windows have been replaced by large semicircles.

Marvilla, Santarem.

All the body of the church of Santa Maria da Marvilla at Santarem is built in the style of Dom João III., that is, the nave arcade has tall Ionic columns and round arches. The rebuilding of the church was ordered by Dom Manoel, but the style called after him is only found in the chancel and in the west door. The chancel, square and vaulted, is entered by a wide and high arch, consisting, like the door to the Sala das Pegas at Cintra, of a series of moulded convex curves. The west door is not unlike that at Gollegã. It has a trefoiled head; with a round moulding at the angle resting on the capitals of thin shafts.

FIG. 52.
PALACE, CINTRA.
PARTS ADDED BY D. MANOEL.

153 Beyond a broad hollow over which straggles a very realistic and thick-stemmed plant is a large round moulding springing from larger shafts and concentric with the inner. As at Gollegã from the outer side of this moulding large cusps project, one on each side, while in the middle it rises up in two curves forming an irregular pentagon with curved sides. Each outward projection of this round moulding ends in a large finial, so that there are five in all, one to each cusp and three to the pentagon. Beyond this moulding a plain flat band runs up the jambs and round the top cutting across the base of the cusps and of the pentagon. The bases of the shafts rest on a moulded plinth and are eight-sided, as are the capitals round which run small wreaths of leaves. Here the upright shafts at the sides are not twisted but run up in three divisions to Gothic pinnacles. (Fig. 53.)

Madre de Deus.

Almost exactly the same is a door in the Franciscan nunnery called Madre de Deus, founded to the east of Lisbon in 1509 by Dona Leonor, the widow of Dom João II. and sister of Dom Manoel. The only difference is that the shafts at the sides are both twisted, that the pentagon at the top is a good deal larger and has in it the royal arms, and that at the sides are shields, one on the right with the arms of Lisbon—the ship guided by ravens in which St. Vincent's body floated from the east of Spain to the cape called after him—and one on the left with a pelican vulning her breast.[107]

The proportions of this door are rather better than those of the door at Santarem, and it looks less clumsy, but it is impossible to admire either the design or the execution. The fat round outer moulding with its projecting curves and cusps is very unpleasing, the shafts at the sides are singularly purposeless, and the carving is coarse. At Gollegã the design was even more outrageous, but there it was pulled together and made into a not displeasing whole by the square framing.

University Chapel, Coimbra.

What has been since 1540 the university at Coimbra was originally the royal palace, and the master of the works there till the time of his death in 1524 was Marcos Pires, who also planned and carried out most of the great church of Santa Cruz. Probably the university chapel is his work, for the windows are not at all unlike those at Santa Cruz. The door in many ways resembles the three last described, but the 154 detail is smaller and all the proportions better. The door is double with a triple shaft in the middle; the two openings have very flat trefoil heads with a small ogee curve to the central leaf. The jambs have on each side two slender shafts between which there is a delicate twisted branch, and beyond them is a band of finely carved foliage and then another shaft. From these side shafts there springs a large trefoil, encompassing both openings. It is crocketed on the outside and has the two usual ogee cusps or projections on the outer side; but, instead of a large curved pentagon in the middle, the mouldings of the projections and of the trefoil then intertwine and rise up to some height forming a kind of wide-spreading cross with hollow curves between the arms. The arms of the cross end in finials, as do the ogee projections; there is a shield on each side below the cross arms, another crowned and charged with the royal arms above the central shaft, and on one side of it the Cross of the Order of Christ, and on the other an armillary sphere. On either side, as usual, on an octagonal base are tall twisted shafts, with a crown round the base of the twisted pinnacles which rise just to the level of the spreading arms of the cross. Like the door at Santarem the whole would be sprawling and ill-composed but that here the white-wash of the wall comes down only to the arms of the cross, so as to give it—built as it is of grey limestone—a simple square outline, broken only by the upper arm and finial of the cross.

The heads of the two windows, one on either side of the door, are half-irregular octagons with convex sides. They are surrounded by a broad hollow splay framed by thin shafts resting on corbels and bearing a head, a flat ogee in shape, but broken by two hanging points; one of the most common shapes for a Manoelino window. (Fig. 54.)

One more doorway before ending this chapter, already too long.

São Julião, Setubal.

The parish church of São Julião at Setubal was built during the early years of the sixteenth century, but was so shattered by the great earthquake of 1755 that only two of the doorways survive of the original building. The western is not of much interest, but that on the north—probably the work of João Fenacho who is mentioned as being a well-known carver working at Setubal in 1513—is one of the most elaborate doorways of that period.

FIG. 53.	FIG. 54.
SANTAREM.	COIMBRA.
W. DOOR, MARVILLA.	UNIVERSITY CHAPEL.

The northern side of the church is now a featureless 155 expanse of whitewashed plaster, scarcely relieved by a few simple square windows up near the cornice; but near the west end, in almost incongruous contrast, the plainness of the plaster is emphasised by the exuberant mouldings and carving of the door. Though in some features related to the doors at Santarem or the Madre de Deus the door here is much more elaborate and even barbaric, but at the same time, being contained within a simple gable-shaped moulding under a plain round arch, with no sprawling projections, the whole design—as is the case with the university chapel at Coimbra—is much more pleasing, and if the large outer twisted shafts with their ogee trefoiled head had been omitted, would even have been really beautiful.

The opening of the door itself has a trefoiled head, whose hollow moulding is enriched with small well-carved roses and flowers. This trefoiled head opens under a round arch, springing from delicate round shafts, shafts and arch-mould being alike enriched with several finely carved rings, while from ring to ring the rounded surface is beautifully wrought with wonderful minutely carved spirals. The bases and caps of these, as of the other larger shafts, are of the usual Manoelino type, round with a hollow eight-sided abacus. Beyond these shafts and their arch, rather larger shafts, ringed in the same way and carved with a

76

delicate diaper, support a larger arch, half-octagonal in shape and with convex sides, all ornamented like its supports, while all round this and outside it there runs a broad band of foliage, half Gothic, half renaissance in character. Beyond these again are the large shafts with their ogee trefoiled arch, which though they spoil the beauty of the design, at the same time do more than all the rest to give that strange character which it possesses. These shafts are much larger than the others, indeed they are made up of several round mouldings twisted together each of the same size as the shaft next them. Base and capital are of course also much larger, and there is only one ring ornament, above which the twisting is reversed. All the mouldings are carved, some with spirals, some with bundles of leaves bound round by a rope, with bunches of grape-like fruit between. The twisted mouldings are carried up beyond the capitals to form a huge trefoil turning up at the top to a large and rather clumsy finial. In this case the upright shafts at the sides are not twisted as in the other doors; they are square in plan, 156 interrupted by a moulding at the level of the capitals, below which they are carved on each face with large square flowers, while above they have a round moulding at the angles. At the top are plain Gothic pinnacles; behind which rises the enclosing arch, due doubtless to the restoration after the earthquake. The gable-shaped moulding runs from the base of these pinnacles to the top of the ogee, and forms the boundary between the stonework and the plaster.

Such then is the Manoelino in its earlier forms, and there can be little doubt that it was gradually evolved from a union of late Gothic and Moorish, owing some peculiarities such as twisted shafts, rounded mouldings, and coupled windows to Moorish, and to Gothic others such as its flowery finials. The curious outlines of its openings may have been derived, the simpler from Gothic, the more complex from Moorish. Steps are wanting to show whence came the sudden growth of naturalism, but it too probably came from late Gothic, which had already provided crockets, finials and carved bands of foliage so that it needed but little change to connect these into one growing plant. Sometimes these Manoelino designs, as in the palace at Cintra, are really beautiful when the parts are small and do not straggle all over the surface, but sometimes as in the Marvilla door at Santarem, or in that of the convent of the Madre de Deus at Lisbon, the mouldings are so clumsy and the design so sprawling and ill-connected, that they can only be looked on as curiosities of architectural aberration. 157

CHAPTER XI
THOMAR AND THE CONQUEST OF INDIA

VASCO DA GAMA set sail from Lisbon in July 1497 with a small fleet to try and make his way to India by sea, and he arrived at Calicut on the Malabar coast nearly a year later, in May 1598. He and his men were well received by the zamorim or ruler of the town—then the most important trade centre in India—and were much helped in their intercourse by a renegade native of Seville who acted as interpreter. After a stay of about two months he started for home with his ships laden with spices, and with a letter to Dom Manoel in which the zamorim said:—

'Vasco da Gama, a nobleman of thy household, has visited my kingdom, and has given me great pleasure. In my kingdom is abundance of cinnamon, cloves, ginger, pepper, and precious stones; what I seek from my country is gold, silver, coral and scarlet.'[108]

Arriving at Lisbon in July 1499, Vasco da Gama met with a splendid reception from king and people; was given 20,000 gold cruzados, a pension of 500 cruzados a year, and the title of Dom; while provision was also made for the families of those who had perished during the voyage; for out of one hundred and forty-eight who started two years earlier only ninety-six lived to see Lisbon again.

So valuable were spices in those days that the profit to the king on this expedition, after all expenses had been paid and all losses deducted, was reckoned as being in the proportion of sixty to one.

No wonder then that another expedition was immediately organised by Dom Manoel. This armada—in which the largest ship was of no more than four hundred tons— sailed 158 from Lisbon under the command of Pedro Alvares Cabral on March 9, 1500.

Being driven out of his course, Cabral after many days saw a high mountain which he took to be an island, but sailing on found that it was part of a great continent. He landed, erected a cross, and took possession of it in the name of his king, thus securing Brazil for Portugal. One ship was sent back to Lisbon with the news, and the rest turned eastwards to make for the Cape of Good Hope. Four were sunk by a great gale, but the rest arrived at Calicut on September 13th.

Here he too was well received by the zamorim and built a factory, but this excited the anger of the Arab traders, who burned it, killing fifty Portuguese. Cabral retorted by burning part of the town and sailed south to Cochin, whose ruler, a vassal of the zamorim, was glad to receive the strangers and to accept their help against his superior. Thence he soon sailed homewards with the three ships which remained out of his fleet of thirteen.

In 1502 Dom Manoel received from the Pope Alexander VI. the title of 'Lord of Navigation, conquests and trade of Ethiopia, Arabia, Persia, and India,' and sent out another great expedition under Vasco da Gama, who, however, with his lieutenant, Vicente Sodre, found legitimate trade less profitable than the capture of pilgrim ships going to and from Mecca, which they rifled and sank with all on board. From the first thus treated they took 12,000 ducats in money and 10,000 ducats' worth in goods, and then blew up the ship with 240 men besides women and children.

Reaching Calicut, the town was again bombarded and sacked, since the zamorim would not or could not expel all the Arab merchants, the richest of his people.

Other expeditions followed every year till in 1509 a great Mohammedan fleet led by the 'Mirocem, the Grand Captain of the Sultan of Grand Cairo and of Babylon,' was defeated off the island of Diu, and next year the second viceroy, Affonso de Albuquerque, moved the seat of the government from Cochin to Gôa, which, captured and held with some difficulty, soon became one of the richest and most splendid cities of the East.

Ormuz at the mouth of the Persian Gulf and the great depot of Persian trade had been captured in 1509, and it was not long before the Portuguese had penetrated to the Straits of Malacca and even to China and Japan. 159

So within twelve years from the time of Vasco da Gama's voyage the foundations of the Portuguese empire in the East had been firmly laid—an empire which, however, existed merely as a great trading concern in which Dom Manoel was practically sole partner and so soon became the richest sovereign of his time.

Seeing therefore how close the intercourse was between Lisbon and India,[109] it is perhaps no wonder that, in his very interesting book on the Renaissance Architecture of Portugal, Albrecht Haupt, struck by the very strange forms used at Thomar and to a lesser degree in the later additions to Batalha, propounded a theory that this strangeness was directly due to the importation of Indian details. That the discovery of a sea route to India had a great influence on the architecture of Portugal cannot be denied, for the direct result of this discovery was to fill the coffers of a splendour-loving king with what was, for the time, untold wealth, and so to enable him to cover the country with innumerable buildings; but tempting as it would be to accept Haupt's theory, it is surely more reasonable to look nearer home for the origin of these peculiar features, and to see in them only the culmination of the Manoelino style and the product of an even more exuberant fancy than that possessed by any other contemporary builder. Of course, when looking for parallels with such a special object in view it is easy enough to find them, and to see resemblances between the cloister windows at Batalha and various screens or panels at Ahmedabad; and when we find that a certain Thomas Fernandes[110] had been sent to India in 1506 as military engineer and architect; that another Fernandes, Diogo of Beja, had in 1513 formed part of an embassy sent to Gujerat and so probably to the capital Ahmedabad; and that Fernandes was also the name of the architects of Batalha, it becomes difficult not to connect these separate facts together and to jump to the quite unwarrantable conclusion that the four men of the same name may have been related and that one of them, probably Diogo, had given his 160 kinsmen sketches or descriptions on which they founded their designs.[111]

With regard to Thomar, where the detail is even more curious and Indian-looking, the temptation to look for Indian models is still stronger, owing to the peculiar position which the Order of Christ at Thomar now held, for the knights of that order had for some time possessed complete spiritual jurisdiction over India and all other foreign conquests.

This being so, it might have seemed appropriate enough for Dom Manoel to decorate the additions he made to the old church with actual Indian detail, as his builder did with corals and other symbols of the strange discoveries then made. The fact also that on the stalls at Santa Cruz in Coimbra are carved imaginary scenes from India and from Brazil might seem to be in favour of the Indian theory, but the towns and forests there depicted are exactly what a mediæval artist would invent for himself, and are not at all like what they were supposed to represent, and so, if they are to be used in the argument at all, would rather go to show how little was actually known of what India was like.

There seems also not to be even a tradition that anything of the sort was done, and if a tradition has survived about the stalls at Coimbra, surely, had there been one, it might have survived at Thomar as well.

At the same time it must be admitted that the bases of the jambs inside the west window in the chapter-house are very unlike anything else, and are to a Western eye like Indian work. However, a most diligent search in the Victoria and Albert Museum through endless photographs of Indian buildings failed to find anything which was really at all like them, and this helped to confirm the belief that this resemblance is more fancied than real; besides, the other strange features, the west window outside, and the south window, now a door, are surely nothing more than Manoelino realism gone a little mad.

Thomar has already been seen in the twelfth century when Dom Gualdim Paes built the sixteen-sided church and the castle, and when he and his Templars withstood the Moorish invaders with such success.

As time went on the Templars in other lands became rich 161 and powerful, and in the fourteenth century Philippe le Bel of France determined to put an end to them as an order and to confiscate their goods. So in 1307 the grand master was imprisoned, and five years later the Council of Vienne, presided over by Clement V.—a Frenchman, Bertrand de Goth—suppressed the order. Philippe seized their property, and in 1314 the grand master was burned.

In Portugal their services against the Moors were still remembered, and although by this time no part of Portugal was under Mohammedan rule, Granada was not far off, and Morocco was still to some extent a danger.

Dom Diniz therefore determined not to exterminate the Templars, but to change them into a new military order, so in 1319 he obtained a bull from John XXII. from Avignon constituting the Order of Christ. At first their headquarters were at Castro-Marim at the mouth of the Guadiana, but soon they returned to their old Templar stronghold at Thomar and were re-granted most of their old possessions.

The Order of Christ soon increased in power, and under the administration of Prince Henry, 1417 to 1460, took a great part in the discoveries and explorations which were to bring such wealth and glory to their country. In 1442, Eugenius IV. confirmed the spiritual jurisdiction of the order over all conquests in Africa, and Nicholas V. and Calixtus III. soon extended this to all other conquests made, or to be made anywhere, so that the knights had spiritual authority over them 'as if they were in Thomar itself.' This boon was obtained by Dom Affonso V. at his uncle Prince Henry's wish.

When Prince Henry died he was succeeded as duke of Vizeu and as governor of the order by his nephew Fernando, the second son of Dom Duarte. Fernando died ten years later and was succeeded by his elder son Diogo, who was murdered fifteen years later by Dom João II. in 1485. Then the title passed to his brother Dom Manoel, and with it the administration of the order, a position which he retained when he ascended the throne, and which has since belonged to all his successors.

Prince Henry finding that the old Templar church with its central altar was unsuited to the religious services of the order, built a chapel or small chancel out from one of the eastern sides and dedicated it to St. Thomas of Canterbury. 162 But as the order advanced in wealth and in power this addition was found to be far too small, and in a general chapter held by Dom Manoel in 1492 it was determined to build a new Coro large enough to hold all the knights and leaving the high altar in its old place in the centre of the round church.

In all the Templar churches in England, when more room was wanted, a chancel was built on to the east, so that the round part, instead of containing the altar, has now become merely a nave or a vestibule. At Thomar, however, probably because it was already common to put the stalls in a gallery over the west door, it was determined to build the new Coro to the west, and this was done by breaking through the two westernmost sides of the sixteen-sided building and inserting a large pointed arch.

Although it was decided to build in 1492, little or nothing can have been done for long, if it is true that João de Castilho who did the work was only born about the year 1490; and that he did it is certain, as he says himself that he 'built the Coro, the chapter-house—under the Coro—the great arch of the church, and the principal door.'

Two stone carvers, Alvaro Rodrigues and Diogo de Arruda, were working there in 1512 and 1513, and the stalls were begun in July 1511, so that some progress must have been made by them. If then João de Castilho did the work he must have been born some time before 1490, as he could hardly have been entrusted with such a work when a boy of scarcely twenty.

João de Castilho, who is said to have been by birth a Biscayan, soon became the most famous architect of his time. He not only was employed on this Coro, but was afterwards summoned to superintend the great Jeronymite monastery of Belem, which he finished. Meanwhile he was charged by João III. with the building of the vast additions made necessary at Thomar when in 1523 the military order was turned into a body of monks. He lived long enough to become a complete convert to the renaissance, for at Belem the Gothic framework is all overlaid with renaissance detail, while in his latest additions at Thomar no trace of Gothic has been left. He died shortly before 1553, as we learn from a document dated January 1st of that year, which states that his daughter Maria de Castilho then began, on the death of her father, to receive a pension of 20,000 reis. 163

The new Coro is about eighty-five feet long inside by thirty wide, and is of three bays. Standing, as does the Templars' church, on the highest point of the hill, it was, till the erection of the surrounding cloisters, clear of any buildings. Originally the round church, being part of the fortifications, could only be entered from the north, but the first thing done by Dom Manoel was to build on the south side a large platform or terrace reached from the garden on the east by a great staircase. This terrace is now bounded on the west by the Cloister dos Filippes, on the south by a high wall and by the chapter-house, begun by Dom Manoel but never finished, and on the north by the round church and by one bay of the Coro; and in this bay is now the chief entrance to the church. The lower part of the two western bays is occupied by the chapter-house, with one window looking west over the cloister of Santa Barbara, and one south, now hidden by the upper Cloister dos Filippes and used as a door. [See plan p. 225.]

Inside, the part over the chapter-house is raised to form the choir, and there, till they were burned in 1810 by the French for firewood, stood the splendid stalls begun in July 1511 by Olivel of Ghent who had already made stalls for São Francisco at Evora.[112] The stalls had large figures carved on their backs, a continuous canopy, and a high and elaborate cresting, while in the centre on the west side the Master's stall ended in a spire which ran up with numberless pinnacles, ribs and finials to a large armillary sphere just under the vaulting.[113] Now the inside is rather bare, with no ornament beyond the intricacy of the finely moulded ribs and the elaborate corbels from which they spring. These are a mass of carving, armillary spheres, acanthus leaves, shields upheld by well-carved figures, crosses, and at the top small cherubs holding the royal crown.

The inner side of the door has a segmental head and on either jamb are tall twisted shafts. A moulded string course running round just above the level once reached by the top of the stalls turns up over the window as a hood-mould. 164

At the same time much was done to enrich the old Templars' church. All the shafts were covered with gilt diaper and the capitals with gold; crockets were fixed to the outer sides of the pointed arches of the central octagon, and inside it were placed figures of saints standing on Gothic corbels under canopies of beautiful tabernacle work. Similar statues stand on the vaulting shafts of the outer polygon and between them, filling in the spaces below the round-headed windows, are large paintings in the Flemish style common to all Portuguese pictures of that time—of the Nativity, of the Visit of the Magi, of the Annunciation, and of the Virgin and Child.

To-day the only part of the south side visible down to the ground level is the eastern bay in which opens the great door. This is one of the works which João de Castilho claims as his, and on one of the jambs there is carved a strap, held by two lion's paws on which are some letters supposed to be his signature, and some figures which have been read as 1515, probably wrongly, for there seems to have been no renaissance work done in Portugal except by Sansovino till the coming of Master Nicolas to Belem in 1517 or later.[114] If it is 1515 and gives the date, it must mean the year when the mere building was finished, not the carving, for the renaissance band can hardly have been done till after his return from Belem.

The doorway is one of great beauty, indeed is one of the most beautiful pieces of work in the kingdom. The opening itself is round-headed with three bands of carving running all round it, separated by slender shafts of which the outermost up to the springing of the arch is a beautiful spiral with four-leaved flowers in the hollows. Of the carved bands the innermost is purely renaissance, with candelabra, medallions, griffins and leaves all most beautifully cut in the warm yellow limestone. On the next band are large curly leaves still Gothic in style and much undercut; and in the last, four-leaved flowers set some distance one from the other.

At the top, the drip-mould grows into a large trefoil with crockets outside and an armillary sphere within. At the sides tall thin buttresses end high above the door in 165 sharp carved pinnacles and bear under elaborate canopies many figures of saints.[115] Two other pinnacles rise from the top of the arch, and between them are more saints. In the middle stands Our Lady, and from her canopy a curious broken and curving moulding runs across the other pinnacles and canopies to the sides.

But that which gives to the whole design its chief beauty is the deep shadow cast by the large arch thrown across from one main buttress to the other just under the parapet. This arch, moulded and enriched with four-leaved flowers, is fringed with elaborate cusps, irregular in size, which with rounded mouldings are given a trefoil shape by small beautifully carved crockets. (Fig. 55.)

Except the two round buttresses at the west end and one on the north side which has Manoelino pinnacles, all are the same, breaking into a cluster of Gothic pinnacles rather more than half-way up and ending in one large square crocketed pinnacle very like those at Batalha. The roof being flat and paved there is no gable at the west end; there is a band of carving for cornice, then a moulding, and above it a parapet of flattened quatrefoils, in each of which is an armillary sphere, and at the top a cresting, alternately of cusped openings and crosses of the Order of Christ, most of which, however, have been broken away. Of the windows all are wide and pointed, without tracery and deeply splayed. The one in the central bay next the porch has niches and canopies at the side for statues and jambs not unlike those designed some years after at Belem. There is also a certain resemblance between the door here and the great south entrance to Belem, though this one is of far greater beauty, being more free from over-elaboration and greatly helped by the shadow of the high arch.

So far the design has shown nothing very abnormal; but for one or two renaissance details it is all of good late Gothic, with scarcely any Manoelino features. It is also more pleasing than any other contemporary building in Portugal, and the detail, though very rich, is more restrained. This may be due to the nationality of João de Castilho, for some of the work is almost Spanish, for example the buttresses, the pinnacles, and the door with its trefoiled drip-mould. 166

If, however, the two eastern bays are good late Gothic, what can be said of the western? Here the fancy of the designer seems to have run quite wild, and here it is that what have been considered to be Indian features are found.

It is hard to believe that João de Castilho, who nowhere, except perhaps in the sacristy door at Alcobaça, shows any love of what is abnormal and outlandish, should have designed these extraordinary details, and so perhaps the local tradition may be so far true, according to which the architect was not João but one Ayres do Quintal. Nothing else seems to be known of Ayres—though a head carved under the west window of the chapter-house is said to be his—but in a country so long illiterate as Portugal, where unwritten stories have been handed down from quite distant times, it is possible that oral tradition may be as true as written records.

Now it is known that João de Castilho was working at Alcobaça in 1519. In 1522 he was busy at Belem, where he may have been since 1517, when for the first time some progress seems to have been made with the building there. What really happened, therefore, may be that when he left Thomar, the Coro was indeed built, and the eastern buttresses finished, but that the carving of the western part was still uncut and so may have been the work of Ayres after João was himself gone.[116] This is, of course, only a conjecture, for Ayres seems to be mentioned in no document, but whoever it was who carved these buttresses and windows was a man of extraordinary originality, and almost mad fancy.

To turn now from the question of the builder to the building itself. The large round buttresses at the west end are fluted at the bottom; at about half their height comes a band of carving about six feet deep seeming to represent a mass of large ropes ending in tasselled fringes or possibly of roots. On one buttress a large chain binds these together, on the others a strap and buckle—probably the Order of the Garter given to Dom Manoel by Henry VII. Above this five large knotty tree-trunks or branches of coral grow up the buttresses uniting in rough trefoiled heads at the top, and having statues between them— Dom Affonso Henriques,

FIG. 55.	FIG. 56.
THOMAR.	THOMAR.
CONVENT OF CHRIST.	OUTSIDE OF W. WINDOW OF CHAPTER HOUSE
S. DOOR.	UNDER HIGH CHOIR IN NAVE.

167 Dom Gualdim Paes, Dom Diniz and Dom Manoel—two on each buttress. Then the buttress becomes eight-sided and smaller, and, surrounded by five thick growths, of which not a square inch is unworked and whose pinnacles are covered with carving, rises with many a strange moulding to a high round pinnacle bearing the cross of the order—a sign, if one may take the coral and the trees to be symbolical of the distant seas crossed and of the new lands visited, of the supreme control exercised by the order over all missions.

Coral-like mouldings too run round the western windows on both north and south sides, and at the bottom these are bound together with basket work.

Strange as are the details of these buttresses, still more strange are the windows of the chapter-house. Since about 1560 the upper cloister of the Filippes has covered the south side of the church so that the south chapter-house window, which now serves as a door, is hidden away in the dark. Still there is light enough to see that in naturalism and in originality it far surpasses anything elsewhere, except the west window of the same chapter-house. Up the jambs grow branches bound round by a broad ribbon. From the spaces between the ribbons there sprout out on either side thick shoots ending in large thistle heads. The top of the opening is low, of complicated curves and fine mouldings, on the outermost of which are cut small curly leaves, but higher up the branches of the jambs with their thistle heads and ribbons with knotted ropes and leaves form a mass of inextricable intricacy, of which little can be seen in the dark except the royal arms.

Inside the vault is Gothic and segmental, but the west window is even more strange than the southern; its inner arch is segmental and there are window seats in the thickness of the wall. The jambs have large round complicated bases of many mouldings, some enriched with leaves, some with thistle heads, some with ribbons, and one with curious projections like small elephants' trunks—in short very much what a Western mind might imagine some Hindu capital, reversed, to be like. On the jamb itself and round the head are three upright mouldings held together by carved basket work of cords, and bearing at intervals thistle heads in threes; beyond is another band of leaf-covered carving, and beyond 168 it an upright strip of wavy lines.[117] The opening has a head like that of the other window and is filled with a bronze grille.

Still more elaborate and extraordinary is the outside of this window, nor would it be possible to find words to describe it.

The jambs are of coral branches, with large round shafts beyond, entirely leaf-covered and budding into thistle heads. Ropes bind them round at the bottom and half-way up great branches are fastened on by chains. At the top are long finials with more chains holding corals on which rest armillary spheres. The head of the window is formed of twisted masses, from which project downwards three large thistle heads. Above this is a great wreath of leaves, hung with two large loops of rope, and twisting up as a sort of cusped ogee trefoil to the royal arms and a large cross of the Order of Christ. A square frame with flamelike border rises to the top of the side finials to enclose a field cut into squares by narrow grooves. Below the window more branches, coral, and ropes knot each other round the head of Ayres just below the rope moulding which runs across from buttress to buttress. Above the top of the opening and about half-way up the whole composition there is an offset, and on it rests a series of disks, set diagonally and strung on another rope. (Fig. 56.)

Although, were the royal arms and the cross removed, the window might not look out of place in some wild Indian temple, yet it is much more likely not to be Indian, but that the shafts at the sides are but the shafts seen in many Manoelino doors, that the window head is an elaboration of other heads,[118] that the coral jambs are another form of common naturalism, and that the great wreath is only the hood-mould rendered more extravagant. In no other work in Portugal or anywhere in the West are these features carved and treated with such wild elaboration, nor anywhere else is there seen a base like that of the jambs inside, but surely there is nothing which a man of imagination could not have evolved from details already existing in the country. |169|

Above the window the details are less strange. A little higher than the cross a string course traverses the front from north to south, crested with pointed cusps. Higher up still, a round window, set far back in a deep splay, lights the church above. Outside the sharp projecting outer moulding of this window are rich curling leaves, inside a rope, while other ropes run spirally across the splay, which seems to swell like a sail, and was perhaps meant to remind all who saw it that it was the sea that had brought the order and its master such riches and power. At the top are the royal arms crowned, and above the spheres of the parapet and the crosses of the cresting another larger cross dominates the whole front.

Such is Dom Manoel's addition to the Templars' church, and outlandish and strange as some of it is, the beautiful rich yellow of the stone under the blue sky and the dark shadows thrown by the brilliant sun make the whole a building of real beauty. Even the wild west window is helped by the compactness of its outline and by the plainness of the wall in which it is set, and only the great coral branches of the round buttresses are actually unpleasing. The size too of the windows and the great thickness of the wall give the Coro a strength and a solidity which agree well with the old church, despite the richness of the one and the severe plainness of the other. There is perhaps no building in Portugal which so well tells of the great increase of wealth which began under Dom Manoel, or which so well recalls the deeds of his heroic captains—their long and terrible voyages, and their successful conquests and discoveries. Well may the emblem of Hope,[119] the armillary sphere, whereby they found their way across the ocean, be carved all round the parapet, over the door, and beside the west window with its wealth of knots and wreaths.

Whether or not Ayres or João de Castilho meant the branches of coral to tell of the distant oceans, the trees of the forests of Brazil, and the ropes of the small ships which underwent such dangers, is of little consequence. To the present generation which knows that all these discoveries were only possible because Prince Henry and his Order of Christ had devoted their time and their wealth to the |170| one object of finding the way to the East, Thomar will always be a fitting memorial of these great deeds, and of the great men, Bartholomeu Diaz, Vasco da Gama, Affonso de Albuquerque, Pedro Cabral, and Tristão da Cunha, by whom Prince Henry's great schemes were brought to a successful issue. |171|

CHAPTER XII
THE ADDITIONS TO BATALHA

LITTLE had been done to the monastery of Batalha since the death of Dom Duarte left his great tomb-chapel unfinished. Dom Affonso v., bent on wasting the lives of the bravest of his people and his country's wealth in the vain pursuit of conquests in Morocco, could spare no money to carry out what his father had begun, and so make it possible to move his parents' bodies from their temporary resting-place before the high altar to the chapel intended to receive them. AffonsoV. himself dying was laid in a temporary tomb of wood in the chapter-house, as were his wife and his grandson, the only child of Dom João II.; while a coffin of wood in one of the side chapels held Dom João himself.

When João died, his widow Dona Leonor is said to have urged her brother, the new king, to finish the work begun by their ancestor and so form a fitting burial-place for her son as well as for himself and his descendants. Dom Manoel therefore determined to finish the Capellas Imperfeitas, and the work was given to the elder Matheus Fernandes, who had till 1480, when he was followed by João Rodrigues, been master of the royal works at Santarem. The first document which speaks of him at Batalha is dated 1503, and mentions him as Matheus Fernandes, vassal of the king, judge in ordinary of the town of Santa Maria da Victoria, and master of the works of the same monastery, named by the king. He died in 1515, and was buried near the west door.[120] He was followed by another Matheus Fernandes, probably his son, who died in 1528, to be succeeded by João de Castilho. But by then Dom Manoel was already dead. He had been buried not here, but in his new foundation of Belem, and his son 172 João III. and João de Castilho himself were too much occupied in finishing Belem and in making great additions to Thomar to be able to do much to the Capellas Imperfeitas. So after building two beautiful but incongruous arches, João de Castilho went back to his work elsewhere, and the chapels remain Imperfeitas to this day.

It will be remembered that the tomb-house begun by Dom Duarte took the form of a vast octagon some seventy-two feet in diameter surrounded by seven apsidal chapels—one on each side except that towards the church—and by eight smaller chapels between the apses. When Matheus Fernandes began his work most of the seven surrounding chapels were finished except for their vaulting, but not all, as in two or three the outer moulding of the entrance arch is enriched by small crosses of the Order of Christ, and by armillary spheres carved in the hollow; while the whole building stood isolated and unconnected with the church.

The first thing, therefore, done by Matheus was to build an entrance hall or pateo uniting the octagon with the church. Unless the walls of the Pateo be older than Dom Manoel's time it is impossible now to tell how Huguet, Dom Duarte's architect, meant to connect the two, perhaps by a low passage running eastwards from the central apse, perhaps not at all.

The plan carried out by Matheus took the form of a rectangular hall enclosing the central apse and the two smaller apses to the north and south, but leaving—now at any rate—a space between it and the side apses. Possibly the original intention may have been to pull down the two side apses, and so to form a square ambulatory behind the high altar leading to the great octagon beyond; but if that were the intention it was never carried out, and now the only entrance is through an insignificant pointed door on the north side.

The walls of the Pateo with their buttresses, string courses and parapet are so exactly like the older work as to suggest that they may really date from the time of Dom Duarte, and that all that Matheus Fernandes did was to build the vault, insert the windows, and form the splendid entrance to the octagon; but in any case the building was well advanced if not finished in 1509, when over the small entrance door was written, 'Perfectum fuit anno Domini 1509.'

Two windows light the Pateo, one looking north and one south. They are both alike, and both are thoroughly 173 Manoelino in style. They are of two lights, with well-moulded jambs, and half-octagonal heads. The drip-mould, instead or merely surrounding the half octagon, is so broken and bent as to project across it at four points, being indeed shaped like half a square with a semicircle on the one complete side, and two quarter circles on the half sides, all enriched by many a small cusp and leaf. The mullion is made of two branches twisting upwards, and the whole window head is filled with curving boughs and leaves forming a most curious piece of naturalistic tracery, to be compared with the tracery of some of the openings in the Claustro Real. (Fig. 58.)

No doubt, while the Pateo was being built, the great entrance to the Imperfect chapels, one of the richest as well as one of the largest doorways in the world, was begun, and it must have taken a long time to build and to carve, for the lower part, on the chapel side especially, seems to be rather earlier in style than the upper. The actual opening to the springing of the arch measures some 17 feet wide by 28 feet high, while including the jambs the whole is about 24 feet wide on the chapel, and considerably more on the Pateo side,— since there the splay is much deeper—by 40 feet high. To take the chapel side first:—Above a complicated base there is up the middle of each jamb a large hollow, in which are two niches one above the other, with canopies and bases of the richest late Gothic; on either side of this hollow are tall thin shafts entirely carved with minute diaper, two on the inner and one on the outer side. Next towards the chapel is another slender shaft, bearing two small statues one above the other, and outside it slender Gothic pinnacles and tabernacle work rise up to the capital. Up the outer side of the jambs are carved sharp pointed leaves, like great acanthus whose stalk bears many large exquisitely carved crockets. On the other side of the central hollow the diapered shaft is separated from the tiers of tiny pinnacles which form the inner angle of the jamb by a broad band of carving, which for beauty of design and for delicacy of carving can scarcely be anywhere surpassed. On the Pateo side the carving is even more wonderful.[121] There are seven shafts in all on each side, some diapered, some covered with spirals of leaves, one with panelling and one with exquisite foliage carved as minutely as on a piece of ivory.

Between each shaft are narrow mouldings, and between the outer five four bands of ivy, not as rich or as elaborately 174 undercut as on the chapel side, but still beautiful, and interesting as the ivy forms many double circles, two hundred and four in all, in each of which are written the words 'Tāyas Erey' or 'Tāya Serey,' Dom Manoel's motto. For years this was a great puzzle. In the seventeenth century the writer of the history of the Dominican Order in Portugal, Frei Luis de Souza, boldly said they were Greek, and in this opinion he was supported by 'persons of great judgment, for "Tanyas" is the accusative of a Greek word "Tanya," which is the same as region, and "erey" is the imperative of the verb "ereo", which signifies to seek, inquire, investigate, so that the meaning is, addressed to Dom Manoel, seek for new regions, new climes.' Of course whatever the meaning may be it is not Greek, indeed at that time in Portugal there was hardly any one who could speak Greek, and Senhora de Vasconcellos—than whom no one has done more for the collecting of inscriptions in Portugal—has come to the very probable conclusion that the words are Portuguese. She holds that 'Tāyas erey' or 'Tāya serey' should be read 'Tanaz serey,' 'I shall be tenacious'—for Tanaz is old Portuguese for Tenaz—and that the Y is nothing but a rebus or picture of a tenaz or pair of pincers, and indeed the Y's are very like pincers. In this opinion she is upheld by the carving of the tenacious ivy round each word, and the fact that Dom Manoel was not really tenacious at all, but rather changeable, makes it all the more likely that he would adopt such a motto.

The carvers were doubtless quite illiterate and may well have thought that the pincers in the drawing from which they were working were a letter and may therefore have mixed them up to the puzzling of future generations.[122] Or since nowhere is 'Tayaz serey' written with the 'z' may not the first 'y' be the final 'z' of Tanaz misplaced?

The arched head of the opening is treated differently on the two sides. Towards the Pateo the two outer mouldings form a large half octagon set diagonally and with curved sides; the next two form a large trefoil. In the spandrels between these are larger wreaths enclosing 'Tanyas erey,' which is also repeated all round these four mouldings.

The trefoils form large hanging cusps in front of the complicated inner arch. This too is more or less trefoil in shape,

FIG. 57.
BATALHA ENTRANCE TO CAPELLAS INPERFEITAS.
FROM A PHOTOGRAPH BY E. BIEL & CO., OPORTO

[175] but with smaller curves between the larger, and all elaborately fringed with cuspings and foliage.

Four mouldings altogether are of this shape, two on each side, and beyond them towards the chapel is that arch or moulding which gives to the whole its most distinctive character. The great trefoil, with large cusps, which forms the head is crossed by another moulding in such a way as to become a cinquefoil, while the second moulding, like the hood of the door at Santarem, forms three large reversed cusps, each ending in splendid acanthus leaves. Further, the whole of these mouldings are on the inner side carved with a delicate spiral of ribbon and small balls, and on the outer with the same acanthus that runs up the jambs.

Now, on the chapel side especially, from the base to the springing there is little that might not be found in late French Gothic work, except perhaps that diapered shafts were not then used in France, and that the bands of carving are rather different in spirit from French work; but as for the head, no opening of that size was made in France of so complicated and, it must be added, so unconstructional a shape. It is the *chef-d'œuvre* of the Manoelino style, and although a foreigner may be inclined at first, from its very strangeness, to call it Eastern, it is really only a true development in the hands of a real artist of what Manoelino was; an expression of Portugal's riches and power, and of the gradual assimilation of such Moors as still remained on this side the Straits. Of course it is easy to say that it is extravagant, overloaded and debased; and so it may be. Yet no one who sees it can help falling a victim to its fascination, for perhaps its only real fault is that the great cusps and finials are on rather too large a scale for the rest. Not even the greatest purist could help admiring the exquisite fineness of the carving—a fineness made possible by the limestone, very soft when new, which gradually hardens and grows to a lovely yellow with exposure to the air. No records tell us so, but considering the difference in style between the upper and the lower part it may perhaps be conjectured that the elder Matheus designed the lower part, and the younger the upper, after his father's death in 1515.

In the great octagon itself the first thing to be done was to build huge piers, which partly encroach on the small sepulchral chapels between the larger apses. These piers now rise nearly to the level of the central aisle of the church where [176] they are cut off unfinished; they must be about 80 or 90 feet in height. On the outer side they are covered with many circular shafts which are banded together by mouldings at nearly regular intervals. Haupt has pointed out that in general appearance they are not unlike the great minar called the Kutub at Old Delhi, and a lively imagination might see a resemblance to the vast piers, once the bases of minars, which flank the great entrance archways of some mosques at Ahmedabad, for example those in the Jumma Musjid. Yet there is no necessity to go so far afield. Manoelino architects had always been fond of bundles of round mouldings and so naturally used them here, nor indeed are the piers at all like either the Kutub or the minars at Ahmedabad. They have not the batter or the sharp angles of the one, nor the innumerable breaks and mouldings of the others.

Between each pier a large window was meant to open, of which unfortunately nothing has been built but part of the jambs.

Inside the vaulting of the apsidal chapels was first finished; all the vaults are elaborate, have well-moulded ribs, and bosses, some carved with crosses of the Order of Christ, some with armillary spheres, others with a cross and the words 'In hoc signo vinces,' or with a sphere and the words 'Espera in Domino.' Where Dom João II. was to be buried is a pelican vulning herself—for that was his device—and in that intended for his father Dom Affonso V. a 'rodisio' or mill-wheel. A little above the entrance arches to the chapels the octagon is surrounded by two carved string courses separated by a broad plain frieze.[123] On the lower string are the beautifully modelled necks and heads of dragons, springing from acanthus leaves and so set as to form a series of M's, and on the upper an exquisite pattern arranged in squares, while on it rests a most remarkable cresting. In this cresting, which is formed of a single bud set on branches between two coupled buds, the forms are most strange and at the same time beautiful.

Inside, the great piers have been much more highly adorned than without. The vaulting shafts in the middle—which, formed of several small round mouldings, have run up 177 quite plain from the ground, only interrupted by shields and their mantling on the frieze—are here broken and twisted. On either side are niches with Gothic canopies, above which are interlacing leaves and branches. Beyond the niches are the window jambs, on which, next the opening, are shafts carved with naturalistic tree-stems, and between these and the niches two bands of ornament separated by thin plain shafts.

In each opening these bands are different. In some is Gothic foliage, in others semi-classic carving like the string below or realistic like the cresting. In others are naturalistic branches, and in the opening over the chapel where Dom Manoel was to lie are cut the letters M in one hand and R in the other; Manoel Rey. (Fig. 59.)

Only the first foot or so of the vaulting has been built, and there is nothing now to show how the great octagon was to be roofed. Murphy[124] gives his idea; the eight piers carried high up and capped with spires, huge Gothic windows between, and the whole covered by a vast pointed roof—presumably of wood—above the vault. Haupt with his Indian prepossessions suggests a dome surrounded by eight great domed pinnacles. Probably neither is right; certainly Murphy's great roof of wood would never have been made, and as for Haupt's dome nothing domed was built in Portugal till long after and that at first only on a small scale.[125]Besides, the well-developed Gothic ribs which are seen springing in each corner clearly show that some kind of Gothic vault was meant, and not a dome; and that the Portuguese could build wonderful vaults had been already shown by the chapter-house here and was soon to be shown by the transept at Belem. So in all probability the roof would have been a great Gothic vault of which the centre would rise very considerably above the sides; for there is no sign of stilting the ribs over the windows. The whole would have been covered with stone slabs, and would have been surrounded by eight groups of pinnacles, most of which would no doubt have been twisted.

Deeply though one must regret that this great chapel has been left unfinished and open to the sky, yet even in its incomplete state it is a treasure-house of beautiful ornament, and it is wonderful how well the more commonplace Gothic 178 of Huguet's work agrees with and even enhances the richness of the detail which Fernandes drew from so many sources, late Gothic, early renaissance, and naturalistic, and which he knew so well how to combine into a beautiful whole.

The great Claustro Real, built by Dom João I., was peculiar among Portuguese cloisters in having, or at least being prepared for, large traceried windows. Probably these had remained blank, and for about a hundred years awaited the tracery which more than any part of the convent shows the skill of Matheus Fernandes.

There seems to be no exact record of when the work was done, but it must have been while additions were being made to the Imperfect chapels, though more fortunate than they, the work here was successfully finished.

The cloister has seven bays on each side, of which the five in the middle are nearly equal, having either five or six lights. In the eastern corners the openings have only three lights, in the south-western they have four, and in the north-western there stands the square two-bayed lavatory. (Fig. 60.)

In all the openings the shafts are alike. They have tall eight-sided and round bases, similar capitals and a moulded ring half-way up, while the whole shaft from ring to base and from ring to capital is carved with the utmost delicacy, with spirals, with diaper patterns, or with leaflike scales. Above the capitals the pointed openings are filled in with veils of tracery of three different patterns. In the central bay, and in the two next but one on either side of it, and so filling nine openings, is what at first seems to be a kind of reticulated tracery. But on looking closer it is found to be built up of leaf-covered curves and of buds very like those forming the cresting in the Capellas Imperfeitas. In the corner bays—except where stands the lavatory—there is another form of reticulated tracery, where the larger curves are formed by branches, whose leaves make the cusps, while filling in the larger spaces are budlike growths like those in the first-mentioned windows.

87

On either side of the central openings the tracery is more naturalistic than elsewhere; here the whole is formed of interlacing and intertwining branches, with leaves and large fruit-like poppy heads, and in the centre the Cross of the Order of Christ. But of all, the most successful is in the lavatory; there the two bays which form each side are high and narrow,

FIG. 58.
BATALHA
WINDOW OF
PATEO.

FIG. 59.
BATALHA
CAPELLAS IMPERFEITAS.
UPPER PART. FROM A PHOTOGRAPH BY E. BIEL & CO.,
OPORTO.

179 with richly cusped pointed arches. Instead of cutting out the cusps and filling the upper part with tracery, Matheus Fernandes has with extraordinary skill thrown a crested transome across the opening and below it woven together a veil of exquisitely carved branches, which, resting on a central shaft, half hide and half reveal the large marble fountain within. (Fig. 61.)

At first, perhaps, accustomed to the ordinary forms of Gothic tracery, these windows seem strange, to some even unpleasing. Soon, however, when they have been studied more closely, when it has been recognised that the brilliant sunshine needs closer tracery and smaller openings than does the cooler North, and that indeed the aim of the designer is to keep out rather than to let in the direct rays of light, no one can be anything but thankful that Matheus Fernandes, instead of trying to adapt Gothic forms to new requirements, as was done by his predecessors in the church, boldly invented new forms for himself; forms which are entirely suited to the sun, the clear air and sky, and which with their creamy lace make a fitting background to the roses and flowers with which the cloister is now planted.

Now the question arises, from whence did Matheus Fernandes draw his inspiration? We have seen that windows with good Gothic tracery are almost unknown in Portugal, for even in the church here at Batalha the larger windows nearly all show a want of knowledge, and a wish to shut out the sun as much as possible, and besides there is really no resemblance between the tracery in the church and that in the cloister.

In the lowest floor of the Torre de São Vicente, begun by Dom João II. and finished by Dom Manoel to defend the channel of the Tagus, the central hall is divided from a passage by a thin wall whose upper part is pierced to form a perforated screen. The original plan for the tower is said to have been furnished by Garcia de Resende, whose house we have seen at Evora, and if this screen, which is built up of heart-shaped curves, is older than the cloister windows at Batalha, he may have suggested to Matheus Fernandes the tracery which has a more or less reticulated form, though on the other hand it may be later and have been suggested by them. Most probably, however, Matheus Fernandes thought out the tracery for himself. He would not have had far to 180 go to see real reticulated panelling, for the church is covered with it; but an even more likely source of this reticulation might be found in the beautiful Moorish panelling which exists on such buildings as the Giralda or the tower at Rabat, and if we find Moors among the workmen at Thomar there may well have been some at Batalha as well. As for the naturalistic tracery, it is clearly only an improvement on such windows as those of the Pateo behind the church, and there is no need to go to Ahmedabad and find there pierced screens to which they have a certain resemblance.

However, whatever may be its origin, this tracery it is which makes the Claustro Real not only the most beautiful cloister in Portugal, but even, as that may not seem very great praise, one of the most beautiful cloisters in the world, and it must have been even more beautiful before a modern restoration crowned all the walls with a pierced Gothic parapet and a spiky cresting, whose angular form and sharp mouldings do not quite harmonise with the rounded and gentle curves of the tracery below.

After the suppression of the monastic orders in 1834, Batalha, which had already suffered terribly from the French invasion—for in 1810 during the retreat under Massena two cloisters were burned and much furniture destroyed—was for a time left to decay.

However, in 1840 the Cortes decreed an annual expenditure of two contos of reis,[126] or about £450 to keep the buildings in repair and to restore such parts as were damaged.

The first director was Senhor Luis d'Albuquerque, and he and his successors have been singularly successful in their efforts, and have carried out a restoration with which little fault can be found, except that they have been too lavish in building pierced parapets, and in filling the windows of the church with wooden fretwork and with hideous green, red and blue glass.

[181]

CHAPTER XIII
BELEM

BELEM or Bethlehem lies close to the shore, after the broad estuary of the Tagus has again grown narrow, about four miles from the centre of Lisbon, and may best be reached by one of the excellent electric cars which now so well connect together the different parts of the town and its wide-spreading suburbs.

Situated where the river mouth is at its narrowest, it is natural that it was chosen as the site of one of the forts built to defend the capital. Here, then, on a sandbank washed once by every high tide, but now joined to the mainland by so unromantic a feature as the gasworks, a tower begun by Dom João II., and designed, it is said, by Garcia de Resende, was finished by Dom Manoel about 1520 and dedicated to São Vicente, the patron of Lisbon.[127]

The tower is not of very great size, perhaps some forty feet square by about one hundred high. It stands free on three sides, but on the south towards the water it is protected by a great projecting bastion, which, rather wider than the tower, ends at the water edge in a polygon.

The tower contains several stories of one room each, none of which are in themselves in any way remarkable except the lowest, in which is the perforated screen mentioned in the last chapter. In the second story the south window opens on to a long balcony running the whole breadth of the tower, and the other windows on to smaller balconies. The third story is finished with a fortified parapet resting on great corbels. The last and fourth, smaller than those below, is fortified with pointed merlons, and with a round corbelled turret at each corner. [182]

On entering, it is found that the bastion contains a sort of cloister with a flat paved roof on to which opens the door of the tower. Under the cloister are horrid damp dungeons, last used by Dom Miguel, who during his usurpation imprisoned in them such of his liberal opponents as he could catch. The whole bastion is fortified with great merlons, rising above a rope moulding, each, like those on the tower, bearing a shield carved with the Cross of the Order of Christ, and by round turrets corbelled out at the corners. These, like all the turrets, are capped with melon-shaped stone roofs, and curious finials. Similar turrets jut out from two corners of the ground floor.

The parapet also of the cloister is interesting. It is divided into squares, in each of which a quatrefoil encloses a cross of the Order of Christ. At intervals down the sides are spiral pinnacles, at the corners columns bearing spheres, and at the south end a tall niche, elaborately carved, under whose strange canopy stand a Virgin and Child.

The most interesting features of the tower are the balconies. That on the south side, borne on huge corbels, has in front an arcade of seven round arches, resting on round shafts with typical Manoelino caps. A continuous sloping stone roof covers the whole, enriched at the bottom by a rope moulding, and marked with curious nicks at the top. The parapet is

89

Gothic and very thin. The other balconies are the same, a pointed tentlike roof ending in a knob, a parapet whose circles enclose crosses of the order, but with only two arches in front.

The third story is lit by two light windows on three sides, and on the south side by two round-headed windows, between which is cut a huge royal coat-of-arms crowned.

Altogether the building is most picturesque, the balconies are charming, and the round turrets and the battlements give it a look of strength and at the same time add greatly to its appearance. The general outline, however, is not altogether pleasing owing to the setting back of the top story. (Fig. 62.)

The detail, however, is most interesting. It is throughout Manoelino, and that too with hardly an admixture of Gothic. There is no naturalism, and hardly any suggestion of the renaissance, and as befits a fort it is without any of the exuberance so common to buildings of this time.

Now here again, as at Thomar and Batalha, Haupt has 183 seen a result of the intercourse with India; both in the balconies and in the turret roofs[128] he sees a likeness to a temple in Gujerat; and it must be admitted that in the example he gives the balconies and roofs are not at all unlike those at Belem. It might further be urged that Garcia de Resende who designed the tower, if he was never in India himself, formed part of Dom Manoel's great embassy to Rome in 1514, when the wonders of the East were displayed before the Pope, that he might easily be familiar with Indian carvings or paintings, and that finally there are no such balconies elsewhere in Portugal. All that may be true, and yet in his own town of Evora there are still many pavilions more like the smaller balconies than are those in India, and it surely did not need very great originality to put such a pavilion on corbels and so give the tower its most distinctive feature. As for the turrets, in Spain there are many, at Medina del Campo or at Coca, which are corbelled out in much the same way, though their roofs are different, and like though the melon-shaped dome of the turrets may be to some in Gujerat, they are more like those at Bacalhôa, and surely some proof of connection between Belem and Gujerat, better than mere likeness, is wanted before the Indian theory can be accepted. That the son of an Indian viceroy should roof his turrets at Bacalhôa with Indian domes might seem natural; but the turrets were certainly built before he bought the Quinta in 1528, and neither they nor the house shows any other trace of Indian influence.

The night of July 7, 1497, the last Vasco da Gama and his captains were to spend on shore before starting on the momentous voyage which ended at Calicut, was passed by them in prayer, in a small chapel built by Prince Henry the Navigator for the use of sailors, and dedicated to Nossa Senhora do Restello.

Two years later he landed again in the Tagus, with a wonderful story of the difficulties overcome and of the vast wealth which he had seen in the East. As a thankoffering Dom Manoel at once determined to found a great monastery for the Order of St. Jerome on the spot where stood Prince Henry's chapel. Little time was lost, and the first stone was laid on April 1 of the next year. 184

The first architect was that Boutaca who, about ten years before, had built the Jesus Church at Setubal for the king's nurse, Justa Rodrigues, and to him is probably due the plan. Boutaca was succeeded in 1511 by Lourenço Fernandes, who in turn gave place to João de Castilho in 1517[129] or 1522.

It is impossible now to say how much each of these different architects contributed to the building as finished. At Setubal Boutaca had built a church with three vaulted aisles of about the same height. The idea was there carried out very clumsily, but it is quite likely that Belem owes its three aisles of equal height to his initiative even though they were actually carried out by some one else.

Judging also from the style, for the windows show many well-known Manoelino features, while the detail of the great south door is more purely Gothic, they too and the walls may be the work of Boutaca or of Lourenço Fernandes, while the great door is almost certainly that of João de Castilho.

In any case, when João de Castilho came the building was not nearly finished, for in 1522 he received a thousand cruzados towards building columns and the transept vault.[130]

90

But even more important to the decoration of the building than either Boutaca or João de Castilho was the coming of Master Nicolas, the Frenchman[131] whom we shall see at work at Coimbra and at São Marcos. Belem seems to have been the first place to which he came after leaving home, and we soon find him at work there on the statues of the great south door, and later on those of the west door, where, with the exception of the Italian door at Cintra, is carved what is probably the earliest piece of renaissance detail in the country.

The south door, except for a band of carving round each entrance, is free of renaissance detail, and so was probably built before Nicolas added the statues, but in the western a few such details begin to appear, and in these, as in the band round the other openings, he may have had a hand. Inside renaissance detail is more in evidence, but since the great piers would not be carved till after they were built, it is more likely that the renaissance work there is due to João de Castilho himself and to what he had learned either from Nicolas or

FIG. 62.	FIG. 63.
TORRE DE SÃO VICENTE.	BELEM
BELEM.	SACRISTY.

[185] from the growing influence of the Coimbra School. It is, of course, also possible that when Nicolas went to Coimbra, where he was already at work in 1524, some French assistant may have stayed behind, yet the carving on the piers is rather coarser than in most French work, and so was more probably done by Portuguese working under Castilho's direction.

The monastic buildings were begun after the church; but although at first renaissance forms seem supreme in the cloisters, closer inspection will show that they are practically confined to the carving on the buttresses and on the parapets of the arches thrown across from buttress to buttress. All the rest, except the door of the chapter-house—the refectory, undertaken by Leonardo Vaz, the chapter-house itself, and the great undercroft of the dormitory stretching 607 feet away opposite the west door, and scarcely begun in 1521, are purely Manoelino, so that the date 1544 on the lower cloister must refer to the finishing of the renaissance additions and not to the actual building, especially as the upper cloister is even more completely Gothic than the lower.

The sacristy, adjoining the north transept, must have been one of the last parts of the original building to be finished, since in it the vault springs in the centre from a beautiful round shaft covered with renaissance carving and standing on a curious base. (Fig. 63.)

The first chancel, which in 1523 was nearly ready, was thought to be too small and so was pulled down, being replaced in 1551 by a rather poor classic structure designed by Diogo de Torralva. In it now lie Dom Manoel, his son Dom João III., and the unfortunate Dom Sebastião, his great-grandson. Vasco da Gama and other national heroes have also found a resting-place in the church, and the chapter-house is nearly filled with the tomb of Herculano, the best historian of his country.

Since the expulsion of the monks in 1834 the monastic buildings have been turned into an excellent orphanage for boys, who to the number of about seven hundred are taught some useful trade and who still use the refectory as their dining-hall. The only other change since 1835 has been the building of an exceedingly poor domed top to the south-west tower instead of its original low spire, the erection of an upper story above the long undercroft, and of a great entrance [186] tower half-way along, with the result that the tower soon fell, destroying the vault below.

O	MOSHEIRO	DES	JERÓNIMOS	DE	STA	MARIA	DE	BELEM.
FOVNDED		BY		DOM		MANOEL	APRIL	21	1500.
BOVTACA		ARCHITECT		TILL		1511.	SVCCEEDED	BY
LOVRENÇO			FERNANDES.		LITTLE		DONE	TILL
1522	WHEN		JOÃO	DE		CASTILHO	SVCCEEDED.

91

CAPELLA MOR REBVILT 1551 BY DIOGO DE TORRALVA.

The plan of the church is simple but original. It consists of a nave of four bays with two oblong towers to the west. The westernmost bay is divided into two floors by a great choir gallery entered from the upper cloister and also extending to the west between the towers, which on the ground floor form chapels. The whole nave with its three aisles of equal height measures from the west door to the transept some 165 feet long by 77 broad and over 80 high. East of the nave the church spreads out into an enormous transept 95 feet long by 65 wide, and since the vast vault is almost barrel-shaped 187 considerably higher than the nave. North and south of this transept are smaller square chapels, and to the east the later chancel, the whole church being some 300 feet long inside. North of the nave is the cloister measuring 175 feet by 185, on its western side the refectory 125 feet by 30, and on the east next the transept a sacristy 48 feet square, and north of it a chapter-house of about the same size, but increased on its northern side by a large apse. In the thickness of the north wall of the nave a stair leads from the transept to the upper cloister, and a series of confessionals open alternately, the one towards the church for the penitent and the next towards the lower cloister for the father confessor. Lastly, separated from the church by an open space once forming a covered porch, there stretches away to the west the great undercroft, 607 feet long by 30 wide.

Taking the outside of the church first. The walls of the transept and of the transept chapel are perfectly plain, without buttresses, with but little cornice and, now at least, without a cresting or parapet. They are only relieved by an elaborate band of ornament which runs along the whole south side of the church, by the tall round-headed windows, and in the main transept by a big rope moulding which carries on the line of the chapel roof. Plain as it is, this part of the church is singularly imposing from its very plainness and from its great height, and were the cornice and cresting complete and the original chancel still standing would equal if not surpass in beauty the more elaborate nave. The windows—one of which lights the main transept on each side of the chancel, and two, facing east and west, the chapel which also has a smaller round window looking south—are of great size, being about thirty-four feet high by over six wide; they are deeply set in the thick wall, are surrounded by two elaborate bands of carving, and have crocketed ogee hood-moulds.

The great band of ornament which is interrupted by the lower part of the windows has a rope moulding at the top above which are carved and interlacing branches, two rope mouldings at the bottom, and between them a band of carving consisting of branches twisted into intertwining S's, ending in leaves at the bottom and buds at the top, the whole being nearly six feet across.

The three eastern bays of the nave are separated by buttresses, square below, polygonal above, and ending in 188 round shafts and pinnacles at the top. The cornice, here complete, is deep with its five carved mouldings, but not of great projection. On it stands the cresting of elaborately branched leaves, nearly six feet high.

The central bay is entirely occupied by the great south door which, with its niches, statues and pinnacles entirely hides the lower part of the buttresses. The outer round arch of the door is thrown across between the two buttresses, which for more than half their height are covered with carved and twisted mouldings, with niches, canopies, corbels, and statues all carved with the utmost elaboration. Immediately above the great arch is a round-headed window, and on either side between it and the buttresses are two rows of statues and niches in tiers separated by elaborate statue-bearing shafts and pinnacles. Statues even occupy niches on the window jamb, and a Virgin and Child stand up in front on the end of the ogee drip-mould of the great arch. (Fig. 64.)

It will be seen later how poorly Diogo de Castilho at Coimbra finished off his window on the west front of Santa Cruz. Here the work was probably finished first, and it is curious that Diogo in copying his brother's design did not also copy the great canopy which overshadows the window and which, rising through the cornice to a great pinnacled niche, so successfully finishes the whole design. Here too the buttresses carry up the design to the top of the wall, and with the strong cornice and rich cresting save it from the weakness which at Coimbra is emphasised by the irregularity of the walling above.

Luckier than the door at Coimbra this one retains its central jamb, on which, on a twisting shaft from whose base look out two charming lions, there stands, most appropriately, Prince Henry the Navigator, without whose enterprise Vasco da Gama would in all probability never have sailed to India and so given occasion for the founding of this church. Round each of the two entrances runs a band of renaissance carving, and the flat reliefs in the divided tympanum are rather like some that may be seen in France,[132] but otherwise the detail is all Gothic. Twisted shafts bearing the corbels, elaborate canopies, crocketed finials, all are rather Gothic than Manoelino. Since the material—a kind of marble—is much less fine than the stone used at Batalha or in Coimbra or Thomar, 189 the carving is naturally less minute and ivory-like than it is there, and this is especially the case with the foliage, which is rather coarse. The statues too—except perhaps Prince Henry's—are a little short and sturdy.

The tall windows in the bays on either side of this great door are like those in the transept, except that round them are three bands of carving instead of two, the one in the centre formed of rods which at intervals of about a foot are broken to cross each other in the middle, and that beyond the jambs tall twisted shafts run up to round finials just under the cornice.

In the next bay to the west, where is the choir gallery inside, there are two windows, one above the other, like the larger ones but smaller, and united by a moulding which runs round both.

The same is the case with the tower, where, however, the upper window is divided into two, the lower being a circle and the upper having three intersecting lights. The drip-mould is also treated in the common Manoelino way with large spreading finials. Above the cornice, which is less elaborate than in the nave, was a short octagonal drum capped by a low spire, now replaced by a poor dome and flying buttresses.

The west door once opened into a three-aisled porch now gone. It is much less elaborate than the great south door, but shows great ingenuity in fitting it in under what was once the porch vault. The twisted and broken curves of the head follow a common Manoelino form, and below the top of the broken hood-mould are two flying angels who support a large corbel on which is grouped the Holy Family. On the jambs are three narrow bands of foliage, and one of figures standing under renaissance canopies. On either side are spreading corbels and large niches with curious bulbous canopies[133] under which kneel Dom Manoel on the left presented by St. Jerome, and on the right, presented by St. John the Baptist, his second wife, Queen Maria—like the first, Queen Isabel, a daughter of Ferdinand and Isabella and the aunt of his third wife, Leonor. These figures are evidently portraits, and even if they were flattered show that they were not a handsome couple.

Below these large corbels, on which are carved large angels, are two smaller niches with figures, one on each side of the twisted shaft. Renaissance curves form the heads of these 190 as they do of larger niches, one on each side of the Holy Family above, which contain the Annunciation and the Visit of the Wise Men.

Beyond Dom Manoel and his wife are square shafts with more niches and figures, and beyond them again flatter niches, half Manoelino, half renaissance. The rest of the west front above the ruined porch is plain except for a large round window lighting the choir gallery. The north-west tower does not rise above the roof.

Outside, the church as a whole is neither well proportioned nor graceful. The great mass of the transept is too overwhelming, the nave not long enough, and above all, the large windows of the nave too large. It would have looked much better had they been only the size of the smaller windows lighting the choir gallery—omitting the one below, and this would further have had the advantage of not cutting up the beautiful band of ornament. But the weakest part of the whole design are the towers, which must always have been too low, and yet would have been too thin for the massive building behind them had they been higher. Now, of course, the one finished with a dome has nothing to recommend it, neither height, nor proportion, nor design. Yet the doorway taken by itself, or together with the bay on either side, is a very successful composition, and on a brilliantly sunny day so blue is the sky and so white the stone that hardly any one would venture to criticise it for being too elaborate and over-charged, though no doubt it might seem so were the stone dingy and the sky grey and dull.

The church of Belem may be ill-proportioned and unsatisfactory outside, but within it is so solemn and vast as to fill one with surprise. Compared with many churches the actual area is not really very great nor is it very high, yet there is perhaps no other building which gives such an impression of space and of freedom. Entering from the brilliant sunlight it seems far darker than, with large windows, should be the case, and however hideous the yellow-and-blue checks with which they are filled may be, they have the advantage of keeping out all brilliant light; the huge transept too is not well lit and gives that feeling of vastness and mystery which, as the supports are few and slender, would otherwise be wanting, while looking westwards the same result is obtained by the dark cavernous space under the gallery. (Fig. 65.)

FIG. 64.	FIG. 65.
BELEM	BELEM
SOUTH SIDE OF CHURCH OF JERONYMOS.	NAVE OF CHURCH LOOKING WEST.

191 On the south side the walls are perfectly plain, broken only by the windows, whose jambs are enriched with empty niches; on the north the small windows are placed very high up, the twisted vaulting shafts only come down a short way to a string course some way below the windows, leaving a great expanse of cliff-like wall. At the bottom are the confessional doors, so small that they add greatly to the scale, and above them tall narrow niches and their canopies. But the nave piers are the most astonishing part of the whole building. Not more than three feet thick, they rise up to a height of nearly seventy feet to support a great stone vault. Four only of the six stand clear from floor to roof, for the two western are embedded at the bottom in the jambs of the gallery arches. From their capitals the vaulting ribs spread out in every direction, being constructively not unlike an English fan vault, and covering the whole roof with a network of lines. The piers are round, stand on round moulded pedestals, and are divided into narrow strips by eight small shafts. The height is divided into four nearly equal parts by well-moulded rings, encircling the whole pier, and in the middle of the second of these divisions are corbels and canopies for statues. The capitals are round and covered with leaves, but scarcely exceed the piers in diameter. Besides all this each strip between the eight thin shafts is covered from top to bottom— except where the empty niches occur—with carving in slight relief, either foliage or, more usually, renaissance arabesques.

Larger piers stand next the transept, cross-shaped, formed of four of the thinner piers set together, and about six feet thick. They are like the others, except that there are corbels and canopies for statues in the angles, and that a capital is formed by a large moulding carved with what is meant for egg and tongue. From this, well moulded and carved arches, round in the central and pointed in the side aisles, cross the nave from side to side, dividing its vault from that of the transept.

This transept vault, perhaps the largest attempted since the days of the Romans—for it covers a space measuring about ninety-five feet by sixty-five—is three bays long from north to south and two wide from east to west; formed of innumerable ribs springing from these points—of which those at the north and south ends are placed immediately above the arches leading to the chapels—it practically assumes in the middle the shape of a flat oblong dome. 192

Now, though the walls are thick, there are no buttresses, and the skill and daring required to build a vault sixty-five feet wide and about a hundred feet high resting on side walls on one side and on piers scarcely six feet thick on the other must not only excite the admiration of every one, especially when it is remembered that no damage was caused by the great earthquake which shook Lisbon to pieces in 1755, but must also raise the wish that what has been so skilfully done here had been also done in the Capellas Imperfeitas at Batalha.

At the north end of the main transept are two doors, one leading to the cloister and one to the sacristy. A straight and curved moulding surrounds their trefoil heads under a double twining hood-mould. Outside, other mouldings rise high above the whole to form a second large trefoil, whose hood-mould curves into two great crocketed circles before rising to a second ogee.

The chancel has a round and the chapels pointed entrance arches, formed, as are the jambs, of two bands of carving and two thick twisted mouldings. Tomb recesses, added later, with strapwork pediments line the chapels, and at the entrance to the chancel are two pulpits, for the Gospel and Epistle. These are rather like João de Ruão's pulpit at Coimbra in outline, but supported on a large capital are quite Gothic, as are the large canopies which rise above them.

Strong arches with cable mouldings lead to the space under the gallery, which is supported by an elaborate vault, elliptical in the central and pointed in the side aisles.

In the gallery itself—only to be entered from the upper cloister—are the choir stalls, of Brazil wood, added in 1560, perhaps from the designs of Diogo da Carta.[134]

With the earlier stalls at Santa Cruz and at Funchal, and the later at Evora, these are almost the only ones left which have not been replaced by rococo extravagances.

The back is divided into large panels three stalls wide, each containing a painting of a saint, and separated by panelled and carved Corinthian pilasters. Below each painting is an oblong panel with, in the centre, a beautifully carved head looking out of a circle, and at the sides bold carvings of leaves, dragons, sirens, or animals, while beautiful figures of saints stand in round-headed niches under the pilasters. 193 At the ends are larger pilasters, and a cornice carried on corbels serves as canopy. Each of the lower stalls has a carved panel under the upper book-board, but the small figures which stood between them on the arms are nearly all gone.

If 1560 be the real date, the carving is extraordinarily early in character; the execution too is excellent, though perhaps the heads under the paintings are on too large a scale for woodwork, still they are not at all coarse, and would be worthy of the best Spanish or French sculptors.

The cloister, nearly, but not quite square, has six bays on each side, of which the four central bays are of four lights each, while narrower ones at the ends have no tracery. In the traceried bays the arches are slightly elliptical, subdivided by two round-headed arches, which in turn enclose two smaller round arches enriched some with trefoil cusps, some with curious hanging pieces of tracery which are put, not in the middle, but a little to the side nearer the central shaft. The shafts are round, very like those at Batalha, and, like every inch of the arch and tracery mouldings, are covered with ornament; some are twisted, some diapered, some covered with renaissance detail. Broad bands too of carving run round the inside and the outside of the main arches, the inner being almost renaissance and the outer purely Manoelino. The vault of many ribs, varying in arrangement in the different walks, is entirely Gothic, while all the doors—except the double opening leading to the chapter-house, which has beautifully carved renaissance panels on the jambs—are Manoelino. The untraceried openings at the ends are fringed with very extraordinary lobed projections, and on the solid pieces of walling at the corners are carved very curious and interesting coats of arms crosses and emblems worked in with beautifully cut leaves and birds. (Figs. 66 and 67.)

Outside, between each bay, wide buttresses project, of which the front—formed into a square pilaster—is enriched with panels of beautiful renaissance work, while the back part is fluted or panelled. From the top mouldings of these pilasters, rather higher than the capitals of the openings, elliptical arches with a vault behind are thrown across from pier to pier with excellent effect. Now, the base mouldings of these panelled pilasters either do not quite fit those of the fluted strips behind, or else are cut off against them, as are also the 194 top mouldings of the fluted part; further, the fluted part runs up rather awkwardly into the vault, so that it seems reasonable to conjecture that these square renaissance pilasters and the arches may be an after-thought, added because it was found that the original buttresses were not quite strong enough for their work, and this too would account for the purely renaissance character of the carving on them, while the rest is almost entirely

Gothic or Manoelino. The arches are carried diagonally across the corners, in a very picturesque manner, and they all help to keep out the direct sunlight and to throw most effective shadows.

The parapet above these arches is carved with very pleasing renaissance details, and above each pier rise a niche and saint.

The upper cloister is simpler than the lower. All the arches are round with a big splay on each side carved with four-leaved flowers. They are cusped at the top, and at the springing two smaller cusped arches are thrown across to a pinnacled shaft in the centre. The buttresses between them are covered with spiral grooves, and are all finished off with twisted pinnacles. Inside the pointed vault is much simpler than in the walks below.

Here the tracery is very much less elaborate than in the Claustro Real at Batalha, but as scarcely a square inch of the whole cloister is left uncarved the effect is much more disturbed and so less pleasing.

Beautiful though most of the ornament is, there is too much of it, and besides, the depressed shape of the lower arches is bad and ungraceful, and the attempt at tracery in the upper walks is more curious than successful.

The chapter-house too, though a large and splendid room, would have looked better with a simpler vault and without the elliptical arches of the apse recesses.

The refectory, without any other ornament than the bold ribs of its vaulted roof, and a dado of late tiles, is far more pleasing.

Altogether, splendid as it is, Belem is far less pleasing, outside at least, than the contemporary work at Batalha or at Thomar, for, like the tower of São Vicente near by, it is wanting in those perfect proportions which more than richness of detail give charm to a building. Inside it is not so, and though many of the vaulting ribs might be criticised as useless

FIG. 66.	FIG. 67.
BELEM	BELEM
CLOISTER.	LOWER CLOISTER.

195 and the whole vault as wanting in simplicity, yet there is no such impressive interior in Portugal and not many elsewhere.

The very over-elaboration which spoils the cloister is only one of the results of all the wealth which flowed in from the East, and so, like the whole monastery, is a worthy memorial of all that had been done to further exploration from the time of Prince Henry, till his efforts were crowned with success by Vasco da Gama.

Conceição, Velha.

There can be little doubt that the transept front of the church of the Conceição Velha was also designed by João de Castilho. The church was built after 1520 on the site of a synagogue, and was almost entirely destroyed by the earthquake of 1755. Only the transept front has survived, robbed of its cornice and cresting, and now framed in plain pilasters and crowned by a pediment. The two windows, very like those at Belem, have beautiful renaissance details and saints in niches on the jambs.

The large door has a round arch with uprights at the sides rising to a horizontal crested moulding. Below, these uprights have a band of renaissance carving on the outer side, and in front a canopied niche with a well-modelled figure. Above they become semicircular and end in sphere-bearing spirelets. The great round arch is filled with two orders of mouldings, one a broad strip of arabesque, the other a series of kneeling angels below and of arabesque above. The actual openings are formed of two round-headed arches whose outer mouldings cross each other on the central jamb. Above them are two reversed semicircles, and then a great tympanum carved with a figure of Our Lady sheltering popes, bishops, and saints under her robe: a carving which seems to have lately taken the place of a large window. (Fig. 68.)

As it now stands the front is not pleasing. It is too wide, and the great spreading pediment is very ugly. Of course it ought not to be judged by its present appearance, and yet it must be admitted that the windows are too large and come too near the ground, and that much of the detail is coarse. Still it is of interest if only because it is the only surviving building closely related to the church of Belem. Built perhaps to commemorate the expulsion of the Jews, it shared the fate of the Jesuits who instigated the expulsion, and was destroyed only a few years before they were driven from the country by the Marques de Pombal. 196

CHAPTER XIV
THE COMING OF THE FOREIGN ARTISTS

IF João de Castilho and his brother Diogo were really natives of one of the Basque provinces, they might rightly be included among the foreign artists who played such an important part in Portugal towards the end of Dom Manoel's reign and the beginning of that of his son, Dom João III. Yet the earlier work of João de Castilho at Thomar shows little trace of that renaissance influence which the foreigners, and especially the Frenchmen, were to do so much to introduce.

Santa Cruz, Coimbra.

A great house of the Canon Regular of St. Augustine had been founded at Coimbra by Dom Affonso Henriques for his friend São Theotonio in 1131. But with the passage of centuries the church and monastic building of Sta. Cruz had become dilapidated, and were no longer deemed worthy of so wealthy and important a body. So in 1502 Dom Manoel determined to rebuild them and to adorn the church, and it was for this adorning that he summoned so many sculptors in stone and in wood to his aid.

The first architect of the church was Marcos Pires, to whom are due the cloister and the whole church except the west door, which was finished by his successor Diogo de Castilho with the help of Master Nicolas, a Frenchman.

One Gregorio Lourenço seems to have been what would now be called master of the works, and from his letters to Dom Manoel we learn how the work was going on. After Dom Manoel's death in 1521 he writes to Dom João III., telling him what, of all the many things his father the late king had ordered, was already finished and what was still undone.

The church consists of a nave of four bays, measuring some 105 feet by 39, with flanking chapels, the whole lined with eighteenth-century tiles, mostly blue and white. There are also a great choir gallery at the west end, a chancel, polygonal

FIG. 68.
LISBON
CONCEIÇÃO VELHA.

197 within but square outside, 54 feet long by 20 broad, with a seventeenth-century sacristy to the south, a cloister to the north, and chapels, one of which was the chapter-house, forming a kind of passage from sacristy to cloister behind the chancel.

PLAN OF STA. CRUZ

By 1518 the church must have been already well advanced, for in January of that year Gregorio Lourenço writes to Dom Manoel saying that 'the wall of the dormitory was shaken and therefore I have sent for "Pere Anes"—Pedro Annes had been master builder of the royal palace, now the university at Coimbra, and being older may have had more experience than Marcos Pires, the designer of the monastery—who had it shored up, and they say that after the vault of the cloister is finished and the wooden floors in it will be quite safe. Also six days ago came the master of the reredos from Seville and set to work at once to finish the great reredos, for which he has worked all the wood—he must surely have brought it with him from Seville—but the glazier has not yet come to finish the windows.'

On 22nd July following he writes again that all but one of the vaults of the cloister were finished—'and Marcos Pirez works well, and the master of the reredos has finished the tabernacle, and the "cadeiras" [that is probably, sedilia] and the bishop has come to see them and they are very good, and the master who is making the tombs of the kings is working at his job, and has already made much stonework.'

These tombs of the kings are the monuments of Dom Affonso Henriques on the north wall of the chancel and of Dom Sancho I. on the south. The two first kings of

97

Portugal had originally been buried in front of the old church, and were now for the first time given monuments worthy of their importance in the history of their country.[198]

In 1521 Dom Manoel died, and next year Gregorio tells his successor what his father had ordered; after speaking of the pavement, the vault of São Theotonio's Chapel, the dormitory with its thirty beds and its fireplace, the refectory, the royal tombs and a great screen twenty-five palms, or about eighteen feet high, he comes to the pulpit—'This, Sir, which is finished, all who see it say, that in Spain there is no piece of stone of better workmanship, for this 20 000 have been paid,' leaving some money still due.

He then speaks of the different reredoses, tombs of two priors, silver candlesticks, a great silver cross made by Eytor Gonsalves, a goldsmith of Lisbon, much other church plate, and then goes on to say that a lectern was ordered for the choir but was not made and was much needed, as was a silver monstrance, and that the monastery had no money to pay Christovam de Figueiredo for painting the great reredos of the high altar and those of the other chapels, 'and, Sir, it is necessary that they should be painted.'

Besides making so many gifts to Sta. Cruz, Dom Manoel endowed it with many privileges. The priors were exempt from the jurisdiction of the bishop, and had themselves complete control over their own dependent churches. All the canons were chaplains to the king, and after the university came back to Coimbra from Lisbon in 1539 Dom João III. made the priors perpetual chancellors.[135]

By 1522 then the church must have been practically ready, though some carving still had to be done.

Marcos Pires died in 1524 and was succeeded by Diogo de Castilho, and in a letter dated from Evora in that year the king orders a hundred gold cruzados to be paid to Diogo and to Master Nicolas[136] for the statues on the west door which were still wanting, and two years later in September another letter granted Diogo the privilege of riding on a mule.[137]

The interest of the church itself is very inferior to that of [199] the different pieces of church furniture, nearly all the work of foreigners, with which it was adorned, and of which some, though not all, survive to the present day.

Inside there is nothing very remarkable in the structure of the church except the fine vaulting with its many moulded ribs, the large windows with their broken Manoelino heads, and the choir gallery which occupies nearly two bays at the west end. Vaulted underneath, it opens to the church by a large elliptical arch which springs from jambs ornamented with beautiful candelabrum shafts.

Of the outside little is to be seen except the west front, one of the least successful designs of that period.

In the centre—now partly blocked up by eighteenth-century additions, and sunk several feet below the street—is a great moulded arch, about eighteen feet across and once divided into two by a central jamb bearing a figure of Our Lord, whence the door was called 'Portal da Majestade'; above the arch a large round-headed window, deeply recessed, lights the choir gallery, and between it and the top of the arch are three renaissance niches, divided by pilasters, and containing three figures—doubtless some of those for which Diogo de Castilho and Master Nicolas were paid one hundred cruzados in 1524. The window with its mouldings is much narrower than the door, and is joined to the tall pinnacles which rise to the right and left of the great opening by Gothic flying buttresses. Between the side pinnacles and the central mass of the window a curious rounded and bent shaft rises from the hood-mould of the door to end in a semi-classic column between two niches, and from the shaft there grow out two branches to support the corbels on which the niche statues stand. All this is very like the great south door of the Jeronymite monastery at Belem, the work of Diogo's brother João de Castilho; both have a wide door below with a narrower window above, surrounded by a mass of pinnacles and statues, but here the lower door is far too wide, and the upper window too small, and besides the wall is set back a foot or two immediately on each side of the window so that the surface is more broken up. Again, instead of the whole rising up with a great pinnacled niche to pierce the cornice and to dominate parapet and cresting, the drip-mould of the window only gives a few ugly twists, and leaves a blank space between the window head and the straight line of the cornice 200 and parapet; a line in no way improved by the tall rustic cross or the four broken pinnacles which rise above it. Straight crested parapets also crown the wall where it is set back, but at the sides the two corners grow into eight-sided turrets ending in low crocketed stone roofs. Of course the whole front has suffered much from the raising of the street level, but it can never have been beautiful, for the setting back of part of the wall looks meaningless, and the turrets are too small for towers and yet far too large for angle pinnacles. (Fig. 69.)

Although the soft stone is terribly perished, greater praise can be given to the smaller details, especially to the figures, which show traces of considerable vigour and skill.

If the church shows that Marcos Pires was not a great architect, the cloister still more marks his inferiority to the Fernandes or to João de Castilho, though with its central fountain and its garden it is eminently picturesque. Part of it is now, and probably all once was, of two stories. The buttresses are picturesque, polygonal below, a cluster of rounded shafts above, and are carried up in front of the upper cloister to end in a large cross. All the openings have segmental pointed heads with rather poor mouldings. Each is subdivided into two lights with segmental round heads, supporting a vesica-like opening. All the shafts are round, with round moulded bases and round Manoelino caps. The central shaft has a ring moulding half-way up, and all, including the flat arches and the vesicae, are either covered with leaves, or are twisted into ropes, but without any of that wonderful delicacy which is so striking at Batalha. Across one corner a vault has been thrown covering a fountain, and though elsewhere the ribs are plainly moulded, here they are covered with leaf carving, and altogether make this north-east corner the most picturesque part of the whole cloister. (Fig. 70.)

The upper walk with its roof of wood is much simpler, there being three flat arches to each bay upheld by short round shafts.

Now to turn from the church itself and its native builders to the beautiful furniture provided for it by foreign skill. Much of it has vanished. The church plate when it became unfashionable was sent to Gôa, the great metal screen made by Antonius Fernandes is gone, and so is the reredos carved by a master from Seville and painted by Christovão de Figueredo.

FIG. 69.	FIG. 70.
COIMBRA	COIMBRA
WEST FRONT OF STA. CRUZ.	CLOISTER OF STA. CRUZ.

There still hang on the wall of the sacristy two or three 201 pictures which may have formed part of this reredos. They are high up and very dirty, but seem to have considerable merit, especially one of 'Pentecost' which is signed 'Velascus.' The 'Pentecost' still has for its frame some pieces of beautiful early renaissance moulding not unlike what may still be seen on the reredos at Funchal, and it is just the size of a panel for a large reredos. Of course 'Velascus' is not Grão Vasco, though the name is the same, nor can he be Christovão de Figueredo, but perhaps the painting spoken of by Gregorio Lourenço as done by Christovão may only have been of the framing and not necessarily of the panels.

These are gone, but there are still left the royal tombs, the choir stalls, the pulpit, and three beautiful carved altar-pieces in the cloister.

The royal tombs are both practically alike. In each the king lies under a great round arch, on a high altar-tomb, on whose front, under an egg and tongue moulding a large scroll bearing an inscription is upheld by winged children. The arch is divided into three bands of carving, one—the widest—carved with early renaissance designs, the next which is also carried down the jambs, with very rich Gothic foliage, and the outermost with more leaves. The back of each tomb is divided into three by tall Gothic pinnacles, and contains three statues on elaborate corbels and under very intricate canopies, of which the central rises in a spire to the top of the arch.

On the jambs, under the renaissance band of carving, are two statues one above the other on Gothic corbels but under renaissance canopies.

Beyond the arch great piers rise up with three faces separated by Gothic pinnacles. On each face there is at the bottom—above the interpenetrating bases—a classic medallion encompassed by Manoelino twisting stems and leaves, and higher up two statues one above the other. Of these the lower stands on a Gothic corbel under a renaissance canopy, and the upper, standing on the canopy, has over it another tall canopy Gothic in style. Higher up the piers rise up to the vault with many pinnacles and buttresses, and between them, above the arch, are other figures in niches and two angels holding the royal arms.

The design of the whole is still very Manoelino, and therefore the master of the royal tombs spoken of by Gregorio 202 Lourenço was probably a Portuguese, but the skill shown in modelling the figures and the renaissance details are something quite new. (Fig. 71.)

Many Frenchmen are known to have worked in Santa Cruz. One, Master Nicolas, has been met already working at Belem and at the west door here, and others—Longuim, Philipo Uduarte, and finally João de Ruão (Jean de Rouen)—are spoken of as having worked at the tombs.

Though the figures are good with well-modelled draperies, their faces, or those of most of them, are rather expressionless, and some of them look too short—all indeed being less successful than those on the pulpit, the work of João de Ruão. It is likely then that the figures are mostly the work of the lesser known men and not of Master Nicolas or of João de Ruão, though João, who came later to Portugal, may have been responsible for some of the renaissance canopies which are not at all unlike some of his work on the pulpit.

The pulpit projects from the north wall of the church between two of the chapels. In shape it is a half-octagon set diagonally, and is upheld by circular corbelling. It was ready by the time Gregorio Lourenço wrote to Dom João III. in 1522, but still wanted a suitable finishing to its door. This Gregorio urged Dom João to add, but it was never done, and now the entrance is only framed by a simple classic architrave.

Now Georges d'Amboise, the second archbishop of that name to hold the see of Rouen, began the beautiful tomb, on which he and his uncle kneel in prayer, in the year 1520, and the pulpit at Coimbra was finished before March 1522.

Among the workmen employed on this tomb a Jean de Rouen is mentioned, but he left in 1521. The detail of the tomb at Rouen and that of the pulpit here are alike in their exceeding fineness and beauty, and a man thought worthy of taking part in the carving of the tomb might well be able to carry out the pulpit; besides, on it are cut initials or signs which have been read as J.R.[138] The J or I is distinct, the R much less so, but the carver of the pulpit was certainly a Frenchman well acquainted with the work of the French renaissance. It may therefore be accepted with perhaps some likelihood, that the Jean de Rouen who left Normandy in 1521, came then to Coimbra, carved this pulpit, and is the same who as João de Ruão is mentioned in later documents as

FIG. 71.	FIG. 72.
COIMBRA, STA. CRUZ.	COIMBRA
TOMB OF D. SANCHO I.	STA. CRUZ.
	PULPIT.

203 still working for Santa Cruz, where he signed a discharge as late as 1549.[139]

The whole pulpit is but small, not more than about five feet high including the corbelled support, and all carved with a minuteness and delicacy not to be surpassed and scarcely to be equalled by such a work as the tomb at Rouen. At the top is a finely moulded cornice enriched with winged heads, tiny egg and tongue and other carving. Below on each of the four sides are niches whose shell tops rest on small pilasters all covered with the finest ornaments, and in each niche sits a Father of the Western Church, St. Augustine, St. Jerome, St. Gregory, and St. Ambrose. Their feet rest on slightly projecting bases, on the front of each of which is a small panel measuring about four inches by two carved with tiny figures and scenes in slight relief. On the shell heads, which project a little in the centre, there stand, above St. Augustine three minute figures of boys with wreaths, the figures being about three or four inches high, above St. Jerome sit two others, with masks hanging from their arms, upholding a shield and a cross of the Order of Christ. Those above St. Gregory support a sphere, and above St. Ambrose one stands alone with a long-necked bird on each side. At each angle two figures, one above the other, each about eight inches high, stand under canopies the delicacy of whose carving could scarcely be surpassed in ivory. They represent, above, Religion with Faith, Hope, and Charity, and below, four prophets. The corbelled support is made up of a great many different mouldings, most of them enriched in different ways.

Near the top under the angles of the pulpit are beautiful cherubs' heads. About half-way down creatures with wings and human heads capped with winged helmets grow out of a mass of flat carving, and at the very bottom is a kind of winged dragon whose five heads stretch up across the lower mouldings. (Fig. 72.)

Altogether the pulpit is well worthy of the praise given it by Gregorio; there may be more elaborate pieces of carving in Spain, but scarcely one so beautiful in design and in execution, and indeed it may almost be doubted whether France itself can produce a finer piece of work. The figure sculpture is worthy of the best French artists, the whole design is elaborate, but not too much so, considering the 204 smallness of the scale, and the execution is such as could only have been carried out in alabaster or the finest limestone, such as that found at Ança not far off, and used at Coimbra for all delicate work.[140]

In the discharge signed by João de Ruão in 1549 reredoses are spoken of as worked by him. There is nothing in the document to show whether these are the three great pieces of sculpture in the cloisters each of which must once have been meant for a reredos. Unfortunately in the seventeenth century they were walled up, and were only restored to view not many years ago, and though much destroyed, enough survives to show that they were once worthy of the pulpit.

They represent 'Christ shown to the people by Pilate,' the 'Bearing of the Cross,' and the 'Entombment.'

In each there is at the bottom a shelf narrower than the carving above, and uniting the two, a broad band wider at the top than at the bottom, most exquisitely carved in very slight relief, with lovely early renaissance scrolls, and with winged boys holding shields or medallions in the centre. Above is a large square framework, flanked at the sides by tall candelabrum shafts on corbels, and finished at the top by a moulding or, above the 'Bearing of the Cross,' by a crested entablature, with beautifully carved frieze. Within this framework the stone is cut back with sloping sides, carved with architectural detail, arches, doors, entablatures in perspective. At the top is a panelled canopy.

In the 'Ecce Homo' on the left is a flight of steps leading up to the judgment seat of Pilate, who sits under a large arch, with Our Lord and a soldier on his right. The other half of the composition has a large arch in the background, and in front a crowd of people some of whom are seen coming through the opening in the sloping side.

In the 'Bearing of the Cross' the background is taken up by the walls and towers of Jerusalem. Our Lord with a great T-shaped cross is in the centre, with St. Veronica on the right and a great crowd of people behind, while other persons look out of the perspective arches at the side. (Fig. 73.)

In all, especially perhaps in the 'Ecce Homo,' the 205 composition is good, and the modelling of the figures excellent. Unfortunately the faces are much decayed and perhaps the figures may be rather wanting in repose, and yet even in their decay they are very beautiful pieces of work, and show that João de Ruão—if he it was who carved them—was as able to design a large composition as to carve a small pulpit. Under the 'Ecce Homo,' in a tablet held by winged boys who grow out of the ends of the scrolls, there is a date which seems to read 1550. The 'Quitaçam' was signed on the 11th of September 1549, and if 1550 is the date here carved it may show when the work was finally completed.[141]

There once stood in the refectory a terra cotta group of the 'Last Supper.' Now nothing is left but a few fragments in the Museum, but there too the figures of the apostles were well modelled and well executed.

Of the other works ordered by Dom Manoel the only one which still remains are the splendid stalls in the western choir gallery. These in two tiers of seats run round the three walls of the gallery except where interrupted by the large west window. They can hardly be the 'cadeiras' or seats mentioned in Gregorio's letter of July 1518, for it is surely impossible that they should have been begun in January and finished in July however active the Seville master may have been, and judging from their carving they seem more Flemish than Spanish, and we know that Flemings had been working not very long before on the cathedral reredos. The lower tier of seats has Gothic panelling below, good Miserere seats, arms, on each of which sits a monster, and on the top between each and supporting the book-board of the upper row, small figures of men, with bowed backs, beggars, pilgrims, men and women all most beautifully carved. The panels behind the upper tier are divided by twisted Manoelino shafts bearing Gothic pinnacles, and the upper part of each panel is enriched with deeply undercut leaves and finials surrounding armillary spheres. Above the panels, except over the end stalls where sat the Dom Prior and the other dignitaries, and which have higher canopies, there runs a continuous canopy panelled with Gothic quatrefoils, and having in front a fringe of interlacing cusps. Between this and the cresting is a beautiful carved cornice of leaves and of crosses of the Order of Christ, and the cresting itself is formed by a number of carved scenes, 206 cities, forests, ships, separated by saintly figures and surmounted by a carved band from which grow up great curling leaves and finials. These scenes are supposed to represent the great discoveries of Vasco da Gama and of Pedro Alvares Cabral in India and in Brazil, but if this is really so the carvers must have been left to their own imagination, for the towns do not look particularly Indian, nor do the forests suggest the tropical luxuriance of Brazil: perhaps the small three-masted ships alone, with their high bows and stern, represent the reality. (Fig. 74.)

As a whole the design is entirely Gothic, only at the ends of each row of stalls is there anything else, and there the panels are carved with renaissance arabesque, which, being gilt like all the other carving, stands out well from the dark brown background.

These are almost the only mediæval stalls left in the country. Those at Thomar were burnt by the French, those in the Carmo at Lisbon destroyed by the earthquake, and those at Alcobaça have disappeared. Only at Funchal are there stalls of the same date, for those at Vizeu seem rather later and are certainly poorer, their chief interest now being derived from the old Chinese stamped paper with which their panels are covered.

Coimbra, Sé Velha.

If the stalls at Santa Cruz are the only examples of this period still left on the mainland, the Sé Velha possesses the only great mediæval reredos. In Spain great structures are found in almost every cathedral rising above the altar to the vault in tier upon tier of niche and panel. Richly gilded, with fine paintings on the panels, with delicate Gothic pinnacles and tabernacle work, they and the metal screens which half hide them do much to make Spanish churches the most interesting in the world. Unfortunately in Portugal the bad taste of the eighteenth century has replaced all those that may have existed by great and heavy erections of elaborately carved wood. All covered with gold, the Corinthian columns, twisted and wreathed with vines, the overloaded arches and elaborate entablatures are now often sadly out of place in some old interior, and make one grieve the more over the loss of the simpler or more appropriate reredos which came before them.

FIG. 73.	FIG. 74.
COIMBRA	COIMBRA.
STA. CRUZ.	STALLS, STA CRUZ.

REREDOS IN CLOISTER.

Dom Jorge d'Almeida held the see of Coimbra and the countship of Arganil—for the bishops are always counts of Arganil— 207 from 1481 till 1543, when he died at the age of eighty-five; during these sixty-two years he did much to beautify his church, and of these additions the oldest is the reredos put up in 1508. This we learn from a 'quitaçã' or discharge granted in that year to 'Mestre Vlimer framengo, ora estante nesta cidada, e seu Parceiro João Dipri,' that is, to 'Master Vlimer a Fleming, now in this city, and to his partner John of Ypres.'

The reredos stands well back in the central apse; it is divided into five upright parts, of which that in the centre is twice as wide as any of the others, while the outermost with the strips of panelling and carving which come beyond them are canted, following the line of the apse wall. Across these five upright divisions and in a straight line is thrown a great flattened trefoil arch joined to the back with Gothic vaulting. In the middle over the large division it is fringed with the intersecting circles of curved branches, while from the top to the blue-painted apse vault with its gilded ribs and stars a forest of pinnacles, arches, twisting and intertwining branches and leaves rises high above the bishop's arms and mitre and the two angels who uphold them.

Below the arch the five parts are separated by pinnacle rising above pinnacle. At the bottom under long canopies of extraordinary elaboration are scenes in high relief. Above them in the middle the apostles watch the Assumption of the Virgin; saints stand in the other divisions, one in each, and over their heads are immense canopies rising across a richly cusped background right up to the vaulting of the arch. Though not so high, the canopy over the Virgin is far more intricate as it forms a great curve made up of seven little cusped arches with innumerable pinnacles and spires. (Fig. 75.)

Being the work of Flemings, the reredos is naturally full of that exuberant Flemish detail which may be seen in a Belgian town-hall or in the work of an early Flemish painter; and if the stalls at Santa Cruz are not by this same Master Vlimer, the intertwining branches on the cresting and the sharply carved leaves on the panels show that he had followers or pupils.

Like most Flemish productions, the reredos is wanting in grace. Though it throws a fine deep shadow the great arch is very ugly in shape and the great canopies are far too large, and yet the mass of gold, well lit by the windows of the 208 lantern and rising to the dim blue vault, makes a singularly fine ending to the old and solemn church.

More important than the reredos in the art history of the country are some other changes made by Dom Jorge, which show that the Frenchmen working at Santa Cruz were soon employed elsewhere.

On the north side of the nave a door leads out of the church, and this these Frenchmen entirely transformed.

At the bottom, between two much decayed Corinthian pilasters, is the door reached by a flight of steps. The arch is of several orders, one supported by thin columns, one by square fluted pilasters. Within these, at right angles to each other, are broad faces carved and resting on piers at whose corners are tiny round columns, in two stories, with carved reliefs between the upper pair. In the tympanum is a beautiful Madonna and Child, and two round medallions with heads adorn the spandrils above the arch. Beyond each pilaster is a canted side joining the porch to the wall and having a large niche and figure near the top. The whole surface has been covered with exquisite arabesques like those below the reredoses in the cloister at Santa Cruz, but they have now almost entirely perished.

Above the entablature a second story rises forming a sort of portico. At the corners are square fluted Corinthian pilasters; between them in front runs a balustrading, divided into three by the pedestals of two slender columns, Corinthian also, and there are others next the pilasters. The entablature has been most delicate, with the finest wreaths carved on the frieze. Over the canted sides are built small round-domed turrets.

Above this the third story reaches nearly up to the top of the wall. In the middle is an arch resting on slender columns and supporting a pediment; on either side are square niches with columns at the sides, beyond them fan-shaped semicircles, and at the corners vases. Behind this there rise to the top of the battlements four panelled Doric pilasters with cornice above, and two deep round-headed niches with figures, one on each side.

Inside the church are pilasters and a wealth of delicate relief.

Perhaps the whole may not be much more fortunate than most attempts to build up a tall composition by piling columns one above the other, and the top part is certainly too heavy

FIG. 75.	FIG. 76.
COIMBRA	COIMBRA.
SÉ VELHA.	SÉ VELHA.
REREDOS.	CHAPEL OF SÃO PEDRO.

103

for what comes below it. Yet the details are or were beautiful, and the portico above the door most graceful and pleasing, though, being unfortunately on the north side, the effect is lost of the deep shadow the sun would have thrown and the delicacy of the mouldings almost wasted.

Less important are the changes made to the north transept door. Fluted pilasters and Corinthian columns were inserted below, a medallion with a figure cut on the tympanum, and small coupled shafts resting on the Doric capitals of the pilasters built to uphold the entablature.

Inside the most important, as well as the most beautiful addition, was a reredos built by Dom Jorge as his monument in the chapel of São Pedro, the small apse to the north of the high altar.

Just above the altar table—which is of stone supported on one central shaft—are three panels filled in high relief with sculptured scenes from the life of St. Peter, the central and widest panel representing his martyrdom, while on the uprights between them are small figures under canopies.

The upper and larger part is arranged somewhat like a Roman triumphal arch. There are three arches, one larger and higher in the middle, with a lower and narrower one on each side, separated by most beautiful tall candelabrum shafts with very delicate half-Ionic capitals. In the centre, in front of the representation of some town, probably Rome, is Our Lord bearing His Cross and St. Peter kneeling at His feet—no doubt the well-known legend 'Domine quo vadis?' In the side arches stand two figures with books: one is St. Paul with a sword, and the other probably St. Peter himself. Above each of the side arches there is a small balustraded loggia, scarcely eighteen inches high, in each of which are two figures, talking, all marvellously lifelike. Beautiful carvings enrich the friezes everywhere, and small heads in medallions all the spandrils. At the top, in a hollow circle upheld by carved supports, crowned and bearing an orb in His left hand, is God the Father Himself. (Fig. 76.)

Less elaborate than the pulpit and less pictorial than the altar-pieces in the cloister of Santa Cruz, this reredos is one of the most successful of all the French works at Coimbra, and its beauty is enhanced by the successful lighting through a large window cut on purpose at the side, and by the beautiful tiles—probably contemporary—with which the chapel is lined.

In front of the altar lies Dom Jorge d'Almeida, under a flat stone, bearing his arms, and this inscription in Latin, 'Here lies Jorge d'Almeida by the goodness of the divine power bishop and count. He lived eighty-five years, and died eight days before the Kalends of Sextillis A.D. 1543, having held both dignities sixty-two years.'

CHAPTER XV
THE INFLUENCE OF THE FOREIGNER

VERY quickly the fame of these French workers spread across the country, and they or their pupils were employed to design tombs, altar-pieces, or chapels outside of Coimbra. Perhaps the da Silvas, lords of Vagos, were among the very first to employ them, and in their chapel of São Marcos, some eight or nine miles from Coimbra, more than one example of their handiwork may still be seen.

Tomb in Nossa Senhora dos Olivaes, Thomar.

However, before visiting São Marcos mention must be made of two tombs, one in Nossa Senhora dos Olivaes at Thomar, and one in the Graça church at Santarem. Both are exceedingly French in design, and both were erected not long after the coming of the foreigners.

The tomb in Thomar is the older. It is that of Diogo Pinheiro, the first bishop of Funchal—which he never visited—who died in 1525. No doubt the monument was put up soon after. It is placed rather high on the north wall of the chancel; at the very bottom is a moulding enriched with egg and tongue, separated by a plain frieze—crossed by a shield with the bishop's arms—from the plinth and from the pedestals of the side shafts and their supporting mouldings. On the plinth under a round arched recess stands a sarcophagus with a tablet in front bearing the date A.D. 1525, while behind in an elegant shell-topped niche is a figure kneeling on a beautiful corbel. The front of this arch is adorned with cherubs' heads, the jambs with arabesques, and heads look out of circles in the spandrils. At the sides are Corinthian pilasters, and in front of them beautiful candelabrum shafts. The cornice with a well-carved frieze is simple, and in the pediment are again carved Dom Diogo's arms, surmounted by his bishop's hat.

At the ends are vase-shaped finials, and another supported by dragons rises from the pediment. (Fig. 77.) 212

This monument is indeed one of the most pleasing pieces of renaissance work in existence, and one would be tempted to attribute it to João de Castilho were it not that it is more French than any of his work, and that in 1525 he can hardly have come back to Thomar, where the Claustro da Micha, the first of the new additions, was only begun in 1528. It will be safer then to attribute it to one of the Coimbra Frenchmen.

Tomb in Graça, Santarem.

The same must be said of the tomb in the Graça church at Santarem. It was built in 1532 in honour of three men already long dead—Pero Carreiro, Gonzalo Gil Barbosa his son-in-law, and Francisco Barbosa his grandson. The design is like that of Bishop Pinheiro's monument, omitting all beneath the plinth, except that the back is plain, the arch elliptical, and the pediment small and round. The coffer has a long inscription,[142] the jambs and arch are covered with arabesques, the side shafts are taller and even more elegant than at Thomar, and in the round pediment is a coat of arms, and on one side the head of a young man wearing a helmet, and on the other the splendidly modelled head of an old man; though much less pleasing as a whole, this head for excellent realism is better than anything found on the bishop's tomb.

If we cannot tell which Frenchman designed these tombs, we know the name of one who worked for the da Silvas at São Marcos, and we can also see there the work of some of their pupils and successors.

São Marcos.

São Marcos, which lies about two miles to the north of the road leading from Coimbra through Tentugal to Figueira de Foz at the mouth of the Mondego, is now unfortunately much ruined. Nothing remains complete but the church, for the monastic buildings were all burned not so long ago by some peasantry to injure the landlord to whom they belonged, and with them perished many a fine piece of carving.

The da Silvas had long had here a manor-house with a chapel, and in 1452 Dona Brites de Menezes, the wife of Ayres Gomes da Silva, the fourth lord of Vagos, founded a small Jeronymite monastery. Of her chapel, designed by

FIG. 77.	FIG. 78.
THOMAR.	SÃO MARCOS.
STA. MARIA DOS OLIVAES.	TOMB IN CHANCEL.
TOMB OF BP. OF	FROM A PHOTOGRAPH BY E. BIEL & CO.,
FUNCHAL.	OPORTO.

213 Gil de Souza, little now remains, for the chancel was rebuilt in the next century and the nave in the seventeenth. Only the tomb of Dona Brites' second son, Fernão Telles de Menezes, still survives, for the west door, with a cusped arch, beautifully undercut foliage, and knotted shafts at the side, was added in 1570.

The tomb of Fernão Telles, which was erected about the year 1471, is still quite Gothic. In the wall there opens a large pointed and cusped arch, within which at the top there hangs a small tent which, passing through a ring, turns into a great stone curtain upheld by hairy wild men. Inside this curtain Dom Fernão lies in armour on a tomb whose front is covered with beautifully carved foliage, and which has a cornice of roses. On it are three coats of arms, Dom Fernão's, those of his wife, Maria de Vilhena, and between them his and hers quartered.

Most of the tombs, five in all, are found in the chancel which was rebuilt by Ayres da Silva, fifth lord of Vagos, the grandson of Dona Brites, in 1522 and 1523. These are, on the north side, first, at the east end, Dona Brites herself, then her son João da Silva in the middle, and her grandson Ayres at the west, the tombs of Ayres and his father being practically identical. Opposite Dona Brites lies the second count of Aveiras, who died in 1672 and whose tomb is without interest, and opposite Ayres, his son João da Silva, sixth lord of Vagos, who died in 1559. At the east end is a great reredos given by Ayres and containing figures of himself and of his wife Dona Guiomar de Castro, while opening from the north side of the nave is a beautiful domed chapel built by Dona Antonia de Vilhena as a tomb-house for her husband, Diogo da Silva, who died in 1556. In it also lies his elder brother Lourenço, seventh lord of Vagos.

The chancel, which is of two bays, one wide, and one to the east narrower, has a low vault with many well-moulded ribs springing from large corbels, some of which are Manoelino, while others have on them shields and figures of the renaissance. It still retains an original window on each side, small, round-headed, with a band of beautiful renaissance carving on the splay.

Dona Brites lies on a plain tomb in front of which there is a long inscription. Above her rises a round arch set in a square frame. Large flowers like Tudor roses are cut on the 214 spandrils, the ogee hood-mould is enriched with huge wonderfully undercut curly crockets, all Gothic, but the band between the two mouldings of the arch is carved with renaissance arabesques. The tomb of Ayres himself and that of his father João are much more elaborate. Each, lying like Dona Brites on an altar-tomb, is clad in full armour. In front are semi-classic mouldings at the top and bottom, and between them a tablet held by cherubs, that on Dom João's bearing a long inscription, while Dom Ayres' has been left blank. The arches over the recumbent figures are slightly elliptical, and like that of the foundress's tomb each is enriched by a band of renaissance carving, but with classic mouldings outside, instead of a simple round, and with a rich fringe of leafy cusps within. At the ends and between the tombs are square buttresses or pilasters ornamented on each face with renaissance corbels and canopies. The background of each recess is covered with delicate flowing leaves in very slight relief, and has in the centre a niche, with rustic shafts and elaborate Gothic base and canopy under which stands a figure of Our Lord holding an orb in His left hand and blessing with His right. The buttresses, on which stand curious vase-shaped finials, are joined by a straight moulded cornice, above which rises a rounded pediment floriated on the outer side. From the pediment there stands out a helmet whose mantling entirely covers the flat surface, and below it hangs a shield, charged with the da Silva arms, a lion rampant. (Fig. 78.)

Here, as in the royal tombs at Coimbra, Manoelino and renaissance forms have been used together, but here the renaissance largely predominates, for even the cusping is not Gothic, although, as is but natural, the general design still is after the older style. Though very elaborate, these tombs cannot be called quite satisfactory. The figure sculpture is poor, and it is only the arabesques which show skill in execution. Probably then it was the work not of one of the well-known Frenchmen, but of one of their pupils.[143]

Raczynski[144] thought that here in São Marcos he had found some works of Sansovino: a battlepiece in relief, a statue of St. Mark, and the reredos. The first two are gone, but if they were as unlike Italian work as is the reredos, one may be sure 215 that they were not by him. A recently found document[145] confirms what its appearance suggests, namely, that it is French. It was in fact the work of Mestre Nicolas, the Nicolas Chantranez who worked first at Belem and then on the Portal da Magestade at Santa Cruz, and who carved an altar-piece in the Pena chapel at Cintra. Though much larger in general design, it is not altogether unlike the altar-piece in the Sé Velha. It is divided into two stories. In the lower are four divisions, with a small tabernacle in the middle, and in each division, which has either a curly broken pediment, or a shell at its head, are sculptured scenes from the life of St. Jerome.

The upper part contains only three divisions, one broad under an arch in the centre, and one narrower and lower on each side. As in the cathedral, slim candelabrum shafts stand between each division and at the ends, but the entablatures are less refined, and the sharp pediments at the two sides are unpleasing, as is the small round one and the vases at the top. The large central arch is filled with a very spirited carving of the 'Deposition.' In front of the three crosses which rise behind with the thieves still hanging to the two at the sides, is a group of people—officials on horseback on the left, and weeping women on the right. In the division to the left kneels Ayres himself presented by St. Jerome, and in the other on the right Dona Guiomar de Castro, his wife, presented by St. Luke. Throughout all the figure sculpture is excellent, as good as anything at Coimbra, but compared with the reredos in the Sé Velha, the architecture is poor in the extreme: the central division is too large, and the different levels of the cornice, rendered necessary of course by the shape of the vault, is most unpleasing. No one, however, can now judge of the true effect, as it has all been carefully and hideously painted with the brightest of colours. (Fig. 79.)

Being architecturally so inferior to the Sé Velha reredos, it is scarcely possible that they should be by the same hand, and therefore it seems likely that both the work in St. Peter's chapel and the pulpit in Santa Cruz may have been executed by the same man, namely by João de Ruão.[146]

Pena Chapel, Cintra.

Leaving São Marcos for a minute to finish with the works 216 of Nicolas Chantranez, we turn to the small chapel of Nossa Senhora da Pena, founded by Dom Manoel in 1503 as a cell of the Jeronymite monastery at Belem. Here in 1532 his son João III. dedicated a reredos of alabaster and black marble as a thankoffering for the birth of a son.[147]

Like Nicolas' work at São Marcos the altar piece is full of exquisite carving, more beautiful than in his older work. In the large central niche, with its fringe of cusps, is the 'Entombment,' where Our Lord is being laid by angels in a beautiful sarcophagus. Above this niche sit the Virgin and Child, on the left are the Annunciation above and the Birth at Bethlehem below, and on the right the Visit of the Magi and the Flight into Egypt. Nothing can exceed the delicacy of these alabaster carvings or of the beautiful little reliefs that form the pradella. Many of the little columns too are beautifully wrought, with good capitals and exquisitely worked drums, and yet, though the separate details may be and are fine, the whole is even more unsatisfactory than is his altar-piece at São Marcos, and one has to look closely and carefully to see its beauties. As the one at São Marcos is spoiled by paint, this one is spoiled by the use of different-coloured marble; besides, the different parts are even worse put together. There is no repose anywhere, for the little columns are all different, and the bad effect is increased by the way the different entablatures are broken out over the many projections.

São Marcos.

Interesting and even beautiful as are the tombs on the north side of the chancel of São Marcos, the chapel dos Reis Magos is even more important historically. This chapel, as stated above, was built by Dona Antonia de Vilhena in 1556 as a monument to her husband. Dona Antonia was in her time noted for her devotion to her husband's memory, and for her patriotism in that she sent her six sons to fight in Morocco, from whence three never returned. Her brother-in-law, Lourenço da Silva, also, who lies on the east side of the same chapel, fell in Africa in the fatal battle of Alcacer-Quebir in 1578, where Portugal lost her king and soon after her independence. 217

The chapel is entered from the nave by a large arch enriched in front with beautiful cherubs' heads and wreaths of flowers, and on the under side with coffered panels. This arch springs from a beautifully modelled entablature borne on either side by a Corinthian pilaster, panelled and carved, and by a column fluted above, and wreathed with hanging fruits and flowers below, while similar arches form recesses on the three remaining sides of the chapel, one—to the north—containing the altar, and the other two the tombs of Diogo and of Lourenço da Silva.

On the nave side, outside the columns, there stands on either side—placed like the columns on a high pedestal—a pilaster, panelled and carved with exquisite arabesques. These pilasters have no capitals, but instead well-moulded corbels, carved with griffin heads, uphold the entablature, and, by a happy innovation, on the projection thus formed are pedestals bearing short Corinthian columns. These support the main entablature whose cornice and frieze are enriched, the one with egg and tongue and with dentils, and the other

107

with strapwork and with leaves. In the spandrils above the arch are medallions surrounding the heads of St. Peter and of St. Paul, St. Peter being especially expressive.

Inside, the background of each tomb recess is covered with strapwork, surrounding in one case an open and in another a blank window, but unfortunately the reredos representing the Visit of the Magi is gone, and its place taken by a very poor picture of Our Lady of Lourdes.

The pendentives with their cherub heads are carried by corbels in the corners, and the dome is divided by bold ribs, themselves enriched with carving, into panels filled with strapwork. (Fig. 80.)

This chapel then is of great interest, not only because of the real beauty of its details but also because it was the first built of a type which was repeated more than once elsewhere, as, for instance, at Marceana near Alemquer, on the Tagus, and in the church of Nossa Senhora dos Anjos at Montemor-o-Velho, not far from São Marcos. Of the chapels at Montemor one at least was built by the same family, and in another where the reredos—a very fine piece of carving—represents a Pietà, small angels are seen to weep as they look from openings high up at the sides.

Perhaps the most successful feature of the design is the 218 happy way in which corbels take the place of capitals on the lower pilasters of the front. By this expedient it was possible to keep the upper column short without having to compare its proportions with those of the pilaster below, and also by projecting these columns to give the upper part an importance and an emphasis it would not otherwise have had.

There is no record of who designed this or the similar chapels, but by 1556 enough time had passed since the coming of the French for native pupils to have learned much from them. There is in the design something which seems to show that it is not from the hand of a Frenchman, but from that of some one who had learned much from Master Nicolas or from João de Ruão, but who had also learned something from elsewhere. While the smaller details remain partly French, the dome with its bold ribs suggests Italy, and it is known that Dom Manoel, and after him Dom João, sent young men to Italy for study. In any case the result is something neither Italian nor French.

Even more Italian is the tomb of Dona Antonia's father-in-law, João da Silva, sixth lord of Vagos, erected in 1559 and probably by the same sculptor. João da Silva lies in armour under a round arch carved with flowers and cherubs. In front of his tomb is a long inscription on a tablet held by beautifully modelled boys. On each side of the arch is a Corinthian pilaster, panelled and carved below and having at the top a shallow niche in which stand saints. On the entablature, enriched with medallions and strapwork, is a frame supported by boys and containing the da Silva arms. But the most interesting and beautiful part of the monument is the back, above the effigy. Here, in the upper part, is a shallow recess flanked by corbel-carried pilasters, and containing a relief of the Assumption of the Virgin. Now, the execution of the Virgin and of the small angels who bear her up may not be of the best, but the character of the whole design is quite Italian, and could only have been carved by some one who knew Italian work. On either side of this recess are round-headed niches containing saints, while boys sit in the spandrils above the arch.

Any one seeing this tomb will be at once struck with the Italian character of the design, especially perhaps with the boys who hold the tablet and with those who sit in the spandrils.[148]219

FIG. 79.
SÃO MARCOS.
CHANCEL.

FIG. 80.
SÃO MARCOS.
CHAPEL OF THE "REYES MAGOS."
FROM A PHOTOGRAPH BY E. BIEL & CO., OPORTO.

Even without leaving their country, Portuguese designers would already have had no great difficulty in finding pieces of real Italian work. Not to speak of the white marble door in the old palace of Cintra, possibly the work of Sansovino himself, with its simple mouldings and the beautiful detail of its architrave, there exist at Evora two doorways originally belonging to the church of São Domingos, which must either be the work of Italians or of some man who knew Italy. (Fig. 81.)

Evora, São Domingos.

Built of white marble from Estremoz and dating from about 1530, the panelled jambs have moulded caps on which rests the arch. Like the jambs, the arch has a splay which is divided into small panels. Above in the spandrils are ribboned circles enclosing well-carved heads. On either side are pilasters with Corinthian capitals of the earlier Italian kind. The entablature is moulded only, and instead of a pediment two curves lead up to a horizontal moulding supporting a shell, and above it a cherub's head.

Such real Italian doors, which would look quite at home in Genoa, seem almost unique, but there are many examples of work which, like the tomb and the chapel at São Marcos, seem to have been influenced not only by the French school at Coimbra, but also by Italian work.

Portalegre.
Tavira.
Lagos.

Not very far from Evora in Portalegre, where a bishop's see was founded by Dom João III. in 1549, there is a very fine monument of this kind to a bishop of the Mello family in the seminary, and also a doorway, while at Tavira in the Algarve the Misericordia has an interesting door, not unlike that at Evora, but more richly ornamented by having a sculptured frieze and a band of bold acanthus leaves joining the two capitals above the arch. There is another somewhat similar, but less successful, in the church of São Sebastião at Lagos.

Goes.
Trofa.

Nearer Coimbra there are some fine monuments to the Silveira family at Goes not far from Louzã, and four less interesting to the Lemos in the little parish church of Trofa near Agueda. At Trofa there is a pair of tombs on each side of the chancel, round-arched, with pilasters and with heads in the spandrils, and covered with arabesques. Each pair is practically alike except that the tombs on the north side, being placed closer together leave no room for a central pilaster and have small shafts instead of panelled jambs, and that the pair on the south have pediments. The best 220 feature is a figure of the founder of the chancel kneeling at prayer with his face turned towards the high altar.

Caminha.

Even in the far north the doors of the church at Caminha show how important had been the coming of the Frenchmen to Coimbra. They seem later than the church, but though very picturesque are clearly the work of some one who was not yet quite familiar with renaissance forms. The south door is the more interesting and picturesque. The arch and jambs are splayed, but there are no capitals; heads look out of circles in the spandrils; and the splay as well as the panels of the side pilasters are enriched with carvings which, partly perhaps owing to the granite in which they are cut, are much less delicate than elsewhere. The Corinthian capitals of the pilasters are distinctly clumsy, as are the mouldings, but the most interesting part of the whole design is the frieze, which is so immensely extended as to leave room for four large niches separated by rather clumsy shafts and containing figures of St. Mark and St. Luke in the middle and of St. Peter and St. Paul at the ends. Above in the pediment are a Virgin and Child with kneeling angels. Besides the innovation of the enlarged frieze, which reminds one of a door in the Certosa near Pavia, the clumsiness of the mouldings and the comparative poorness of the sculpture, though the figures are much better than any previously worked by native artists, suggest that the designer and workmen were Portuguese.

The same applies to the west door, which is wider and where the capitals are of a much better shape, though the pilasters are rather too tall. The sculpture frieze is a little wider than usual, and instead of a pediment there is a picturesque cresting, above which are cut four extraordinary monsters. (Fig. 82.)

Moncorvo.

A somewhat similar but much plainer door has been built against the older and round-arched entrance of the Misericordia at Moncorvo in Traz os Montes. The parish church of the same place begun in 1544 is both outside and in a curious mixture of Gothic and Classic. The three aisles are of the same height with round-arched Gothic vaults, but the columns are large and round with bases and capitals evidently copied from Roman doric, though the abacis have been made circular.

Outside the buttresses are still Gothic in form, but the west door is of the fully developed renaissance.

FIG. 81.   **FIG. 82.**

PALACE, CINTRA.   **W DOOR, CAMINHA.**

DOOR BY SANSOVINO.

The opening is 221 flanked by coupled columns which support an entablature on which rest four other shorter columns separating three white marble niches. Above this is a window flanked by single columns which carry a pediment. Though built of granite, the detail is good and the whole doorway not unpleasing.[149]

But, that it was not only such details as doors and monuments that began to show the result of the coming of the Frenchmen is seen in the work of João de Castilho, after he first left Thomar for Belem. There he had found Master Nicolas Chantranez already at work, and there he learned, perhaps from him, so to change his style that by the time he returned to Thomar to work for Dom João III. in 1528 he was able to design buildings practically free from that Gothic spirit which is still found in his latest work at Belem. 222

CHAPTER XVI

LATER WORK OF JOÃO DE CASTILHO AND THE EARLIER CLASSIC

TO Dom Manoel, who died in 1521, had succeeded his son Dom João III. The father had been renowned for his munificence and his splendour, the son cared more for the Church and for the suppression of heresy. By him the Inquisition was introduced in 1536 to the gradual crushing of all independent thought, and so by degrees to the degradation of his country. He reigned for thirty-six years, a time of wealth and luxury, but before he died the nation had begun to suffer from this very luxury; with all freedom of thought forbidden, with the most brave and adventurous of her sons sailing east to the Indies or west to Brazil, most of them never to return, Portugal was ready to fall an easy prey to Philip of Spain when in 1580 there died the old Cardinal King Henry, last surviving son of Dom Manoel, once called the Fortunate King.

With the death of Dom Manoel, or at least with the finishing of the great work which he had begun, the most brilliant and interesting period in the history of Portuguese architecture comes to an end. When the younger Fernandes died seven years after his master in 1538, or when João de Castilho saw the last vault built at Belem, Gothic, even as represented by Manoelino, disappeared for ever, and renaissance architecture, taught by the French school at Coimbra, or learned in Italy by those sent there by Dom Manoel, became universal, to flourish for a time, and then to fall even lower than in any other country.

Except the Frenchmen at Coimbra no one played a greater part in this change than João de Castilho, who, no doubt, first learned about the renaissance from Master Nicolas at Belem; Thomar also, his own home, lies about half-way between 223 Lisbon and Coimbra, so that he may well have visited his brother Diogo at Santa Cruz and seen what other Frenchmen were doing there and so become acquainted with better architects than Master Nicolas; but in any case, who ever it may have been who taught him, he planned at Thomar, after his return there, the first buildings which are wholly in the style of the renaissance and are not merely decorated with renaissance details.

Alcobaça.

But before following him back to Thomar, his additions to the abbey of Alcobaça must be mentioned, as there for the last time, except in some parts of Belem, he allowed himself to follow the older methods, though even at this early date—1518 and 1519— renaissance forms are beginning to creep in.

110

On the southern side of the ambulatory one of the radiating chapels was pulled down in 1519 to form a passage, irregular in shape and roofed with a vault of many ribs. From this two doors lead, one on the north to the sacristy, and one on the south to a chapel. Unfortunately both sacristy and chapel have been rebuilt and now contain nothing of interest, except, in the sacristy, some fine presses inlaid with ivory, now fast falling to pieces. The two doors are alike, and show that João de Castilho was as able as any of his contemporaries to design a piece of extreme realism. On the jambs is carved renaissance ornament, but nowhere else is there anything to show that João and Nicolas had met at Belem some two years before. The head of the arch is wavy and formed mostly of convex curves. Beyond the strip of carving there grows up on either side a round tree, with roots and bark all shown; at the top there are some leaves for capitals, and then each tree grows up to meet in the centre and so form a great ogee, from which grow out many cut-off branches, all sprouting into great curly leaves.

This is realism carried to excess, and yet the leaves are so finely carved, the whole design so compact, and the surrounding whitewashed wall with its dado of tiles so plain, that the effect is quite good. (Fig. 83.)

The year before he had begun for Cardinal Henry, afterwards king, and then commendator of the abbey, a second story to the great cloister of Dom Diniz. Reached by a picturesque stair on the south side, the three-centred arches each enclose two or three smaller round arches, with the 224 spandrils merely pierced or sometimes cusped. The mouldings are simple but not at all classic. The shafts which support these round arches are all carried down across the parapet through the rope moulding at the top to the floor level, and are of three or more patterns. Those at the jambs are plain with hollow chamfered edges, as are also a few of the others. They are, however, mostly either twisted, having four round mouldings separated by four hollows, or else shaped like a rather fat baluster; most of the capitals with curious volutes at the corner are evidently borrowed from Corinthian capitals, but are quite unorthodox in their arrangement.

Though this upper cloister adds much to the picturesqueness of the whole it is not very pleasing in itself, as the three-centred arches are often too wide and flat, and yet it is of great interest as showing how João de Castilho was in 1518 beginning to accept renaissance forms though still making them assume a Manoelino dress.

Batalha, Santa Cruz.

But in the door of the little parish church of Sta. Cruz at Batalha, also built by João de Castilho, Manoelino and renaissance details are used side by side with the happiest result. On each jamb are three round shafts and two bands of renaissance carving; of these the inner band is carried round the broken and curved head of the opening, while the outer runs high up to form a square framing. Of the three shafts the inner is carried round the head, the outer round the outside of the framing, while the one in the centre divides into two, one part running round the head, while the other forms the inner edge of the framing, and also forms a great trefoil on the flat field above the opening. In the two corners between the trefoils and the framing are circles enclosing shields, one charged with the Cross of the Order of Christ, the other with the armillary sphere.

The inner side of the trefoil is cusped, crockets and finials enrich the outer moulding of the opening, while beyond the jambs are niches, now empty. (Fig. 84.)

It is not too much to say that, except the great entrance to the Capellas Imperfeitas, this is the most beautiful of all Manoelino doorways; in no other is the detail so refined nor has any other so satisfactory a framing. Unfortunately the construction has not been good, so that the upper part is now all full of cracks and gaping joints.

FIG. 83.	FIG. 84.
ALCOBAÇA.	W DOOR, STA. CRUZ.
SACRISTY DOOR.	BATALHA.
Thomar.	

Since Dom João III. was more devoted to the Church than 225 to anything else he determined in 1524 to change the great Order of Christ from a body of military knights bound, as had been the Templars, by certain vows, into a monastic order of regulars. This

111

necessitated great additions to the buildings at Thomar, for the knights had not been compelled to live in common like monks.

Accordingly João de Castilho was summoned back from Belem and by 1528 had got to work.

All these additions were made to the west of the existing buildings, and to make room for them Dom João had to buy several houses and gardens, which together formed a suburb called São Martinho, and some of which were the property of João de Castilho, who received for them 463 000 or about £100.[150]

PLAN OF THOMAR

These great additions, which took quite twenty-five years to build, cover an immense area, measuring more than 300 feet long by 300 wide and containing five cloisters. Immediately to the west of the Coro of the church, then probably scarcely finished, is the small cloister of Sta. Barbara; to the north of this is the larger Claustro da Hospedaria, begun about 1539, while to the south and hiding the lower part of the Coro is the splendid two-storied Claustro, miscalled 'dos Filippes,' begun 226 in its present form in 1557 by Diogo de Torralva some time after de Castilho's death.

Further west are two other large cloisters, do Mixo or da Micha to the north and dos Corvos to the south, and west of the Corvos a sort of farmyard called the Pateo dos Carrascos—that is of the evergreen oaks, or since Carrasco also means a hangman, it may be that the executioners of the Inquisition had their quarters there.

Between these cloisters, and dividing the three on the east from the two on the west, is an immense corridor nearly three hundred feet long from which small cells open on each side; in the centre it is crossed by another similar corridor stretching over one hundred and fifty feet to the west, separating the two western cloisters, and with a small chapel to the east.

North of all the cloisters are more corridors and rooms extending eastwards almost to the Templars' castle, but there the outer face dates mostly from the seventeenth century or later.

The first part to be begun was the Claustro da Micha, or loaf, so called from the bread distributed there to the poor. Outside it was begun in 1528, but inside an inscription over the door says it was begun in 1534 and finished in 1546. Being the kitchen cloister it is very plain, with simple round-headed arches. Only the entrance door is adorned with a Corinthian column on either side; its straight head rests on well-carved corbels, and above it is a large inscribed tablet upheld by small boys.

Under the pavement of the cloister as well as under the Claustro dos Corvos is a great cistern. On the south was the kitchen and the oil cellar, on the east the dispensary, and on the west a great oven and wood-store with three large halls above, which seem to have been used by the Inquisition.[151] The lodgings of the Dom Prior were above the cloister to the north.

Like the Claustro da Micha, the Claustro dos Corvos has plain round arches resting on round columns and set usually in pairs with a buttress between each pair. On the south side, below, were the cellars, finished in 1539, and above the library, on the west, various vaulted stores with a passage above leading to the library from the dormitory. 227

The whole of the east side is occupied by the refectory, about 100 feet long by 30 wide. On each of the long sides there is a pulpit, one bearing the date 1536, enriched with arabesques, angels, and small columns. At the south end are two windows, and at the north a hatch communicating with the kitchen.

The Claustro da Hospedaria, as its name denotes, was where strangers were lodged; like the Claustro dos Corvos each pair of arches is divided by a buttress, and the round columns have simple but effective capitals, in which nothing of the regular Corinthian is left but the abacus, and a large plain leaf at each corner. Still, though plain, this cloister is very picturesque. Its floor, like those of all the cloisters, lies deep below the level of the church, and looking eastward from one of the cell windows the Coro and the round church are seen towering high above the brown tile roofs of the rooms beyond the cloister and of the simple upper cloister, which runs across the eastern walk. (Fig. 85.)

This part of the building, begun about 1539, must have been carried on during João de Castilho's absence, as in 1541 he was sent to Mazagão on the Moroccan coast to build fortifications; there he made a bastion 'so strong as to be able not only to resist the Shariff, but also the Turk, so strong was it.'[152]

The small cloister of Santa Barbara is the most pleasing of all those which João de Castilho was able to finish. In order not to hide the west front of the church its arches had to be kept very low. They are three-centred and almost flat, while the vault is even flatter, the bays being divided by a stone beam resting on beautifully carved brackets. The upper cloister is not carried across the east side next the church; but in its south-west corner an opening with a good entablature, resting on two columns with fine Corinthian capitals, leads to one of those twisting stairs without a newel 228 of which builders of this time were so fond. Going up this stair one reaches the cloister of the Filippes which João did not live to carry out.

More interesting than any of these cloisters are the long dormitory passages. The walls for about one-third of the height are lined with tiles, which with the red paving tiles were bought for about £33 from one Aleixo Antunes. The roofs are throughout of dark panelled wood and semicircular in shape. The only windows—except at the crossing—are at the ends of the three long arms. There is a small round-headed window above, and below one, flat-headed, with a column in the centre and one at each side, the window on the north end having on it the date 1541, eight years after the chapel in the centre had been built.

On this chapel at the crossing has been expended far more ornament than on any other part of the passages. Leading to each arm of the passage an arch, curiously enriched with narrow bands which twice cross each other leaving diamond-shaped hollows, rests on Corinthian pilasters, which have only four flutes, but are adorned with niches, whose elegant canopies mark the level of the springing of the chapel vault. This vault, considerably lower than the passage arches, is semicircular and coffered. Between it and the cornice which runs all round the square above the passage arches is a large oblong panel, in the middle of which is a small round window. Beautifully carved figures which, instead of having legs, end in great acanthus-leaf volutes with dragons in the centre, hold a beautifully carved wreath round this window. In the middle of the architrave below, a tablet, held by exquisite little winged boys, gives the date, 'Era de 1533.' Above the cornice there rises a simple vault with a narrow round-headed window on each side.

This carving over the chapel is one of the finest examples of renaissance work left in the country. It is much bolder than any of the French work left at Coimbra, being in much higher relief than was usual in the early French renaissance, and yet the figures and leaves are carved with the utmost delicacy and refinement. (Fig. 86.)

The same delicacy characterises such small parts of the cloister dos Filippes as were built by João de Castilho before he retired in 1551. These are now confined to two stairs leading from the upper to the lower cloister.

FIG. 85. THOMAR.
CONVENT OF CHRIST.
CLAUSTRO DA HOSPEDARIA.

FIG. 86.
THOMAR.
CHAPEL IN DORMITORY PASSAGE.

These stairs 229 are adorned with pilasters or thin columns against the walls, delicate cornices, medallions, figures, and foliage; in one are square-headed built-up doors or doorlike spaces, with well-moulded architraves, and always in the centre above the opening small figures are carved, in one an exquisite little Cupid holding a torch. At the bottom of the eastern stair, which is decorated with scenes from the life of St. Jerome and with the head of Frei Antonio of Lisbon, first prior of the reformed order, a door led into the lower floor of the unfinished chapter-house. On this same stair there is a date 1545, so the work was probably going on till the very end of João's tenure of office, and fine as the present cloister is, it is a pity that he was not able himself to finish it, for it is the chief cloister in the whole building, and on it he would no doubt have employed all the resources of his art. (Fig. 87.)

It is not without interest to learn that, like architects of the present day, João de Castilho often found very great difficulties in carrying out his work. Till well within the last hundred years Portugal was an almost roadless country, and four centuries ago, as now, most of the heavy carting was done by oxen, which are able to drag clumsy carts heavily laden up and down the most impassable lanes. Several times does he write to the king of the difficulty of getting oxen. On 4th March 1548 he says:

'I have written some days ago to Pero Carvalho to tell him of the want of carts, since those which we had were away carrying stone for the works at Cardiga and at Almeirim'—a palace now destroyed opposite Santarem—'the works of Thomar remaining without stone these three months. And for want of a hundred cart-loads of stone which I had worked at the quarry—doors and windows—I have not finished the students' studies'—probably in the noviciate near the Claustro da Micha. 'The studies are raised to more than half their height and in eight days' work I shall finish them if only I had oxen, for those I had have died.

'I would ask 20 000 [about £4, 10s.] to buy five oxen, and with three which I have I could manage the carriage of a thousand cart-loads of worked stone, besides that of which I speak of to your Highness, and since there are no carts the men can bring nothing, even were they given 60 reis [about 3d.] a cartload there is no one to do carting....

[230]

' ... And if your Highness will give me these oxen I shall finish the work very quickly, that when your Highness comes here you may find something to see and have contentment of it.'

Later he again complains of transport difficulties, for the few carts there were in the town were all being used by the Dom Prior; and in the year when he retired, 1551, he writes in despair asking the king for 'a very strong edict [Alvará] that no one of any condition whatever might be excused, because in this place those who have something of their own are excused by favour, and the poor men do service, which to them seems a great aggravation and oppression. May your Highness believe that I write this as a desperate man, since I cannot serve as I desire, and may this provision be sent to the magistrate and judge that they may have it executed by their officer, since the mayor [Alcaide] here is always away and never in his place.'[153]

These letters make it possible to understand how buildings in those days took such a long time to finish, and how João de Castilho—though it was at least begun in 1545—was able to do so little to the Claustro dos Filippes in the following six years.

The last letter also seems to show that some at least of the labour was forced.

Leaving the Claustro dos Filippes for the present, we must return to Batalha for a little, and then mention some buildings in which the early renaissance details recall some of the work at Thomar.

Batalha.

The younger Fernandes had died in 1528, leaving the Capellas Imperfeitas very much in the state in which they still remain. Though so much more interested in his monastery at Thomar, Dom João ordered João de Castilho to go on with the chapels, and in 1533 the loggia over the great entrance door had been finished. Beautiful though it is it did not please the king, and is not in harmony with the older work, and so nothing more was done.

In place of the large Manoelino window, which was begun on all the other seven sides, João de Castilho here built two renaissance arches, each of two orders, of which the broader springs from the square pilasters and the narrower from candelabrum shafts. In front there run up to the cornice three beautiful shafts standing on high pedestals which rest

FIG. 87.	FIG. 88.
THOMAR.	THOMAR.
CONVENTO DE CHRISTO.	CHAPEL OF THE CONCEIÇÃO.
STAIR IN CLAUSTRO DOS FILIPPES.	

[231] on corbels; the frieze of the cornice is carved much after the manner of the window panel in the dormitory corridor at Thomar, and with long masks where it projects over the shafts.

Below, the carved cornice and architrave are carried across the opening as they are round the whole octagon, but the frieze is open and filled with balusters. Behind, the whole space is spanned by a three-centred arch, panelled like the passage arches at Thomar.

114

All the work is most exquisite, but it is not easy to see how the horizontal cornice was to be brought into harmony with the higher windows intended on the other seven sides, nor does the renaissance detail, beautiful though it is, agree very well with the exuberant Manoelino of the rest.

With the beginning of the Claustro dos Filippes the work of João de Castilho comes to an end. He had been actively employed for about forty years, beginning and ending at Thomar, finishing Belem, and adding to Alcobaça, besides improving the now vanished royal palace and even fortifying Mazagão on the Moroccan coast, where perhaps his work may still survive. In these forty years his style went through more than one complete change. Beginning with late Gothic he was soon influenced by the surrounding Manoelino; at Belem he first met renaissance artists, at Alcobaça he either used Manoelino and renaissance side by side or else treated renaissance in a way of his own, though shortly after, at Belem again, he came to use renaissance details more and more fully. A little later at Thomar, having a free hand—for at Belem he had had to follow out the lines laid down by Boutaca—he discarded Manoelino and Gothic alike in favour of renaissance.

In this final adoption of the renaissance he was soon followed by many others, even before he laid down his charge at Thomar in 1551.

In most of these buildings, however, it is not so much his work at Thomar which is followed—except in the case of cloisters—but rather the chapel of the Conceição, also at Thomar. Like it they are free from the more exuberant details so common in France and in Spain, and yet they cannot be called Italian.

Thomar, Conceição.

There is unfortunately no proof that the Conceição chapel is João's work; indeed the date inscribed inside is 1572, 232 twenty-one years after his retirement, and nineteen after his death. Still this date is probably a mistake, and some of the detail is so like what is found in the great convent on the hill above that probably it was really designed by him.

This small chapel stands on a projecting spur of the hill half-way down between the convent and the town.

Inside the whole building is about sixty feet long by thirty wide, and consists of a nave with aisles about thirty feet long, a transept the width of the central aisle but barely projecting beyond the walls, a square choir with a chapel on each side, followed by an apse; east of the north choir chapel is a small sacristy, and east of the south a newel-less stair—like that in the Claustro de Sta. Barbara—leading up to the roof and down to some vestries under the choir. Owing to the sacristy and stair the eastern part of the chancel, which is rather narrower than the nave, is square, showing outside no signs of the apse.

The outside is very plain: Ionic pilasters at the angles support a simple cornice which runs round the whole building; the west end and transepts have pediments with small semicircular windows. The tile roofs are surmounted by a low square tower crowned by a flat plastered dome at the crossing and by the domed stair turret at the south-east corner. The west door is plain with a simple architrave. The square-headed windows have a deep splay—the wall being very thick—their architraves as well as their cornices and pediments rest on small brackets set not at right angles with the wall, but crooked so as to give an appearance of false perspective.

The inside is very much more pleasing, indeed it is one of the most beautiful interiors to be found anywhere. (Fig. 88.)

On each side of the central aisle there are three Corinthian columns, with very correct proportions, and exquisite capitals, beautifully carved if not quite orthodox. Corresponding pilasters stand against the walls, as well as at the entrance to the choir, and at the beginning of the apse. These and the columns support a beautifully modelled entablature, enriched only with a dentil course. Central aisle, transepts and choir are all roofed with a larger and the side aisles with a smaller barrel vault, divided into bays by shallow arches. In choir and transepts the vault is coffered, but in the nave each bay is ornamented with three sets of four square panels, set in the shape of a cross, each panel having in it another panel set 233 diagonally to form a diamond. At the crossing, which is crowned by a square coffered dome, the spandrils are filled with curious winged heads, while the semi-dome of the apse is covered with narrow ribs. The windows are exactly like those outside, but the west door has over it a very refined though plain pediment.

So far, beyond the great refinement of the details, there has been nothing very characteristic of João de Castilho, but when we find that the pilasters of the choir and apse, as well as the choir and transept arches, are panelled in that very curious way—with strips crossing each other at long intervals to form diamonds—which João employed in the passage arches in the Thomar dormitory and in the loggia at Batalha, it would be natural enough to conclude that this chapel is his work, and indeed the best example of what he could do with classic details.

Now under the west window of the north aisle there is a small tablet with the following inscription in Portuguese[154]:—'This chapel was erected in A.D. 1572, but profaned in 1810 was restored in 1848 by L. L. d'Abreu,' etc.

Of course in 1572 João de Castilho had been long dead, but the inscription was put up in 1848, and it is quite likely that by then L. L. d'Abreu and his friends had forgotten or did not know that even as late as the sixteenth century dates were sometimes still reckoned by the era of Cæsar, so finding it recorded that the chapel had been built in the year 1572 they took for granted that it was A.D. 1572, whereas it may just as well have been E.C. 1572, that is A.D. 1534, just the very time when João de Castilho was building the dormitory in the convent and using there the same curious panelling. Besides in 1572 this form of renaissance had long been given up and been replaced by a heavier and more classic style brought from Italy. It seems therefore not unreasonable to claim this as João de Castilho's work, and to see in it one of the earliest as well as the most complete example of this form of renaissance architecture, a form which prevailed side by side with the 234 work of the Frenchmen and their pupils for about fifteen years.

Now in some respects this chapel recalls some of the earlier renaissance buildings in Italy, and yet no part of it is quite Italian, nor can it be called Spanish. The barrel vault here and in the dormitory chapel in the convent are Italian features, but they have not been treated exactly as was done there, or as was to be done in Portugal some fifty years later, so that it seems more likely that João de Castilho got his knowledge of Italian work at second-hand, perhaps from one of the men sent there by Dom Manoel, and not by having been there himself.

No other building in this style can be surely ascribed to him, and no other is quite so pleasing, yet there are several in which refined classic detail of a similar nature is used, and one of the best of these is the small church of the Milagre at Santarem. As for the cloisters which are mentioned later, they have much in common with João de Castilho's work at Thomar, as, for instance, in the Claustros da Micha, or the Claustro da Hospedaria; in the latter especially the upper story suggests the arrangement which became so common.

This placing of a second story with horizontal architrave on the top of an arched cloister is very common in Spain, and might have been suggested by such as are found at Lupiana or at Alcalá de Henares,[155] but these are not divided into bays by buttresses, so it is more likely that they were borrowed from such a cloister as that of Sta. Cruz at Coimbra, where the buttresses run up to the roof of the upper story and where the arches of that story are almost flat.

Santarem, Milagre.

The Milagre or Miracle church at Santarem is so called because it stands near where the body of St. Irene, martyred by the Romans at Nabantia, now Thomar, after floating down the Nabão, the Zezere, and the Tagus, came to shore and so gave her name to Santarem.

The church is small, being about sixty-five feet long by forty wide. It has three aisles, wooden panelled roofs, an arcade resting on Doric columns, and at the east a sort of transept followed by an apse. The piers to the west side 235 of this transept are made up of four pilasters, all of different heights. The highest, the one on the west side, has a Corinthian capital and is enriched in front by a statue under a canopy standing on a corbel upheld by a slender baluster shaft. The second in height is plain, and supports the arch which crosses the central aisle. The arches opening from the aisles into the transept chapel are lower still, and rest, not on capitals, but on corbels. Like the nave arch, on their spandrels heads are carved looking out of circles. Lowest of all—owing to the barrel vault which covers the central aisle at the crossing—are the arches leading north and south to the chapels. They too spring from corbels and are quite plain.

Santarem, Marvilla.

Up in the town on the top of the hill the nave of the church of the Marvilla—whose Manoelino door and chancel have already been mentioned—is of about the same date. This nave is about one hundred feet long by fifty-five wide, has three aisles with wooden ceilings; the arcades of round arches with simple moulded architrave rest on the beautiful Ionic capitals of columns over twenty-six feet high. These capitals, of Corinthian rather than of Ionic proportions, with simple fluting instead of acanthus leaves, have curious double volutes at each angle, and small winged heads in the middle of each side of the abacus.

Altogether the arcades are most stately, and the beauty of the church is further enhanced by the exceptionally fine tiles with which the walls as well as the spandrels above the arches are lined. Up to about the height of fifteen feet, above a stone bench, the tiles, blue, yellow, and orange, are arranged in panels, two different patterns being used alternatively, with beautiful borders, while in each spandrel towards the central aisle an Emblem of the Virgin, Tower of Ivory, Star of the Sea, and so on, is surrounded by blue and yellow intertwining leaves. Above these, as above the panels on the walls, the whole is covered with dark and light tiles arranged in checks, and added as stated by a date over the chancel arch in 1617. The lower tiles are probably of much the same date or a little earlier.

Against one of the nave columns there stands a very elegant little pulpit. It rests on the Corinthian capital of a very bulbous baluster, is square, and has on each side four beautiful little Corinthian columns, fluted and surrounded with large acanthus leaves at the bottom. Almost exactly like it, 236 but round and with balusters instead of columns, is the pulpit in the church of Nossa Senhora dos Olivaes at Thomar. (Fig. 89.)

Elvas, São Domingos.

The most original in plan as well as in decoration of all the buildings of this time is the church of the nunnery of São Domingos at Elvas, like nearly all nunneries in the kingdom now fast falling to pieces. In plan it is an octagon about forty-two feet across with three apses to the east and a smaller octagonal dome in the middle standing on eight white marble columns with Doric capitals. The columns, the architrave below the dome, the arches of the apses and their vaults, are all of white marble covered with exquisite carved ornament partly gilt, while all the walls and the other vaults are lined with tiles, blue and yellow patterns on a white ground. The abacus of each column is set diagonally to the diameter of the octagon, and between it and the lower side of the architrave are interposed thin blocks of stone rounded at the ends.

Like the Conceição at Thomar this too dates from near the end of Dom João's reign, having been founded about 1550.

Cintra, Penha Longa and Penha Verde.

Capitals very like those in the nave of the Marvilla, but with a ring of leaves instead of flutes, are found in the cloister of the church at Penha Longa near Cintra, and in the little round chapel at Penha Verde not far off, where lies the heart of Dom João de Castro, fourth viceroy of India. Built about 1535, it is a simple little round building with a square recess for the altar opposite the door. Inside, the dome springs from a cornice resting on six columns whose capitals are of the same kind.

Others nearly the same are found in the house of the Conde de São Vicente at Lisbon, only there the volutes are replaced by winged figures, as is also the case in the arcades of the Misericordia at Tavira, the door of which has been mentioned above.

Vizeu, Cloister.

Still more like the Marvilla capitals are those of the lower cloister of the cathedral of Vizeu. This, the most pleasing of all the renaissance cloisters in Portugal, has four arches on each side resting on fluted columns which though taller than usual in cloisters, have no entasis. The capitals are exactly like those at Santarem, but being of granite are much coarser, with roses instead of winged heads on the unmoulded abaci. At the angles two columns are placed together and a shallow strip is carried up above them all to the cornice. Somewhere in the lower cloister are the arms of Bishop Miguel da Silva, who is

FIG. 89.   **FIG. 90.**

SANTAREM   **VIZEU**

CHURCH OF THE MARVILLA.   **CATHEDRAL CLOISTER.**

237 said to have built it about 1524, but that is an impossibly early date, as even in far less remote places such classical columns were not used till at least ten years later. Yet the cloister must probably have been built some time before 1550. An upper unarched cloister, with an architrave resting on simple Doric columns, was added, *sede vacante*, between 1720 and 1742, and greatly increases the picturesqueness of the whole. (Fig. 90.)

Lamego, Cloister.

A similar but much lower second story was added by Bishop Manoel Noronha[156] in 1557 to the cloister of Lamego Cathedral. The lower cloister with its round arches and eight-sided shafts is interesting, as most of its capitals are late Gothic, some moulded, a few with leaves, though some have been replaced by very good capitals of the Corinthian type but retaining the Gothic abacus.[157]

Coimbra, São Thomaz.
Carmo.
Cintra, Penha Longa.
Faro, São Bento.
Lorvão.

Most, however, of the cloisters of this period do not have a continuous arcade like that of Vizeu, but have arches set in pairs in the lower story with big buttresses between each pair. Such is the cloister of the college of São Thomaz at Coimbra, founded in 1540, where the arches of the lower cloister rest on Ionic capitals, while the architrave of the upper is upheld by thin Doric columns; of the Carmo, also at Coimbra, founded in 1542, where the cloister is almost exactly like that of São Thomaz, except that there are twice as many columns in the upper story; of Penha Longa near Cintra, where the two stories are of equal height and the lower, with arches, has moulded and the upper, with horizontal architrave, Ionic capitals, and of São Bento at Faro, where the lower capitals are like those in the Marvilla, but without volutes, while the upper are Ionic. In all these the big square buttress is carried right up to the roof of the upper cloister, as it was also at Lorvão near Coimbra. There the arches below are much wider, so that above the number of supports has been doubled.[158]

Amarante.

In one of the cloisters of São Gonçalvo at Amarante on 238 the Tamega—famous for the battle on the bridge during the French invasion—there is only one arch to each bay below, and it springs from jambs, not from columns, and is very plain. The buttresses do not rise above the lower cornice and have Ionic capitals, as have also the rather stout columns of the upper story. The lower cloister is roofed with a beautiful three-centred vault with many ribs, and several of the doors are good examples of early renaissance.

Santarem, Sta. Clara.

More like the other cloisters, but probably somewhat later in date, is that of Sta. Clara at Santarem, fast falling to pieces. In it there are three arches, here three-centred, to each bay, and instead of projecting buttresses wide pilasters, like the columns, Doric below, Ionic above.

Guarda, Reredos.

On first seeing the great reredos in the cathedral of Guarda, the tendency is to attribute it to a period but little later than the works of Master Nicolas at São Marcos or of João de Ruão at Coimbra. But on looking closer it is seen that a good deal of the ornament—the decoration of the pilasters and of the friezes—as well as the appearance of the figures, betray a later date—a date perhaps as late as the end of the reign of Dom João III. (Fig. 91.)

Though the reredos is very much larger and of finer design, the figures have sufficient resemblance to those in the chapel of the Holy Sacrament in the Sé Velha at Coimbra, put

118

up in 1566, to show that they must be more or less contemporary, the Guarda reredos being probably the older.[159]

Filling the whole of the east end of the apse of the Capella Mor, the structure rises in a curve up to the level of the windows. Without the beautiful colouring of Master Vlimer's work at Coimbra, or the charm of the reredos at Funchal, with figures distinctly inferior to those by Master Nicolas at São Marcos, this Guarda reredos is yet a very fine piece of work, and is indeed the only large one of its kind which still survives.

It is divided into three stories, each about ten feet high, with a half-story below resting on a plain plinth.

Each story is divided into large square panels by pilasters or columns set pretty close together, the topmost story having candelabrum shafts, the one below it Corinthian columns, the lowest Doric pilasters, and the half-story below pedestals for these pilasters. Entablatures with ornamental friezes divide 239 each story, while at the top the centre is raised to admit of an arch, an arrangement probably copied from João de Ruão's altar-piece.

In the half-story at the bottom are half-figures of the twelve Apostles, four under each of the square panels at the sides, and one between each pair of pilasters.

Above is represented, on the left the Annunciation, on the right the Nativity; in the centre, now hidden by a hideous wooden erection, there is a beautiful little tabernacle between two angels. Between the pilasters, as between the columns above, stand large figures of prophets.

In the next story the scenes are, on the left the Magi, on the right the Presentation, and in the centre the Assumption of the Virgin.

The whole of the top is taken up with the Story of the Crucifixion, our Lord bearing the Cross on the left, the Crucifixion under the arch, and the Deposition on the right.

Although the whole is infinitely superior in design to anything by Master Nicolas, it must be admitted that the sculpture is very inferior to his, and also to João de Ruão's. The best are the Crucifixion scenes, where the grouping is better and the action freer, but everywhere the faces are rather expressionless and the figures stiff.

As everything is painted, white for the background and an ugly yellow for the figures and detail, it is not possible to see whether stone or terra cotta is the material; if terra cotta the sculptor may have been a pupil of Filipe Eduard, who in the time of Dom Manoel wrought the Last Supper in terra cotta, fragments of which still survive at Coimbra. 240

CHAPTER XVII
THE LATER RENAISSANCE AND THE SPANISH USURPATION

THIS earlier style did not, however, last very long. Even before the death of Dom João more strictly classical forms began to come in from Italy, brought by some of the many pupils who had been sent to study there. Once when staying at Almeirim the king had been much interested in a model of the Colosseum brought to him by Gonçalo Bayão, whom he charged to reproduce some of the monuments he had seen in Rome.

Whether he did reproduce them or not is unknown, but in the Claustro dos Filippes at Thomar this new and thoroughly Italian style is seen fully developed.

Thomar, Claustro dos Filippes.

Diogo de Torralva had been nominated to direct the works in Thomar in 1554, but did nothing to this cloister till 1557 after Dom João's death, when his widow, Dona Catharina, regent for her grandson, Dom Sebastião, ordered him to pull down what was already built, as it was unsafe, and to build another of the same size about one hundred and fifteen feet square, but making the lower story rather higher.

The work must have been carried out quickly, since on the vault of the upper cloister there is the date 1562—a date which shows that the whole must have been practically finished some eighteen years before Philip of Spain secured the throne of Portugal, and that therefore the cloister should rather be called after Dona Catharina, who ordered it, than after the 'Reis Intrusos,' whose only connection with Thomar is that the first was there elected king.

Between each of the three large arches which form a side of the lower cloister stand two Roman Doric columns of considerable size. They are placed some distance apart leaving

119

room between them for an opening, while another window-like opening occurs above the moulding from which the arches spring.

FIG. 91.   FIG. 92.
GUARDA   THOMAR
REREDOS IN CATHEDRAL.   CLAUSTRO DOS FILIPPES.

241 In the four corners the space between the columns, as well as the entablature, is set diagonally, leaving room in one instance for a circular stair. The cornice is enriched with dentils and the frieze with raised squares. On the entablature more columns of about the same height as those below, but with Ionic capitals, stand in pairs. Stairs lead up in each corner to the flat roof, above which they rise in a short dome-bearing drum. In this upper cloister the arches are much narrower, springing from square Ionic pilasters, two on each side, set one behind the other, and leaving an open space beyond so that the whole takes the form of a Venetian window. The small upper window between the columns is round instead of square, and the cornice is carried on large corbels. In front of all the openings is a balustrade. Two windows look south down the hillside over rich orchards and gardens, while immediately below them a water channel, the end of a great aqueduct built under Philip I. of Portugal, II. of Spain, by the Italian Filippo Terzi,[160] cools the air, and, overflowing, clothes the arches with maidenhair fern. Another window opening on to the Claustro de Sta. Barbara gives a very good view of the curious west front of the church. There is not and there probably never was any parapet to the flat paved roof, from where one can look down on the surrounding cloisters, and on the paved terrace before the church door where Philip was elected king in April 1580. (Fig. 92.)

This cloister, the first example in Portugal of the matured Italian renaissance, is also, with the exception of the church of São Vicente de Fora at Lisbon, the most successful, for all is well proportioned, and shows that Diogo de Torralva really understood classic detail and how to use it. He was much less successful in the chancel of Belem, while about the cathedral which he built at Miranda de Douro it is difficult to find out anything, so remote and inaccessible is it, except that it stands magnificently on a high rock above the river.[161]

The reigns of Dom Sebastião and of his grand-uncle, the Cardinal-King, were noted for no great activity in building. Only at Evora, where he so long filled the position of archbishop before succeeding to the throne, was the cardinal able 242 to do much. The most important architectural event in Dom Sebastião's reign was the coming of Filippo Terzi from Italy to build São Roque, the church of the Jesuits in Lisbon, and the consequent school of architects, the Alvares, Tinouco, Turianno, and others who were so active during the reign of Philip.

But before speaking of the work of this school some of Cardinal Henry's buildings at Evora must be mentioned, and then the story told of how Philip succeeded in uniting the whole Peninsula under his rule.

Evora, Graça.

A little to the south of the cathedral of Evora, and a little lower down the hill, stands the Graça or church of the canons of St. Augustine. Begun during the reign of Dom João III., the nave and chancel, in which there is a fine tomb, have many details which recall the Conceicão at Thomar, such as windows set in sham perspective. But they were long in building, and the now broken down barrel vault and the curious porch were not added till the reign of Dom Sebastião, while the monastic buildings were finished about the same time.

This porch is most extraordinary. Below, there are in front four well-proportioned and well-designed Doric columns; beyond them and next the outer columns are large projecting pilasters forming buttresses, not unlike the buttresses in some of the earlier cloisters. Above the entablature, which runs round these buttresses, there stand on the two central columns two tall Ionic semi-columns, surmounted by an entablature and pointed pediment, and enclosing a large window set back in sham perspective. On either side large solid square panels are filled by huge rosettes several feet across, and above them half-pediments filled with shields reach up to the central pediment but at a lower level. Above these pediments another raking moulding runs up supported on square blocks, while on the top of the upper buttresses there sit figures of giant boys with globes on their backs; winged figures also kneel on the central pediment.

It will be seen that this is one of the most extraordinary erections in the world. Though built of granite some of the detail is quite fine, and the lower columns are well proportioned; but the upper part is ridiculously heavy and out of keeping with the rest, and inconceivably ill-designed. The different parts also are ill put together and look as if they had belonged to distinct buildings designed on a totally different scale. 243

Evora University.

Not much need be said of the Jesuit University founded at Evora by the Cardinal in 1559 and suppressed by the Marques de Pombal. Now partly a school and partly an orphanage, the great hall for conferring degrees is in ruins, but the courtyard with its two ranges of galleries still stands. The court is very large, and the galleries have round arches and white marble columns, but is somehow wanting in interest. The church too is very poor, though the private chapel with barrel vault and white marble dome is better, yet the whole building shows, like the Graça porch, that classic architecture was not yet fully understood, for Diogo de Torralva had not yet finished his cloister at Thomar, nor had Terzi begun to work in Lisbon.

When Dom João III. died in 1557 he was succeeded by his grandson Sebastião, who was then only three years old. At first his grandmother, Dona Catharina, was regent, but she was thoroughly Spanish, and so unpopular. For five years she withstood the intrigues of her brother-in-law, Cardinal Henry, but at last in 1562 retired to Spain in disgust. The Cardinal then became regent, but the country was really governed by two brothers, of whom the elder, Luis Gonçalves da Câmara, a Jesuit, was confessor to the young king.

Between them Dom Sebastião grew up a dreamy bigot whose one ambition was to lead a crusade against the Moors—an ambition in which popular rumour said he was encouraged by the Jesuits at the instigation of his cousin, Philip of Spain, who would profit so much by his death.

Since the wealth of the Indies had begun to fill the royal treasury, the Cortes had not been summoned, so there was no one able to oppose his will, when at last an expedition sailed in 1578.

At this time the country had been nearly drained of men by India and Brazil, so a large part of the army consisted of mercenaries; peculation too had emptied the treasury, and there was great difficulty in finding money to pay the troops.

Yet the expedition started, and landing first at Tangier afterwards moved on to Azila, which Mulay Ahmed, a pretender to the Moorish umbrella, had handed over.

On July 29th, Dom Sebastião rashly started to march inland from Azila. The army suffered terribly from heat and thirst, and was quite worn out before it met the reigning 244 amir, Abd-el-Melik, at Alcacer-Quebir, or El-Kasar-el-Kebir, 'the great castle,' on the 3rd of August.

Next morning the battle began, and though Abd-el-Melik died almost at once, the Moors, surrounding the small Christian army, were soon victorious. Nine thousand were killed, and of the rest all were taken prisoners except fifty. Both the Pretender and Dom Sebastião fell, and with his death and the destruction of his army the greatness of Portugal disappeared.

For two years, till 1580, his feeble old grand-uncle the Cardinal Henry sat on the throne, but when he died without nominating an heir none of Dom Manoel's descendants were strong enough to oppose Philip II. of Spain. Philip was indeed a grandson of Dom Manoel through his mother Isabel, but the duchess of Braganza, daughter of Dom Duarte, duke of Guimarães, Cardinal Henry's youngest brother, had really a better claim.

But the spirit of the nation was changed, she dared not press her claims, and few supported the prior of Crato, whose right was at least as good as had been that of Dom João I., and so Philip was elected at Thomar in April 1580.

Besides losing her independence Portugal lost her trade, for Holland and England both now regarded her as part of their great enemy, Spain, and so harried her ports and captured her treasure ships. Brazil was nearly lost to the Dutch, who also succeeded in expelling the Portuguese from Ceylon and from the islands of the East Indies, so that when the sixty years' captivity was over and the Spaniards expelled, Portugal found it impossible to recover the place she had lost.

It is then no wonder that almost before the end of the century money for building began to fail, and that some of the churches begun then were never finished; and yet for about the first twenty or thirty years of the Spanish occupation building went on actively, especially in Lisbon and at Coimbra, where many churches were planned by Filippo Terzi, or by the two Alvares and others. Filippo Terzi seems first to have been employed at Lisbon by the Jesuits in building their church of São Roque, begun about 1570.[162]

Lisbon, São Roque.

Outside the church is as plain as possible; the front is divided into three by single Doric pilasters set one on each 245 side of the main door and two at each corner. Similar pilasters stand on these, separated from them only by a shallow cornice. The main cornice is larger, but the pediment is perfectly plain. Three windows, one with a pointed and two with round pediments, occupy the spaces left between the upper pilasters. The inside is richer; the wooden ceiling is painted, the shallow chancel and the side chapels vaulted with barrel vaults, of which those in the chapels are enriched with elaborate strapwork. Above the chapels are square-headed windows, and then a corbelled cornice. Even this is plain, and it owes most of its richness to the paintings and to the beautiful tiles which cover part of the walls.[163]

The three other great churches which were probably also designed by Terzi are Santo Antão, Sta. Maria do Desterro, and São Vicente de Fora.

Of these the great earthquake of 1755 almost entirely destroyed the first two and knocked down the dome of the last.

São Vicente de Fora.

Though not the first to be built, São Vicente being the least injured may be taken before the others. It is a large church, being altogether about 236 feet long by 75 wide, and consists of a nave of three bays with connected chapels on each side, a transept with the fallen dome at the crossing, a square chancel, a retro-choir for the monks about 45 feet deep behind the chancel, and to the west a porch between two tall towers.

On the south side are two large square cloisters of no great interest with a sacristy between—in which all the kings of the House of Braganza lie in velvet-covered coffins—and the various monastic buildings now inhabited by the patriarch of Lisbon.

The outside is plain, except for the west front, which stands at the top of a great flight of steps. On the west front two orders of pilasters are placed one above the other. Of these the lower is Doric, of more slender proportions than usual, while the upper has no true capitals beyond the projecting entablature and corbels on the frieze. Single pilasters divide the centre of the front into three equal parts and coupled pilasters stand at the corners of the towers. In the central part three plain arches open on to the porch, with a pedimented niche above each. In the tower the niches are placed lower with oblong openings above and below. 246

Above the entablature of the lower order there are three windows in the middle flanked by Ionic pilasters and surmounted by pediments, while in the tower are large round-headed niches with pediments. (Fig. 93.)

The entablature of the upper order is carried straight across the whole front, with nothing above it in the centre but a balustrading interrupted by obelisk-bearing pedestals, **PLAN OF SÃO VICENTE** but at the ends the towers rise in one more square story flanked with short Doric pilasters. Round-arched openings for bells occur on each side, and within the crowning balustrade with its obelisks a stone dome rises to an eight-sided domed lantern.

Like all the church, the front is built of beautiful limestone, rivalling Carrara marble in whiteness, and seen down the narrow street which runs uphill from across the small *praça* the whole building is most imposing. It would have been even more satisfactory had the central part been a little narrower, and had there been something to mark the barrel vault within; the omission too of the lower order, which is so much taller than the upper, would have been an improvement, but even with these defects the design is most stately, and refreshingly free of all the fussy over-elaboration and the fantastic piling up of pediments which soon became too common.

But if the outside deserves such praise, the inside is worthy of far more. The great stone barrel vault is simply coffered with square panels. The chapel arches are singularly plain, and spring from a good moulding which projects nearly to the face of the pilasters.

<table>
<tr><td style="text-align:center">FIG. 93.</td><td style="text-align:center">FIG. 94.</td></tr>
<tr><td style="text-align:center">LISBON</td><td style="text-align:center">LISBON</td></tr>
<tr><td style="text-align:center">SÃO VICENTE DE FORA.</td><td style="text-align:center">SÃO VICENTE DE FORA.</td></tr>
</table>

247 Two of these stand between each chapel, and have very beautiful capitals founded on the Doric but with a long fluted neck ornamented in front by a bunch of crossed arrows and at the corners with acanthus leaves, and with egg and tongue carved on the moulding below the Corinthian abacus. Of the entablature, only the frieze and architrave is broken round the pilasters; for the cornice with its great mutules runs straight round the whole church, supported over the chapels by carving out the triglyphs—of which there is one over each pilaster, and two in the space between each pair of pilasters—so as to form corbels.

Only the pendentives of the dome and the panelled drum remain; the rest was replaced after the earthquake by wooden ceiling pierced with skylights. (Fig. 94.)

Though so simple—there is no carved ornament except in the beautiful capitals—the interior is one of the most imposing to be seen anywhere, and though not really very large gives a wonderful impression of space and size, being in this respect one of the most successful of classic churches. It is only necessary to compare São Vicente de Fora with the great clumsy cathedral which Herrera had begun to build five years earlier at Valladolid to see how immensely superior Terzi was to his Spanish contemporary. Even in his masterpiece, the church of the Escorial, Herrera did not succeed in giving such spacious greatness, for, though half as large again, the Escorial church is imposing rather from its stupendous weight and from the massiveness of its granite piers than from the beauty of its proportions.

Philip took a great interest in the building of the Escorial, and also had the plans of São Vicente submitted to him in 1590. This plan, signed by him in November 1590, was drawn by João Nunes Tinouco, so that it is possible that Tinouco was the actual designer and not Terzi, but Tinouco was still alive sixty years later when he published a plan of Lisbon, and so must have been very young in 1590. It is probable, therefore, that tradition is right in assigning São Vicente to Terzi, and even if it be actually the work of Tinouco, he has here done little but copy what his master had already done elsewhere.

Lisbon, Santo Antão.

After São Roque the first church begun by Terzi was Santo Antão, now attached to the hospital of São José. Begun in 1579 it was not finished till 1652, only to be destroyed by 248 the earthquake in 1755. As at São Vicente, the west front has a lower order of huge Doric pilasters nearly fifty feet high. There is no porch, but three doors with poor windows above which look as if they had been built after the earthquake.

Unfortunately, nearly all above the lower entablature is gone, but enough is left to show that the upper order was Ionic and very short, and that the towers were to rise behind buttress-like curves descending from the central part to two obelisks placed above the coupled corner pilasters.

The inside was almost exactly like São Vicente, but larger.

Lisbon, Santa Maria do Desterro.

Santa Maria do Desterro was begun later than either of the last two, in 1591. Unlike them the two orders of the west front are short and of almost equal size, Doric below and Ionic above. The arches of the porch reach up to the lower entablature, and the windows above are rather squat; it looks as if there was to have been a third order above, but it is all gone.

The inside was of the usual pattern, except that the pilasters were not coupled between the chapels, that they were panelled, and that above the low chapel arches there are square windows looking into a gallery.

Torreão do Paço.

Besides these churches Terzi built for Philip a large addition to the royal palace in the shape of a great square tower or pavilion, called the Torreão. The palace then stood to the west of what is now called the Praça do Commercio, and the Torreão jutted out over the Tagus. It seems to have had five windows on the longer and four on the shorter sides, to have been two stories in height, and to have been covered by a great square dome-shaped roof, with a lantern at the top and turrets at the corners. Pilasters stood singly between each window and in pairs at the corners, and the windows all had pediments. Now, not a stone of it is left, as it was in the palace square, the Terreno do Paço da Ribeira, that the earthquake was at its worst, swallowing up the palace and overwhelming thousands of people in the waves of the river.

Coimbra, Sé Nova.

Meanwhile the great Jesuit church at Coimbra, now the Sé Nova or new cathedral, had been gradually rising. Founded by Dom João III. in 1552, and dedicated to the Onze mil Virgems, it cannot have been begun in its present form till much later, till about 1580, while the main, or south, front seems even later still.[164]249

Inside, the church consists of a nave of four bays with side chapels—in one of which there is a beautiful Manoelino font—transepts and chancel with a drumless dome over the crossing. In some respects the likeness to São Vicente is very considerable; there are coupled Doric pilasters between the chapels, the barrel vault is coffered, and the chapel arches are extremely plain. But here the likeness ends. The pilasters are panelled and have very simple moulded capitals; the entablature is quite ordinary, without triglyphs or mutules, and is broken round each pair of pilasters; the coffers on the vault are very deep, and are scarcely moulded; and, above all, the proportions are quite different as the nave is too wide for its height, and the drum is terribly needed to lift up the dome. In short, the architect seems to have copied the dispositions of Santo Antão and has done his best to spoil them, and yet he has at the same time succeeded in making the interior look large, though with an almost Herrera-like clumsiness.

The south front is even more like Santo Antão. As there, three doors take the place of the porch, and the only difference below is that each Doric pilaster is flanked by half pilasters. Above the entablature the front breaks out into a wild up-piling of various pediments, but even here the likeness to Santo Antão is preserved, in that a great curve comes down from the outer Ionic pilasters of the central part, to end, however, not in obelisks, but in a great volute: the small towers too are set much further back. Above, as below, the central part is divided into three. Of these the two outer, flanked by Ionic pilasters on pedestals, are finished off above with curved pediments broken to admit of obelisks. The part between these has a large window below, a huge coat of arms above, and rises high above the sides to a pediment so arranged that while the lower mouldings form an angle the upper form a curve on which stand two finials and a huge cross. (Fig. 95.)

Oporto, Collegio Novo.

Very soon this fantastic way of piling up pieces of pediment and of entablature became only too popular, being copied for instance in the Collegio Novo at Oporto, where, however, the design is not quite so bad as the towers are brought forward and are carried up considerably higher. But apart from this horrid misuse of classic details the greatest fault of the façade at Coimbra is the disproportionate size of 250 some of the details; the obelisks and the cherubs' heads on which they stand, the statues at the ends, and the central cross, and above all the colossal acanthus leaves in the great scrolls are of such a size as entirely to dwarf all the rest.

From what remains of the front of Santo Antão, it looks as if it and the front of the Sé Velha had been very much alike. Santo Antão was not quite finished till 1652, so that it is probable that the upper part of the west front dates from the seventeenth century, long after

Terzi's death, and that the Sé Nova at Coimbra was finished about the same time, and perhaps copied from it.

Coimbra, Misericordia.

But it was not only Terzi's churches which were copied at Coimbra. While the Sé Nova, then, and for nearly two hundred years more, the church of the Jesuits, was still being built, the architect of the chief pateo of the Misericordia took Diogo de Torralva's cloister at Thomar as his model.

It was in the year 1590 that Cardinal Affonso de Castello Branco began to build the headquarters of the Misericordia of Coimbra, founded in 1500 as a simple confraternity. The various offices of the institution, including a church, the halls whose ceilings have been already mentioned, and hospital dormitories—all now turned into an orphanage—are built round two courtyards, one only of which calls for special notice, for nearly everything else has been rebuilt or altered. In this court or cloister, the plan of the Claustro dos Filippes has been followed in that there are three wide arches on each side, and between them—but not in the corners, and further apart than at Thomar—a pair of columns. In this case the space occupied by one arch is scarcely wider than that occupied by the two fluted Doric columns and the square-headed openings between them. Another change is that the complete entablature with triglyphs and metopes is only found above the columns, for the arches rise too high to leave room for more than the cornice. (Fig. 96.)

The upper story is quite different, for it has only square-headed windows, though the line of the columns is carried up by slender and short Ionic columns; a sloping tile roof rests immediately on the upper cornice, above which rise small obelisks placed over the columns.

Coimbra, Episcopal Palace.

At about the same time the Cardinal built a long loggia on the west side of the entrance court of his palace at Coimbra. The hill on which the palace is built being extremely

FIG. 95.   **FIG. 96.**

SÉ NOVA, COIMBRA.   **COIMBRA**
MISERICORDIA.

251 steep, an immense retaining wall, some fifty or sixty feet high, bounds the courtyard on the west, and it is on the top of this wall that the loggia is built forming a covered way two stories in height and uniting the Manoelino palace on the north with some offices which bound the yard on the south. This covered way is formed by two rows of seven arches, each resting on Doric columns, with a balustrading between the outer columns on the top of the great wall. The ceiling is of wood and forms the floor of the upper story, where the columns are Ionic and support a continuous architrave. The whole is quite simple and unadorned, but at the same time singularly picturesque, since the view through the arches, over the old cathedral and the steeply descending town, down to the convent of Santa Clara and the wooded hills beyond the Mondego, is most beautiful; besides, the courtyard itself is not without interest. In the centre stands a fountain, and on the south side a stair, carried on a flying half-arch, leads up to a small porch whose steep pointed roof rests on two walls, and on one small column.

Coimbra, Sé Velha Sacristy.

The same bishop also built the sacristy of the old cathedral. Entered by a passage from the south transept, and built across the back of the apse, it is an oblong room with coffered barrel vault, lit by a large semicircular window at the north end. The cornice, of which the frieze is adorned with eight masks, rests on corbels. On a black-and-white marble lavatory is the date 1593 and the Cardinal's arms. The two ends are divided into three tiled panels by Doric columns, and on the longer sides are presses.

Altogether it is very like the sacristy of Santa Cruz built some thirty years later, but plainer.

By 1590 or so several Portuguese followers of Terzi had begun to build churches, founded on his work, but in some respects less like than is the Sé Nova at Coimbra. Such churches are best seen at Coimbra, where many were built, all now more or less deserted and turned to base uses. Three at least of these stand on either side of the long Rua Sophia which leads northwards from the town.

Coimbra, São Domingos.

The oldest seems to be the church of São Domingos, founded by the dukes of Aveiro, but never finished. Only the chancel with its flanking chapels and the transept have been built. Two of the churches at Lisbon and the Sé Nova of Coimbra are noted for their extremely long Doric pilasters. 252 Here, in the chancel the pilasters and the half columns in the transept are Ionic, and even more disproportionately tall. The architrave is unadorned, the frieze has corbels set in pairs, and between the pairs curious shields and strapwork, and the cornice is enriched with dentils, egg and tongue and modillions. Most elaborate of all is the barrel vault, where each coffer is filled with round or square panels surrounded with strapwork.

This vault and the cornice were probably not finished till well on in the seventeenth century, for on the lower, and probably earlier vaults, of the side chapels the ornamentation is much finer and more delicate.

The transepts were to have been covered with groined vaults of which only the springing has been built. In the north transept and in one of the chapels there still stand great stone reredoses once much gilt, but now all broken and dusty and almost hidden behind the diligences and cabs with which the church is filled. The great fault in São Domingos is the use of the same order both for the tall pilasters in the chancel, and for the shorter ones in the side chapels; so that the taller, which are twice as long and of about the same diameter, are ridiculously lanky and thin.

Coimbra, Carmo.

Almost opposite São Domingos is the church of the Carmo, begun by Frey Amador Arraes, bishop of Portalegre about 1597. The church is an oblong hall about 135 feet long, including the chancel, by nearly 40 wide, roofed with a coffered barrel vault. On each side of the nave are two rectangular and one semicircular chapel; the vaults of the chapel are beautifully enriched with sunk panels of various shapes. The great reredos covers the whole east wall with two stories of coupled columns, niches and painted panels.

Coimbra, Graça.

Almost exactly the same is the Graça church next door, both very plain and almost devoid of interest outside.

São Bento.

Equally plain is the unfinished front of the church of São Bento up on the hill near the botanical gardens. It was designed by Baltazar Alvares for Dom Diogo de Murça, rector of the University in 1600, but not consecrated till thirty-four years later. The church, which inside is about 164 feet long, consists of a nave with side chapels, measuring 60 feet by about 35, a transept of the same width, and a square chancel. Besides there is a deep porch in front between two oblong towers, which have never been carried up above the roof. 253

The porch is entered by three arches, one in the middle wider and higher than the others. Above are three niches with shell heads, and then three windows, two oblong and one round, all set in rectangular frames. At the sides there are broad pilasters below, with the usual lanky Doric pilasters above reaching to the main cornice, above which there now rises only an unfinished gable end. The inside is much more pleasing. The barrel vaults of the chapels are beautifully panelled and enriched with egg and tongue; between each, two pilasters rise only to the moulding from which the chapel arches spring, and support smaller pilasters with a niche between. In the spandrels of the arches are rather badly carved angels holding shields, and on the arches themselves, as at São Marcos, are cherubs' heads. A plain entablature runs along immediately above these arches, and from it to the main cornice, the walls, covered with blue and white tiles, are perfectly blank, broken only by square-headed windows. Only at the crossing do pilasters run up to the vault, and they are of the usual attenuated Doric form. As usual the roof is covered with plain coffers, as is also the drumless dome.

This is very like the Carmo and the Graça, which repeat the fault of leaving a blank tiled wall above the chapels, and it is quite possible that they too may have been built by Alvares; the plan is evidently founded on that of one of Terzi's churches, as São Vicente, or on that of the Sé Nova, but though some of the detail is charming there is a want of unity

126

between the upper and lower parts which is found in none of Terzi's work, nor even in the heavier Sé Nova.[165]

Lisbon, São Bento.

Baltazar Alvares seems to have been specially employed by the order of St. Benedict, for not only did he build their monasteries at Coimbra but also São Bento, now the Cortes in Lisbon, as well as São Bento da Victoria at Oporto, his greatest and most successful work.

Oporto, São Bento.

The plan is practically the same as that of São Bento at Coimbra, but larger. Here, however, there are no windows over the chapel arches, nor any dome at the crossing. Built of grey granite, a certain heaviness seems suitable enough, and the great coffered vault is not without grandeur, while the gloom of the inside is lit up by huge carved and gilt altar-pieces and by the elaborate stalls in the choir gallery. 254

CHAPTER XVIII
OTHER BUILDINGS OF THE LATER RENAISSANCE, TILL THE EXPULSION OF THE SPANIARDS

IN the last chapter the most important works of Terzi and of his pupils have been described, and it is now necessary to go back and tell of various buildings which do not conform to his plan of a great barrel-vaulted nave with flanking chapels, though the designers of some of these buildings have copied such peculiarities as the tall and narrow pilasters of which his school was so fond, and which, as will be seen, ultimately degenerated into mere pilaster strips.

Vianna do Castello, Misericordia.

But before speaking of the basilican and other churches of this time, the Misericordia at Vianna do Castello must be described.[166]

The Misericordia of Vianna stands on the north side of the chief square of the town, and was built in 1589 by one João Lopez, whose father had designed the beautiful fountain which stands near by.

It is a building of very considerable interest, as there seems to be nothing else like it in the country. The church of the Misericordia, a much older building ruined by later alteration, is now only remarkable for the fine blue and white tile decoration with which its walls are covered. Just to the west of it, and at the corner of the broad street in which is a fine Manoelino house belonging to the Visconde de Carreira, stands the building designed by Lopez. The front towards the street is plain, but that overlooking the square highly decorated.

At the two corners are broad rusticated bands which run up uninterrupted to the cornice; between them the front is divided into three stories of open loggias. Of these the lowest has five round arches resting on Ionic columns; in

FIG. 97.
VIANNA DO CASTELLO.
MISERICORDIA.

255 the second, on a solid parapet, stand four whole and two half 'terms' or atlantes which support an entablature with wreath-enriched frieze; corbels above the heads of the figures cross the frieze, and others above them the low blocking course, and on them are other terms supporting the main cornice, which is not of great projection. A simple pediment rises above the four central figures, surmounted by a crucifix and containing a carving of a sun on a strapwork shield. (Fig. 97.)

The whole is of granite and the figures and mouldings are distinctly rude, and yet it is eminently picturesque and original, and shows that Lopez was a skilled designer if but a poor sculptor.

Beja, São Thiago.

Coming now to the basilican churches. That of São Thiago at Beja was begun in 1590 by Jorge Rodrigues for Archbishop Theotonio of Evora. It has a nave and aisles of six bays covered with groined vaults resting on Doric columns, a transept and three shallow rectangular chapels to the east. The clerestory windows are round.

Azeitão, São Simão.

127

Much the same plan had been followed a little earlier by Affonso de Albuquerque, son of the great viceroy of India, when about 1570 he built the church of São Simão close to his country house of Bacalhôa, at Azeitão not far from Setubal. São Simão is a small church with nave and aisles of five bays, the latter only being vaulted, with arcades resting on Doric columns; at first there was a tower at each corner, but they fell in 1755, and only one has been rebuilt. Most noticeable in the church are the very fine tiles put up in 1648, with saintly figures over each arch. They are practically the same as those in the parish church of Alvito.

Evora, Cartuxa.

Another basilican church of this date is that of the Cartuxa or Charter House,[167] founded by the same Archbishop Theotonio in 1587, a few miles out of Evora. Only the west front, built about 1594 of black and white marble, deserves mention. Below there is a porch, spreading beyond the church, and arranged exactly like the lower Claustro dos Filippes at Thomar, with round arches separated by two Doric columns on pedestals, but with a continuous entablature carried above the arches on large corbelled keystones. Behind rises the front in two stories. The lower has three windows, square-headed and separated by Ionic columns, two on each side, with niches between. Single Ionic columns also stand at the outer angles of the aisles. In the upper story 256 the central part is carried up to a pediment by Corinthian columns resting on the Ionic below; between them is a large statued niche surrounded by panels.

Unfortunately the simplicity of the design is spoilt by the broken and curly volutes which sprawl across the aisles, by ugly finials at the corners, and by a rather clumsy balustrading to the porch.

Beja, Misericordia.

The interior of the Misericordia at Beja, a square, divided into nine smaller vaulted squares by arches resting on fine Corinthian columns, with altar recesses beyond, looks as if it belonged to the time of Dom João III., but if so the front must have been added later. This is very simple, but at the same time strong and unique. The triple division inside is marked by three great rusticated Doric pilasters on which rest a simple entablature and parapet. Between are three round arches, enclosing three doors of which the central has a pointed pediment, while over the others a small round window lights the interior.

Oporto, Nossa Senhora da Serra do Pilar.

But by far the most original of all the buildings of this later renaissance is the monastery of Nossa Senhora da Serra do Pilar in Villa Nova de Gaya, the suburb of Oporto which lies south of the Douro. Standing on a high granite knoll, which rises some fifty feet above the country to the south, and descends by an abrupt precipice on the north to the deep-flowing river, here some two hundred yards wide, and running in a narrow gorge, the monastery and its hill have more than once played an important part in history. From there Wellington, in 1809, was able to reconnoitre the French position across the river while his army lay hidden behind the rocks; and it was from a creek just a little to the east that the first barges started for the north bank with the men who seized the unfinished seminary and held it till enough were across to make Soult see he must retreat or be cut off. Later, in 1832, the convent, defended for Queen Maria da Gloria, was much knocked about by the besieging army of Dom Miguel.

The Augustinians had begun to build on the hill in 1540, but none of the present monastery can be earlier than the seventeenth century, the date 1602 being found in the cloister.

The plan of the whole building is most unusual and original: the nave is a circle some seventy-two feet in diameter, surmounted by a dome, and surrounded by eight shallow chapels, of which one contains the entrance and another is 257 prolonged to form a narrow chancel. This chancel leads to a larger square choir behind the high altar, and east of it is a round cloister sixty-five feet across. The various monastic buildings are grouped round the choir and cloister, leaving the round nave standing free. The outside of the circle is two stories in height, divided by a plain cornice carried round the pilasters which mark the recessed chapels within. The face of the wall above this cornice is set a little back, and the pilaster strips are carried up a short distance to form a kind of pedestal, and are then set back

128

with a volute and obelisk masking the offset. The main cornice has two large corbels to each bay, and carries a picturesque balustrading within which rises a tile roof covering the dome and crowned by a small lantern at the top. The west door has two Ionic columns on each side; a curious niche with corbelled sides rises above it to the lower cornice; and the church is lit by a square-headed window pierced through the upper part of each bay. Only the pilasters, cornices, door and window dressings are of granite ashlar, all the rest being of rubble plastered and whitewashed.

PLAN OF NOSSA SENHORA DO PILAR

Now the eucalyptus-trees planted round the church have grown so tall that only the parapet can be seen rising above the tree-tops.

Though much of the detail of the outside is far from being classical or correct, the whole is well proportioned and well put together, but the same cannot be said of the inside. Pilasters of inordinate height have been seen in some of the Lisbon churches, but compared with these which here stand in couples between the chapels they are short and well proportioned. These pilasters, which are quite seventeen diameters high, have for capitals coarse copies of those in São Vicente de Fora in Lisbon. In São Vicente the cornice was carried on corbels crossing the frieze, and so was continuous 258 and unbroken. Here all the lower mouldings of the cornice are carried round the corbels and the pilasters so that only the two upper are continuous, an arrangement which is anything but an improvement. Another unpleasing feature are the three niches which, with hideous painted figures, are placed one above the other between the pilasters. The chancel arch reaches up to the main cornice, but those of the door and chapel recesses are low enough to leave room for the windows. The dome is divided into panels of various shapes by broad flat ribs with coarse mouldings. The chancel and choir beyond have barrel vaults divided into simple square panels.

The church then, though interesting from its plan, is—inside especially—remarkably unpleasing, though it is perhaps only fair to attribute a considerable part of this disagreeable effect to the state of decay into which it has fallen—a state which has only advanced far enough to be squalid and dirty without being in the least picturesque. Far more pleasing than the church is the round cloister behind. In it the thirty-six Ionic columns are much better proportioned, and the capitals better carved; on the cornice stands an attic, rendered necessary by the barrel vault, heavy indeed, but not too heavy for the columns below. This attic is panelled, and on it stand obelisk-bearing pedestals, one above each column, and between them pediments of strapwork. (Fig. 98.)

Had this cloister been square it would have been in no way very remarkable, but its round shape as well as the fig-trees that now grow in the garth, and the many plants which sprout from joints in the cornice, make it one of the most picturesque buildings in the country. The rest of the monastic buildings have been in ruins since the siege of 1832.

Coimbra, Santa Cruz Sacristy.

The sacristy of Santa Cruz at Coimbra must have been begun before Nossa Senhora da Serra had been finished. Though so much later—for it is dated 1622—the architect of this sacristy has followed much more closely the good Italian forms introduced by Terzi. Like that of the Sé Velha, the sacristy of Santa Cruz is a rectangular building, and measures about 52 feet long by 26 wide; each of the longer sides is divided into three bays by Doric pilasters which have good capitals, but are themselves cut up into many small panels. The cornice is partly carried on corbels as in the Serra church, but here the effect is much better. There are large semicircular windows, divided into three lights at each end, and

FIG. 99.
COIMBRA
SACRISTY OF STA. CRUZ.

FIG. 98.
OPORTO
CLOISTER, NOSSA SENHORA DA SERRA DO PILAR.

259 the barrel vault is covered with deep eight-sided coffers. One curious feature is the way the pilasters in the north-east corner are carried on corbels, so as to leave room for two doors, one of which leads into the chapter-house behind the chancel. (Fig. 99.)

Lisbon, Santa Engracia.

129

Twenty years later was begun the church of Santa Engracia in Lisbon. It was planned on a great scale; a vast dome in the centre surrounded by four equal apses, and by four square towers. It has never been finished, and now only rises to the level of the main cornice; but had the dome been built it would undoubtedly have been one of the very finest of the renaissance buildings in the country.

Like the Serra church it is, outside, two stories in height having Doric pilasters below—coupled at the angles of the towers—and Ionic above. In the western apse, the pilasters are replaced by tall detached Doric columns, and the Ionic pilasters above by buttresses which grow out of voluted curves. Large, simply moulded windows are placed between the upper pilasters, with smaller blank windows above them, while in the western apse arches with niches set between pediment-bearing pilasters lead into the church.

Here, in Santa Engracia, is a church designed in the simplest and most severe classic form, and absolutely free of all the fantastic misuse of fragments of classic detail which had by that time become so common, and which characterise such fronts as those of the Sé Nova at Coimbra or the Collegio Novo at Oporto. The niches over the entrance arches are severe but well designed, as are the windows in the towers and all the mouldings. Perhaps the only fault of the detail is that the Doric pilasters and columns are too tall.

Now in its unfinished state the whole is heavy and clumsy, but at the same time imposing and stately from its great size; but it is scarcely fair to judge so unfinished a building, which would have been very different had its dome and four encompassing towers risen high above the surrounding apses and the red roofs of the houses which climb steeply up the hillside.

Coimbra, Santa Clara.

The new convent of Santa Clara at Coimbra was begun about the same time—in 1640—on the hillside overlooking the Mondego and the old church which the stream has almost buried; and, more fortunate than Santa Engracia, it has been finished, but unlike it is a building of little interest.

The church is a rectangle with huge Doric pilasters on 260 either side supporting a heavy coffered roof. There are no aisles, but shallow altar recesses with square-headed windows above. The chancel at the south end is like the nave but narrower; the two-storied nuns' choir is to the north. As the convent is still occupied it cannot be visited, but contains the tomb of St. Isabel, brought from the old church, in the lower choir, and her silver shrine in the upper. Except for the cloister, which, designed after the manner of the Claustro dos Filippes at Thomar, has coupled Doric columns between the arches, and above, niches flanked by Ionic columns between square windows, the rest of the nunnery is even heavier and more barrack-like than the church. Indeed almost the only interest of the church is the use of the huge Doric pilasters, since from that time onward such pilasters, usually as clumsy and as large, are found in almost every church.

This fondness for Doric is probably due to the influence of Terzi, who seems to have preferred it to all the other orders, though he always gave his pilasters a beautiful and intricate capital. In any case from about 1580 onwards scarcely any other order on a large scale is used either inside or outside, and by 1640 it had grown to the ugly size used in Santa Clara and in nearly all later buildings, the only real exception being perhaps in the work of the German who designed Mafra and rebuilt the Capella Mor at Evora. Such pilasters are found forming piers in the church built about 1600 to be the cathedral of Leiria, in the west front of the cathedral of Portalegre, where they are piled above each other in three stories, huge and tall below, short and thinner above, and in endless churches all over the country. Later still they degenerated into mere angle strips, as in the cathedral of Angra do Heroismo in the Azores and elsewhere.

Such a building as Santa Engracia is the real ending of Architecture in Portugal, and its unfinished state is typical of the poverty which had overtaken the country during the Spanish usurpation, when robbed of her commerce by Holland and by England, united against her will to a decaying power, she was unable to finish her last great work, while such buildings as she did herself finish—for it must not be forgotten that Mafra was designed by a foreigner—show a meanness of invention and design scarcely to be equalled in any other

130

land, a strange contrast to the exuberance of fancy lavished on the buildings of a happier age. 261

CHAPTER XIX
THE RESTORATION AND THE EIGHTEENTH CENTURY

WHEN elected at Thomar in 1580, Philip II. of Spain had sworn to govern Portugal only through Portuguese ministers, a promise which he seems to have kept. He was fully alive to the importance of commanding the mouth of the Tagus and the splendid harbour of Lisbon, and had he fixed his capital there instead of at Madrid it is quite possible that the two countries might have remained united.

For sixty years the people endured the ever-growing oppression and misgovernment. The duque de Lerma, minister to Philip III., or II. of Portugal, and still more the Conde duque de Olivares under Philip IV., treated Portugal as if it were a conquered province.

In 1640, the very year in which Santa Engracia was begun, the regent was Margaret of Savoy, whose ministers, with hardly an exception, were Spaniards.

It will be remembered that when Philip II. was elected in 1580, Dona Catharina, duchess of Braganza and daughter of Dom Manoel's sixth son, Duarte, duke of Guimarães, had been the real heir to the throne of her uncle, the Cardinal King. Her Philip had bought off by a promise of the sovereignty of Brazil, a promise which he never kept, and now in 1640 her grandson Dom João, eighth duke of Braganza and direct descendant of Affonso, a bastard son of Dom João I., had succeeded to all her rights.

He was an unambitious and weak man, fond only of hunting and music, so Olivares had thought it safe to restore to him his ancestral lands; and to bind him still closer to Spain had given him a Spanish wife, Luisa Guzman, daughter of the duke of Medina Sidonia. Matters, however, turned out very differently from what he had expected. A gypsy had once told Dona Luisa that she would be a queen, and a queen 262 she was determined to be. With difficulty she persuaded her husband to become the nominal head of the conspiracy for the expulsion of the Spaniards, and on the 1st of December 1640 the first blow was struck by the capture of the regent and her ministers in the palace at Lisbon. Next day, December 2nd, the duke of Braganza was saluted as King Dom João IV. at Villa Viçosa, his country home beyond Evora.

The moment of the revolution was well chosen, for Spain was at that time struggling with a revolt which had broken out in Cataluña, and so was unable to send any large force to crush Dom João. All the Indian and African colonies at once drove out the Spaniards, and in Brazil the Dutch garrisons which had been established there by Count Maurice of Nassau were soon expelled.

Though a victory was soon gained over the Spaniards at Montijo, the war dragged on for twenty-eight years, and it was only some years after Don John of Austria 168 had been defeated at Almeixial by Schomberg (who afterwards took service under William of Orange) that peace was finally made in 1668. Portugal then ceded Ceuta, and Spain acknowledged the independence of the revolted kingdom, and granted to its sovereign the title of Majesty.

It is no great wonder, then, that with such a long-continued war and an exhausted treasury a building like Santa Engracia should have remained unfinished, and it would have been well for the architecture of the country had this state of poverty continued, for then far more old buildings would have survived unaltered and unspoiled.

Unfortunately by the end of the seventeenth century trade had revived, and the discovery of diamonds and of gold in Brazil had again brought much wealth to the king.

Of the innumerable churches and palaces built during the eighteenth century scarcely any are worthy of mention, for perhaps the great convent palace of Mafra and the Capella Mor of the Sé at Evora are the only exceptions.

In the early years of that century King João V. made a vow that if a son was born to him, he would, on the site of the poorest monastery in the country, build the largest and the richest. At the same time anxious to emulate the glories of the Escorial, he determined that his building should contain a palace as well as a monastery—indeed it may almost be said 263 to contain two palaces, one for the king on the south, and one on the north for the queen.

Mafra.

A son was born, and the poorest monastery in the kingdom was found at Mafra, where a few Franciscans lived in some miserable buildings. Having found his site, King João had next to find an architect able to carry out his great scheme, and so low had native talent fallen, that the architect chosen was a foreigner, Frederic Ludovici or Ludwig, a German.

The first stone of the vast building was laid in 1717, and the church was dedicated thirteen years later, in 1730.[169]

The whole building may be divided into two main parts. One to the east, measuring some 560 feet by 350, and built round a large square courtyard, was devoted to the friars, and contained the convent entrance, the refectory, chapter-house, kitchen, and cells for two hundred and eighty brothers, as well as a vast library on the first floor.

The other and more extensive part to the west comprises the king's apartments on the south side, the queen's on the north, and between them the church.

It is not without interest to compare the plan of this palace or monastery with the more famous Escorial. Both cover almost exactly the same area,[170] but while in the Escorial the church is thrust back at the end of a vast patio, here it is brought forward to the very front. There the royal palace occupies only a comparatively small area in the north-west corner of the site, and the monastic part the whole lying south of the entrance patio and of the church; here the monastic part is thrust back almost out of sight, and the palace stretches all along the west front except where it is interrupted in the middle by the church.

Indeed the two buildings differ from one another much as did the characters of their builders. The gloomy fanaticism of Philip of Spain is exemplified by the preponderance of the monastic buildings no less than by his own small dark bed-closet opening only to the church close to the high altar. João V., pleasure-loving and luxurious, pushed the friars to the back, and made his own and the queen's rooms the most 264 prominent part of the whole building, and one cannot but feel that, though a monastery had to be built to fulfil a vow, the king was actuated not so much by religious zeal as by an ostentatious megalomania which led him to try and surpass the size of the Escorial.

PLAN OF MAFRA

To take the plan rather more in detail. The west front, about 740 feet long, is flanked by huge square projecting pavilions. The king's and the queen's apartments are each entered by rather low and insignificant doorways in the middle of the long straight blocks which join these pavilions to the church. These doors lead under the palace to large square courtyards, one on each side of the church, and forming on 265 the ground floor a cloister with a well-designed arcading of round arches, separated by Roman Doric shafts. The king's and the queen's blocks are practically identical, except that in the king's a great oval hall called the Sala dos actos takes the place of some smaller rooms between the cloister and the outer wall.

Between these blocks stands the church reached by a great flight of steps. It has a nave and aisles of three large and one small bay, a dome at the crossing, and transepts and chancel ending in apses. In front, flanking towers projecting beyond the aisles are united by a long entrance porch.

Between the secular and the monastic parts a great corridor runs north and south, and immediately beyond it a range of great halls, including the refectory at the north end and the chapter-house at the south. Further east the great central court with its surrounding cells divides the monastic entrance and great stair from such domestic buildings as the kitchen, the bakery, and the lavatory. Four stories of cells occupy the whole east side.

Though some parts of the palace and monastery such as the two entrance courts, the library, and the interior of the church, may be better than might have been expected from the date, it is quite impossible to speak at all highly of the building as a whole.

It is nearly all of the same height with flat paved roofs; indeed the only breaks are the corner pavilions and the towers and dome of the church.

The west side consists of two monotonous blocks, one on each side of the church, with three stories of windows. At either end is a great square projecting mass, rusticated on the lowest floor, with short pilaster strips between the windows on the first, and Corinthian pilasters on the second. The poor cornice is surmounted by a low attic, within which rises a hideous ogee plastered roof. (Fig. 100.)

The church in the centre loses much by not rising above the rest of the front, and the two towers, though graceful enough in outline, are poor in detail, and are finished off with a very ugly combination of hollow curves and bulbous domes.

The centre dome, too, is very poor in outline with a drum and lantern far too tall for its size; though of course, had the drum been of a better proportion, it would hardly have shown above the palace roof. 266

Still more monotonous are the other sides with endless rows of windows set in a pink plastered wall.

Very different is the outline of the Escorial, whose very plainness and want of detail suits well the rugged mountain side in which it is set. The main front with its high corner towers and their steep slate roofs, and with its high centre-piece, is far more impressive, and the mere reiteration of its endless featureless windows gives the Escorial an appearance of size quite wanting to Mafra. Above all the great church with massive dome and towers rises high above all the rest, and gives the whole a sense of unity and completeness which the smaller church of Mafra, though in a far more prominent place, entirely fails to do.

Poor though the church at Mafra is outside, inside there is much to admire, and but little to betray the late date. The porch has an effective vault of black and white marble, and domes with black and white panels cover the spaces under the towers. Inside the church is all built of white marble with panels and pilasters of pink marble from Pero Pinheiro on the road to Cintra. (Fig. 101.)

The whole church measures about 200 feet long by 100 wide, with a nave also 100 feet long. The central aisle is over 40 feet wide, and has two very well-proportioned Corinthian pilasters between each bay. Almost the only trace of the eighteenth century is found in the mouldings of the pendentive panels, and in the marble vault, but on the whole the church is stately and the detail refined and restrained.

The refectory, a very plain room with plastered barrel vault, 160 feet long by 40 wide, is remarkable only for the splendid slabs of Brazil wood which form the tables, and for the beautiful brass lamps which hang from the ceiling.

Much more interesting is the library which occupies the central part of the floor above. Over 200 feet long, it has a dome-surmounted transept in the middle, and a barrel vault divided into panels. All the walls are lined with bookcases painted white like the barrel vault and like the projecting gallery from which the upper shelves are reached. One half is devoted to religious, and one half to secular books, and in the latter each country has a space more or less large allotted to it. As scarcely any books seem to have been added since the building was finished, it should contain many a rare and valuable volume, and as all seem to be in excellent condition, they might well deserve a visit from some learned book-lover.

FIG. 100.	FIG. 101.
MAFRA	MAFRA
W. FRONT OF PALACE.	INTERIOR OF CHURCH.

267

Mafra does not seem to have ever had any interesting history. Within the lines of Torres Vedras, the palace escaped the worst ravages of the French invasion. In 1834 the two hundred and eighty friars were turned out, and since then most of the vast building has been turned into barracks, while the palace is but occasionally inhabited by the king when he comes to shoot in the great wooded *tapada* or enclosure which stretches back towards the east.

Evora, Capella Mor.

Just about the time that João V. was beginning his great palace at Mafra, the chapter of the cathedral of Evora came to the conclusion that the old Capella Mor was too small, and altogether unworthy of the dignity of an archiepiscopal see. So they determined to pull it

133

down, and naturally enough employed Ludovici to design the new one. The first stone was laid in 1717, and the chancel was consecrated in 1746 at the cost of about £27,000.

The outside, of white marble, is enriched with two orders of pilasters, Corinthian and Composite. Inside, white, pink and black marbles are used, the columns are composite, but the whole design is far poorer than anything at Mafra.

King João V. died in 1750 after a long and prosperous reign. Besides building Mafra he gave great sums of money to the Pope, and obtained in return the division of Lisbon into two bishoprics, and the title of Patriarch for the archbishop of Lisboa Oriental, or Eastern Lisbon.

When he died he was succeeded by Dom José, whose reign is noted for the terrible earthquake of 1755, and for the administration of the great Marques de Pombal. It was on the 1st of November, when the population of Lisbon was assembled in the churches for the services of All Saints' day, that the first shock was felt. This was soon followed by two others which laid the city in ruins, killing many people. Most who had escaped rushed to the river bank, where they with the splendid palace at the water's edge were all overwhelmed by an immense tidal wave.

The damage done to the city was almost incalculable. Scarcely a house remained uninjured, and of the churches nearly all were ruined. The cathedral was almost entirely destroyed, leaving only the low chapels and the romanesque nave and transepts standing, and of the later churches all were 268 ruined, and only São Roque and São Vicente de Fora—which lost its dome—remained to show what manner of churches were built at the end of the sixteenth century.

This is not the place to tell of the administration of the Marques de Pombal, who rose to eminence owing to the great ability he showed after this awful calamity, or to give a history of how he expelled the Jesuits, subdued the nobles, attempted to make Portugal a manufacturing country, abolished slavery and the differences between the *Old* and the *New Christians*, reformed the administration and the teaching of the University of Coimbra, and robbed the Inquisition of half its terrors by making its trials public. In Lisbon he rebuilt the central part of the town, laying out parallel streets, and surrounding the Praça do Commercio with great arcaded government offices; buildings remarkable rather for the fine white stone of which they are made, than for any architectural beauty. Indeed it is impossible to admire any of the buildings erected in Portugal since the earthquake; the palaces of the Necessidades and the Ajuda are but great masses of pink-washed plaster pierced with endless windows, and without any beauty of detail or of design.

Lisbon, Estrella.

Nor does the church of the Coração de Jesus, usually called the Estrella, call for any admiration. It copies the faults of Mafra, the tall drum, the poor dome, and the towers with bulbous tops.

Oporto, Torre dos Clerigos.

More vicious, indeed, than the Estrella, but much more original and picturesque, is the Torre dos Clerigos at Oporto, built by the clergy in 1755. It stands at the top of a steep hill leading down to the busiest part of the town. The tower is a square with rounded corners, and is of very considerable height. The main part is four stories in height, of which the lowest is the tallest and the one above it the shortest. All are adorned with pilasters or pilaster strips, and the third, in which is a large belfry window, has an elaborate cornice, rising over the window in a rounded pediment to enclose a great shield of arms. The fourth story is finished by a globe-bearing parapet, within which the tower rises to another parapet much corbelled out. The last or sixth story is set still further back and ends in a fantastic dome-shaped roof. In short, the tower is a good example of the wonderful and ingenious way in which the eighteenth-century builders of Portugal often contrived the strangest results by a use—or 269 misuse—of pieces of classic detail, forming a whole often more Chinese than Western in appearance, but at the same time not unpicturesque.[171]

Oporto, Quinta do Freixo.

A much more pleasing example of the same school—a school doubtless influenced by the bad example of Churriguera in Spain—is the house called the Quinta do Freixo on

134

the Douro a mile or so above the town. Here the four towers with their pointed slate roofs rise in so picturesque a way at the four corners, and the whole house blends so well with the parapets and terraces of the garden, that one can almost forgive the broken pediments which form so strange a gable over the door, and the still more strange shapes of the windows. Now that factory chimneys rise close on either side the charm is spoiled, but once the house, with its turrets, its vase-laden parapets, its rococo windows, and the slates painted pale blue that cover its walls, must have been a fit setting for the artificial civilisation of a hundred and fifty years ago, and for the ladies in dresses of silk brocade and gentlemen in flowered waistcoats and powdered hair who once must have gone up and down the terrace steps, or sat in the shell grottoes of the garden.

Queluz.

Though less picturesque and fantastic, the royal palace at Queluz, between Lisbon and Cintra, is another really pleasing example of the more sober rococo. Built by Dom Pedro III. about 1780, the palace is a long building with a low tiled roof, and the gardens are rich in fountains and statues.

Guimarães, Quinta.

Somewhat similar, but unfinished, and enriched with niches and statues, is a Quinta near the station at Guimarães. Standing on a slope, the garden descends northwards in beautiful terraces, whose fronts are covered with tiles. Being well cared for, it is rich in beautiful trees and shrubs.

Oporto, Hospital and Factory.

Much more correct, and it must be said commonplace, are the hospital and the English factory—or club-house—in Oporto. The plans of both have clearly been sent out from England, the hospital especially being thoroughly English in design. Planned on so vast a scale that it has never been completed, with the pediment of its Doric portico unfinished, the hospital is yet a fine building, simple and severe, not unlike what might have been designed by some pupil of Chambers.

The main front has a rusticated ground floor with round-headed windows and doors. On this in the centre stands a 270 Doric portico of six columns, and at the ends narrower colonnades of four shafts each. Between them stretches a long range of windows with simple, well-designed architraves. The only thing, apart from its unfinished condition, which shows that the hospital is not in England, are some colossal figures of saints which stand above the cornice, and are entirely un-English in style.

Of later buildings little can be said. Many country houses are pleasing from their complete simplicity; plastered, and washed pink, yellow, or white, they are devoid of all architectural pretension, and their low roofs of red pantiles look much more natural than do the steep slated roofs of some of the more modern villas.

The only unusual point about these Portuguese houses is that, as a rule, they have sash windows, a form of window so rare in the South that one is tempted to see in them one of the results of the Methuen Treaty and of the long intercourse with England. The chimneys, too, are often interesting. Near Lisbon they are long, narrow oblongs, with a curved top—not unlike a tombstone in shape—from which the smoke escapes by a long narrow slit. Elsewhere the smoke escapes through a picturesque arrangement of tiles, and hardly anywhere is there to be seen a simple straight shaft with a chimney can at the top.

For twenty years after the end of the Peninsular War the country was in a more or less disturbed state. And it was only after Dom Miguel had been defeated and expelled, and the more liberal party who supported Dona Maria II. had won the day, that Portugal again began to revive.

In 1834, the year which saw Dom Miguel's surrender, all monasteries throughout the country were suppressed, and the monks turned out. Even more melancholy was the fate of the nuns, for they were allowed to stay on till the last should have died. In some cases one or two survived nearly seventy years, watching the gradual decay of their homes, a decay they were powerless to arrest, till, when their death at last set the convents free, they were found, with leaking roofs, and rotten floors, almost too ruinous to be put to any use.

135

The Gothic revival has not been altogether without its effects in Portugal. Batalha has been, and Alcobaça is being, saved from ruin. The Sé Velha at Coimbra has been purged—too drastically perhaps—of all the additions and disfigurements 271 of the eighteenth century, and the same is being done with the cathedral of Lisbon.

Such new buildings as have been put up are usually much less successful. Nothing can exceed the ugliness of the new domed tower of the church of Belem, or of the upper story imposed on the long undercroft. Nor can the new railway station in the Manoelino style be admired.

Probably the best of such attempts to copy the art of Portugal's greatest age is found at Bussaco, where the hotel, with its arcaded galleries and its great sphere-bearing spire, is not unworthy of the sixteenth century, and where the carving, usually the spontaneous work of uninstructed men, shows that some of the mediæval skill, as well as some of the mediæval methods, have survived till the present century. 272

BOOKS CONSULTED

- Hieronymi Osorii Lusitani, Silvensis in Algarviis Episcopi: *De rebus Emmanuelis, etc.* Cologne, 1597.

- Padre Ignacio da Piedade e Vasconcellos: *Historia de Santarem Edificada.* Lisboa Occidental, 1790.

- J. Murphy: *History and Description of the Royal Convent of Batalha.* London, 1792.

- Raczynski: *Les Arts en Portugal.* Paris, 1846.

- Raczynski: *Diccionaire Historico-Artistique du Portugal.* Paris, 1847.

- J. C. Robinson: 'Portuguese School of Painting' in the *Fine Arts Quarterly Review.* 1866.

- Simões, A. F.: *Architectura Religiosa em Coimbra na Idade Meia.*

- Ignacio de Vilhena Barbosa: *Monumentos de Portugal Historicos, etc.* Lisboa, 1886.

- Oliveira Martims: *Historia de Portugal.*

- Pinho Leal: *Diccionario Geographico de Portugal.*

- Albrecht Haupt: *Die Baukunst der Renaissance in Portugal.* Frankfurt A.M., 1890.

- Visconde de Condeixa: *O Mosteiro da Batalha em Portugal.* Lisboa & Paris.

- Justi: 'Die Portugiesische Malerei des 16ten Jahrhunderts' in the *Jahrbuch der K. Preuss. Kunstsammlung,* vol. ix. Berlin, 1888.

- Joaquim Rasteiro: *Quinta e Palacio de Bacalhôa em Azeitão.* Lisboa, 1895.

- Joaquim de Vasconcellos: 'Batalha' & 'São Marcos' from *A Arte e a Natureza em Portugal.* Ed. E. Biel e Cie. Porto.

- L. R. D.: *Roteiro Illustrado do Viajante em Coimbra.* Coimbra, 1894.

- Caetano da Camara Manoel: *Atravez a Cidade de Evora, etc.* Evora, 1900.

- Conde de Sabugosa: *O Paço de Cintra.* Lisboa, 1903.

- Augusto Fuschini: *A Architectura Religiosa da Edade Média.* Lisboa, 1904.

- José Queiroz: *Ceramica Portugueza.* Lisboa, 1907.

273

INDEX

136

137

138

139

140

141

142

144

145

147

148

149

150

152

153

FOOTNOTES:

1. |1|The most noticeable difference in pronunciation, the Castilian guttural soft G and J, and the lisping of the Z or soft C seems to be of comparatively modern origin. However different such words as 'chave' and 'llave,' 'filho' and 'hijo,' 'mão' and 'mano' may seem they are really the same in origin and derived from *clavis, filius*, and *manus*.

2. |2|From the name of this dynasty Moabitin, which means fanatic, is derived the word Maravedi or Morabitino, long given in the Peninsula to a coin which was first struck in Morocco.

3. |3|The last nun in a convent at Evora only died in 1903, which must have been at least seventy years after she had taken the veil.

4. |4|A narcissus triandrus with a white perianth and yellow cup is found near Lamego and at Louzã, not far from Coimbra.

5. |5|See article by C. Justi, 'Die Portugesische Malerei des xvi. Jahrhunderts,' in vol. ix. of the *Jahrbuch der K. Preussischen Kunstsammlungen.*

6. |6|Raczynski, *Les Arts en Portugal.*

7. |7|These are the 'Annunciation,' the 'Risen Lord appearing to His Mother,' the 'Ascension,' the 'Assumption,' the 'Good Shepherd,' and perhaps a 'Pentecost' and a 'Nativity.'

8. |8|V. Guimarães, *A Ordem de Christo*, p. 155.

9. |9|A. Hapt, *Die Baukunst, etc., in Portugal*, vol. ii. p. 36.

10. |10|These may perhaps be by the so-called Master of São Bento, to whom are attributed a 'Visitation'—in which Chastity, Poverty, and Humility follow the Virgin—and a 'Presentation,' both now in Lisbon. Some paintings in São Francisco Evora seem to be by the same hand.

11. |11|Misericordia=the corporation that owns and manages all the hospitals, asylums, and other charitable institutions in the town. There is one in almost every town in the country.

12. |12|She seems almost too old to be Dona Leonor and may be Dona Maria.

13. |13|His first wife was Dona Isabel, eldest daughter and heiress to the Catholic Kings. She died in 1498 leaving an infant son Dom Miguel, heir to Castile and Aragon as well as to Portugal. He died two years later when Dom Manoel married his first wife's sister, Dona Maria, by whom he had six sons and two daughters. She died in 1517, and next year he married her niece Dona Leonor, sister of Charles V. and daughter of Mad Juana. She had at first been betrothed to his eldest son Dom João. All these marriages were made in the hope of succeeding to the Spanish throne.

14. |14|Some authorities doubt the identification of the king and queen. But there is a distinct likeness between the figures of Dom Manoel and his queen which adorn the west door of the church at Belem, and the portrait of the king and queen in this picture.

15. |15|It has been reproduced by the Arundel Society, but the copyist has entirely missed the splendid solemnity of St. Peter's face.

16. |16|See 'Portuguese School of Painting,' by J. C. Robinson, in the *Fine Arts Quarterly* of 1866.

17. |17|Vieira Guimarães, *A Ordem de Christo*, p. 150.

18. |18|*Ibid.*, p. 157.

154

19. [19]Carriage hire is still cheap in Portugal, for in 1904 only 6 000 was paid for a carriage from Thomar to Leiria, a distance of over thirty-five miles, though the driver and horses had to stay at Leiria all night and return next day. 6 000 was then barely over twenty shillings.

20. [20]It was the gift of Bishop Affonso of Portugal who held the see from 1485 to 1522.

21. [21]This monstrance was given by Bishop Dom Jorge d'Almeida who died in 1543, having governed the see for sixty-two years. (Fig. 7.)

22. [22]Presented by Canon Gonçalo Annes in 1534.

23. [23]D. Francisco Simonet, professor of Arabic at Granada. Note in *Paço de Cintra*, p. 206.

24. [24]See Miss I. Savory, *In the Tail of the Peacock*.

25. [25]A common pattern found at Bacalhôa, near Setubal, in the Museum at Oporto, and in the Corporation Galleries of Glasgow, where it is said to have come from Valencia in Spain.

26. [26]Joaquim Rasteiro, *Palacio e Quinta de Bacalhôa em Azeitão*. Lisbon, 1895.

27. [27]Columns with corbel capitals support a house on the right. Such capitals were common in Spain, so it is just possible that these tiles may have been made in Spain.

28. [28]Antonio ab Oliva=Antonio de Oliveira Bernardes, who also painted the tiles in São Pedro de Rates.

29. [29]*E.g.* in the church of the Misericordia Vianna do Castello, the cloister at Oporto, the Graça Santarem, Sta. Cruz Coimbra, the Sé, Lisbon, and in many other places.

30. [30]Paço de Cintra, *Cond. de Sabugosa*. Lisbon, 1903.

31. [31]These yokes are about 4 or 5 feet long by 18 inches or 2 feet broad, are made of walnut, and covered with the most intricate pierced patterns. Each parish or district, though no two are ever exactly alike, has its own design. The most elaborate, which are also often painted bright red, green, and yellow are found south of the Douro near Espinho. Further north at Villa do Conde they are much less elaborate, the piercings being fewer and larger. Nor do they extend far up the Douro as in the wine country in Tras-os-Montes the oxen, darker and with shorter horns, pull not from the shoulder but from the forehead, to which are fastened large black leather cushions trimmed with red wool.

32. [32]Originally there was a bell-gable above the narthex door, since replaced by a low square tower resting on the north-west corner of the narthex and capped by a plastered spire.

33. [33]

Theodomir				rex			gloriosus
v.	erex.	&	contrux.	hoc.	monast.	can.	B. Aug.
ad.	Gl.	D. et	V.M.G.D.	&	B. Martini	et	fecit ita so:
lemnit:	sacrari	ab	Lucrec.	ep.	Brac.	et	alliis sub.
J. III.	P.	M. Prid.	Idus.	Nov.	an.	D. DLIX. Post	id. rex
in	hac	eccl. ab.	eod.	ep.	palam	bapt. et	fil. Ariamir
cum	magnat.	suis. omnes	conversi	ad	fid.	ob. v.	reg. &
mirab.	in	fil. ex	sacr.	reliq.	B.M.	a Galiis	eo. reg. postul

translatis & hic asservatis Kal. Jan. An. D. DLX.

34. [34]From M. Bernardes, *Tratados Varios*, vol. ii. p. 4. The same story is told of the monastery of San Salvador de Leyre in Navarre, whose abbot, Virila, wondering how it could be possible to listen to the heavenly choirs for ever without weariness, sat down to rest by a spring which may still be seen, and there listened, enchanted, to the singing of a bird for three hundred years.

35. [35]*E.g.* the west door of Ste. Croix, Bordeaux, though it is of course very much more elaborate.

36. [36]Namely, to give back some Galician towns which had been captured.

37. [37]Bayona is one of the most curious and unusual churches in the north of Spain. Unfortunately, during a restoration made a few years ago a plaster groined vault was added hiding the old wooden roof.

38. [38]

The	tomb	is	inscribed:	Hic	requiescit	Fys:
Dei:		Egas:		Monis:		Vir:
Inclitus:			era:			millesima:

centesima: LXXXII

i.e. Era of Caesar 1182, A.D. 1144.

39. [39]He died soon after at Medinaceli, and a Christian contemporary writer records the fact saying: 'This day died Al-Mansor. He desecrated Santiago, and destroyed Pampluna, Leon and Barcelona. He was buried in Hell.'

40. [40]Another cloister-like building of even earlier date is to be found behind the fourteenth-century church of Leça de Balio: it was built probably after the decayed church had been granted to the Knights of St. John of Jerusalem. (Fig. 17.)

41. [41]A careful restoration is now being carried out under the direction of Senhor Fuschini.

42. [42]The inscription is mutilated at both ends and seems to read, 'Ahmed-ben-Ishmael built it strongly by order of ...'

43. [43]It is a pity that the difference in date makes it impossible to identify this Bernardo with the Bernardo who built Santiago. For the work Dom Miguel gave 500 morabitinos, besides a yoke of oxen worth 12, also silver altar fronts made by Master Ptolomeu. Besides the money Bernardo received a suit of clothes worth 3 morabitinos and food at the episcopal table, while Soeiro his successor got a suit of clothes, a quintal of wine, and a mora of bread. The bishop also gave a great deal of church plate showing that the cathedral was practically finished before his death.

44. [44]Compare the doorlike window of Nossa Senhora da Oliveira at Guimarães.

45. [45]The small church of São Salvador has also an old door, plainer and smaller than São Thiago.

46. [46]The five small shields with the Wounds of Christ on the Portuguese coat are supposed to have been adopted because on the eve of this battle Christ crucified appeared to Affonso and promised him victory, and because five kings were defeated.

47. [47]Andre de Rezende, a fifteenth-century antiquary, says, quoting from an old 'book of anniversaries': 'Each year an anniversary is held in memory of Bishop D. Payo on St. Mark's Day, that is May 21st, on which day he laid the first stone for the foundation of this cathedral, on the spot where now is St. Mark's Altar, and he lies behind the said place and altar in the Chapel of St. John. This church was founded Era 1224,' *i.e.* 1186 A.D. D. Payo became bishop in 1181. Another stone in the chancel records the death, in era 1321, *i.e.* 1283 A.D., of Bishop D. Durando, 'who built and enriched this cathedral with his alms,' but probably he only made some additions, perhaps the central lantern.

48. [48]It was built 1718-1746 by Ludovici or Ludwig the architect of Mafra and cost 160:000 000 or about £30,000.

49. [49]The whole inscription, the first part occurring also on a stone in the castle, runs thus:—

E (i.e. Era) MC : LX. VIII. regnant : Afonso : illustrisimo rege Portugalis : magister : galdinus : Portugalensium : Militum Templi : cum fratribus suis Primo : die : Marcii : cepit edificari : hoc : castellu : nme Thomar : qod : prefatus rex obtulit : Deo : et militibus : Templi : E. M. CC. XX. VIII : III. mens. : Julii : venit rex de maroqis ducens : CCCC milia equitu : et quingenta milia : peditum : et obsedit castrum istud : per sex Dies : et delevit : quantum extra : murum : invenit : castellu : et prefatus : magister : cu : fratribus suis liberavit Deus : de manibus : suis Idem : rex : remeavit : in patria : sua : cu : innumerabili : detrimento : hominu et bestiarum.

50. [50]Cf. Templar church at Segovia, Old Castile, where, however, the interior octagon is nearly solid with very small openings, and a vault over the lower story; it has also three eastern apses.

51. [51]There is a corbel table like it but more elaborate at Vezelay in Burgundy.

52. [52]*E.g.* in S. Martino al Cimino near Viterbo.

53. [53]So says Murray. Vilhena Barbosa says 1676. 1770 seems the more probable.

54. |54|Indeed to the end the native builders have been very chary of building churches with a high-groined vault and a well-developed clerestory. The nave of Batalha and of the cathedral of Guarda seem to be almost the only examples which have survived, for Lisbon choir was destroyed by the great earthquake of 1755, as was also the church of the Carmo in the same city, which perhaps shows that they were right in rejecting such a method of construction in a country so liable to be shaken.

55. |55|Cf. similar corbel capitals in the nave of the cathedral of Orense in Galicia.

56. |56|Before the Black Death, which reduced the number to eight, there are said to have sometimes been as many as 999 monks!

57. |57|It was a monk of Alcobaça who came to General Wellesley on the night of 16th August 1808, and told him that if he wished to catch the French he must be quick as they meant to retire early in the morning, thus enabling him to win the battle of Roliça, the first fight of the Peninsular War.

58. |58|Cf. the clerestory windows of Burgos Cathedral, or those at Dunblane, where as at Guimarães the circle merely rests on the lights below without being properly united with them.

59. |59|From the north-east corner of the narthex a door leads to the cloisters, which have a row of coupled shafts and small pointed arches. From the east walk a good doorway of Dom Manoel's time led into the chapter-house, now the barrack kitchen, the smoke from which has entirely blackened alike the doorway and the cloister near.

60. |60|Compare the horseshoe moulding on the south door of the cathedral of Orense, Galicia, begun 1120, where, however, each horseshoe is separated from the next by a deep groove.

61. |61|The town having much decayed owing to fevers and to the gradual shallowing of the river the see was transferred to Faro in 1579. The cathedral there, sacked by Essex in 1596, and shattered by the earthquake of 1755, has little left of its original work except the stump of a west tower standing on a porch open on three sides with plain pointed arches, and leading to the church on the fourth by a door only remarkable for the dog-tooth of its hood-mould.

62. |62|The towers stand quite separate from the walls and are united to them by wide round arches.

63. |63|In the dilapidated courtyard of the castle there is one very picturesque window of Dom Manoel's time (his father the duke of Beja is buried in the church of the Conceição in the town).

64. |64|An inscription says:—

'Era 1362 |i.e. A.D. 1324| anos foi
esta tore co (meçad) a (aos) 8
dias demaio. é mandou a faze (r
o muito) nobre Dom Diniz
rei de P...'

65. |65|Just outside the castle there is a good romanesque door belonging to a now desecrated church.

66. |66|Some of the distinctive features of Norman such as cushion capitals seem to be unknown in Normandy and not to be found any nearer than Lombardy.

67. |67|Sub Era MCCCXLVIII. idus Aprilis, Dnus Nuni Abbas monasterij de Alcobatie posuit primam lapidem in fundamento Claustri ejusdem loci. presente Dominico Dominici magistro operis dicti Claustri. Era 1348 = A.D. 1310.

68. |68|It is interesting to notice that the master builder was called Domingo Domingues, who, if Domingues was already a proper name and not still merely a patronymic, may have been the ancestor of Affonso Domingues who built Batalha some eighty years later and died 1402.

69. |69|In this cloister are kept in a cage some unhappy ravens in memory of their ancestors having guided the boat which miraculously brought St. Vincent's body to the Tagus.

70. |70|Cf. the aisle windows of Sta. Maria dos Olivaes at Thomar.

71. [71]It was at Leça that Dom Fernando in 1372 announced his marriage with Dona Leonor Telles de Menezes, the wife of João Lourenço da Cunha, whom he had seen at his sister's wedding, and whom he married though he was himself betrothed to a daughter of the Castilian king, and though Dona Leonor's husband was still alive: a marriage which nearly ruined Portugal, and caused the extinction of the legitimate branch of the house of Burgundy.

72. [72]Opening off the north-west corner of the cathedral is an apsidal chapel of about the same period, entered by a fine pointed door, one of whose mouldings is enriched by an early-looking chevron, but whose real date is shown by the leaf-carving of its capitals.

73. [73]A note in Sir H. Maxwell's *Life of Wellington*, vol. i. p. 215, says of Alcobaça: 'They had burned what they could and destroyed the remainder with an immense deal of trouble. The embalmed kings and queens were taken out of their tombs, and I saw them lying in as great preservation as the day they were interred. The fine tesselated pavement, from the entrance to the Altar, was picked up, the facings of the stone pillars were destroyed nearly to the top, scaffolding having been erected for that purpose. An orderly book found near the place showed that regular parties had been ordered for the purpose' (Tomkinson, 77).

74. [74]There is in the Carmo Museum at Lisbon a fine tomb to Dom Fernando, Dom Pedro's unfortunate successor. It was brought from São Francisco at Santarem, but is very much less elaborate, having three panels on each side filled with variously shaped cuspings, enclosing shields, all beautifully wrought.

75. [75]Another trophy is now at Alcobaça in the shape of a huge copper caldron some four feet in diameter.

76. [76]This site at Pinhal was bought from one Egas Coelho.

77. [77]Though a good deal larger than most Portuguese churches, except of course Alcobaça, the church is not really very large. Its total length is about 265 feet with a transept of about 109 feet long. The central aisle is about 25 feet wide by 106 high—an unusual proportion anywhere.

78. [78]Albrecht Haupt, *Die Baukunst der Renaissance in Portugal*, says that 'Der Plan durchaus englisch ist (Lang-und Querschiff fast ganz identisch mit dener der Kathedral zu Canterbury, nur thurmlos).'

79. [79]This spire has been rebuilt since the earthquake of 1755, and so may be quite different from that originally intended.

80. [80]In his book on Batalha, Murphy, who stayed in the abbey for some months towards the end of the eighteenth century, gives an engraving of an open-work spire on this chapel, saying it had been destroyed in 1755.

81. [81]Huguet witnessed a document dated December 7, 1402, concerning a piece of land belonging to Margarida Annes, servant to Affonso Domingues, master of the works, and his name also occurs in a document of 1450 as having had a house granted to him by Dom Duarte, but he must have been dead some time before that as his successor as master of the works, Master Vasquez, was already dead before 1448. Probably Huguet died about 1440.

82. [82]Caspar Estaço, writing in the sixteenth century, says that this triptych was made of the silver against which King João weighed himself, but the story of its capture at Aljubarrota seems the older tradition.

83. [83]These capitals have the distinctive Manoelino feature of the moulding just under the eight-sided abacus, being twisted like a rope or like two interlacing branches.

84. [84]The church was about 236 feet long with a transept of over 100 feet, which is about the length of the Batalha transept.

85. [85]She also sent the beautiful bronze tomb in which her eldest brother Affonso, who died young, lies in the cathedral, Braga. The bronze effigy lies on the top of an altar-tomb under a canopy upheld by two slender bronze shafts. Unfortunately it is much damaged and stands in so dark a corner that it can scarcely be seen.

86. [86]In one transept there is a very large blue tile picture.

87. [87]The Aleo is still at Ceuta. In the cathedral Our Lady of Africa holds it in her hand, and it is given to each new governor on his arrival as a symbol of office.

158

88. [88]The inscription is:—

Memoria de D. Duarte de Menezes Terceiro conde de Viana, Tronco dos condes de Tarouca. Primeiro Capitão de Alcacer-Seguer, em Africa, que com quinhentos soldados defendeu esta praça contra cemmil Mouros, com os quaes teve muitos encontros, ficando n'elles com grande honra e gloria. Morreu na serra de Bonacofú per salvar a vida do seu rei D. Affonso o Quinto.

89. [89]When the tomb was moved from São Francisco, only one tooth, not a finger, was found inside.

90. [90]Besides the church there is in Caminha a street in which most of the houses have charming doors and windows of about the same date as the church.

91. [91]1524 seems too early by some forty years.

92. [92]The rest of the west front was rebuilt and the inside altered by Archbishop Dom José de Braganza, a son of Dom Pedro II., about two hundred years ago.

93. [93]A chapel was added at the back, and at a higher level some time during the seventeenth century to cover in one of the statues, that of St. Anthony of Padua, who was then becoming very popular.

94. [94]This winding stair was built by Dom Manoel: cf. some stairs at Thomar.

95. [95]A 'pelourinho' is a market cross.

96. [96]The kitchens in the houses at Marrakesh and elsewhere in Morocco have somewhat similar chimneys. See B. Meakin, *The Land of the Moors*.

97. [97]'Esta fortaleza se começou a xiij dagosto de mil cccc.l. P[N. of T. horizonal line through it] iiij por mãdado del Rey dõ Joam o segundo nosso sõr e acabouse em tpõ del Rey dom Manoel o primeiro nosso Sñor fela per seus mãdados dom Diogo Lobo baram dalvito.'

98. [98]The house of the duke of Cadaval called 'Agua de Peixes,' not very far off, has several windows in the same Moorish style.

99. [99]Vilhena Barbosa, *Monumentos de Portugal*, p. 324.

100. [100]Though the grammar seems a little doubtful this seems to mean

Since these by service were
And loyal efforts gained,
By these and others like to them
They ought to be maintained.

101. [101]One blank space in one of the corners is pointed out as having contained the arms of the Duque d'Aveiro beheaded for conspiracy in 1758. In reality it was painted with the arms of the Coelhos, but the old boarding fell out and has never been replaced.

102. [102]Affonso de Albuquerque took Ormuz in 1509 and Gôa next year.

103. [103]Sumatra was visited in 1509.

104. [104]Fernão Peres de Andrade established himself at Canton in 1517 and reached Pekin in 1521.

105. [105]Compare the elaborate outlines of some Arab arches at the Alhambra or in Morocco.

106. [106]Some have supposed that Boutaca was a foreigner, but there is a place called Boutaca near Batalha, so he probably came from there.

107. [107]Once the Madre de Deus was adorned with several della Robbia placques. They are now all gone.

108. [108]Danver's *Portuguese in India*, vol. i.

109. [109]See in Oliveira Martims' *Historia de Portugal*, vol. II. ch. i., the account of the Embassy sent to Pope Leo IX. by Dom Manoel in 1514. No such procession had been seen since the days of the Roman Empire. There were besides endless wealth, leopards from India, also an elephant which, on reaching the Castle of S. Angelo, filled its trunk with

scented water and 'asperged' first the Pope and then the people. These with a horse from Ormuz represented the East. Unfortunately the representative of Africa, a rhinoceros, died on the way.

110. [110]Danver's *Portuguese in India*, vol. i.

111. [111]Unfortunately Fernandes was one of the commonest of names. In his list of Portuguese artists, Count Raczynski mentions an enormous number.

112. [112]In the year 1512 Olivel was paid 25 000. He had previously received 12 000 a month. He died soon after and his widow undertook to finish his work with the help of his assistant Muñoz.

113. [113]See the drawing in *A Ordem de Christo* by Vieira Guimarães.

114. [114]The last two figures look like 15 but the first two are scarcely legible; it may not be a date at all.

115. [115]All the statues are rather Northern in appearance, not unlike those on the royal tombs in Santa Cruz, Coimbra, and may be the work of the two Flemings mentioned among those employed at Thomar, Antonio and Gabriel.

116. [116]The door—notwithstanding the supposed date, 1515—was probably finished by João after 1523.

117. [117]Cf. the carving on the jambs of the Allah-ud-din gate at Delhi.

118. [118]Such heads of many curves may have been derived from such elaborate Moorish arches as may be seen in the Alhambra, or, for example, in the Hasan tower at Rabat in Morocco, and it is worth noticing that there were men with Moorish names among the workmen at Thomar—Omar, Mafamede, Bugimaa, and Bebedim.

119. [119]Esp(h)era=*sphere*; Espera=*hope*, present imperative.

120. [120]The inscription says: 'Aqui jaz Matheus Fernandes mestre que foi destas obras, e sua mulher Izabel Guilherme e levou-o nosso Senhor a dez dias de Abril de 1515. Ella levou-a a....'

121. [121]Fig. 57.

122. [122]*As Capellas Imperfeitas e a lenda das devisas Gregas.* Por Caroline Michaëlis de Vasconcellos. Porto, 1905.

123. [123]The frieze is now filled up and plastered, but not long ago was empty and recessed as if prepared for letting in reliefs. Can these have been of terra cotta of the della Robbia school? Dom Manoel imported many which are now all gone but one in the Museum at Lisbon. There are also some della Robbia medallions at the Quinta de Bacalhôa at Azeitão near Setubal.

124. [124]J. Murphy, *History of the Royal Convent of Batalha.* London, 1792.

125. [125]One of the first was probably the chapel dos Reys Magos at São Marcos near Coimbra.

126. [126]A conto = 1.000 000.

127. [127]It is no use telling a tramway conductor to stop near the Torre de São Vicente. He has never heard of it, but if one says 'Fabrica de Gas' the car will stop at the right place.

128. [128]Similar roofs cap the larger angle turrets in the house of the Quinta de Bacalhôa near Setubal, built by Dona Brites, mother of Dom Manoel, about 1490, and rebuilt or altered by the younger Albuquerque after 1528 when he bought the Quinta.

129. [129]Raczynski says 1517, Haupt 1522.

130. [130]According to Raczynski, João de Castilho in 1517 undertook to carry on the work for 140 000 per month, at the rate of 50 per day per man. 140 000=now about £31.

131. [131]Nicolas was the first of the French renaissance artists to come to Portugal.

132. [132]*E.g.* on the Hotel Bourgthéroulde, Rouen.

133. [133]Cf. the top of a turret at St. Wulfram, Abbeville.

134. [134]Haupt.

135. [135]The university was first accommodated in Sta. Cruz, till Dom João gave up the palace where it still is. It was after the return of the university to Coimbra that George Buchanan was for a time professor. He got into difficulties with the Inquisition and had to leave.

136. [136]Nicolas the Frenchman is first mentioned in 1517 as working at Belem. He therefore was probably the first to introduce the renaissance into Portugal, for Sansovino had no lasting influence.

137. [137]'To give room and licence to Dioguo de Castylho, master of the work of my palace at Coimbra, to ride on a mule and a nag seeing that he has no horse, and notwithstanding my decrees to the contrary.'—Sept. 18, 1526.

138. [138]*Vilhena Barbosa Monumentes de Portugal*, p. 411.

139. [139]Other men from Rouen are also mentioned, Jeronymo and Simão.

140. [140]The stone used at Batalha and at Alcobaça is of similar fineness, but seems better able to stand exposure, as the front of Santa Cruz at Coimbra is much more decayed than are any parts of the buildings at either Batalha or Alcobaça. The stone resembles Caen stone, but is even finer.

141. [141]João de Ruão also made some bookcases for the monastery library.

142. [142]'Aqui jas o muito honrado Pero Rodrigues Porto Carreiro, ayo que foy do Conde D. Henrique, Cavalleiro da Ordem de San Tiago, e o muyto honrado Gonzalo Gil Barbosa seu genro, Cavalleiro da Ordem de^to, e assim o muito honrado seu filho Francisco Barbosa: os quaes forão trasladados a esta sepultura no anno de 1532.'—Fr. *Historia de Santarem edificada*. By Ignacio da Piedade e Vasconcellos. Lisboa Occidental, MDCCXXXX.

143. [143]The date 1522 is found on a tablet on Ayres' tomb, so the three must have been worked while the chancel was being built.

144. [144]*Les Arts en Portugal:* letters to the Berlin Academy of Arts. Paris, 1846.

145. [145]*São Marcos:* E. Biel. Porto, in *A arte e a natureza em Portugal:* text by J. de Vasconcellos.

146. [146]There is also a fine reredos of somewhat later date in the church of Varziella near Cantanhede not far off: but it belongs rather to the school of the chapel dos Reis Magos; there is another in the Matriz of Cantanhede itself.

147. [147]Johannis III. Emanuelis filius, Ferdinandi nep. Eduardi pronep. Johannis I. abnep. Portugal. et Alg. rex. Affric. Aethiop. arabic. persic. Indi. ob felicem partum Catherinae reginae conjugis incomparabilis suscepto Emanuele filio principi, aram cum signis pos. dedicavitque anno MDXXXII. Divae Mariae Virgini et Matri sac.

148. [148]The only other object of any interest in the São Marcos is a small early renaissance pulpit on the north side of the nave, not unlike that at Caminha.

149. [149]During the French invasion much church plate was hidden on the top of capitals and so escaped discovery.

150. [150]João then bought a house in the Rua de Corredoura for 80 000 or nearly £18.—Vieira Guimarães, *A Ordem de Christo*, p. 167.

151. [151]There is preserved in the Torre do Tombo at Lisbon a long account of the trial of a 'new Christian' of Thomar, Jorge Manuel, begun on July 15, 1543, in the office of the Holy Inquisition within the convent of Thomar.—Vieira Guimarães, p. 179.

152. [152]From book 34 of João III.'s Chancery a 'quitaçã' or discharge given to João de Castilho for all the work done for Dom João or for his father, viz.—'In Monastery of Belem; in palace by the sea—swallowed up by the earthquake in 1755—balconies in hall, stair, chapel, and rooms of Queen Catherine, chapel of monastery of São Francisco in Lisbon, foundation of Arsenal Chapel; a balcony at Santos, and divers other lesser works. Then a door, window, well balustrade, garden repairs; work in pest house; stone buildings at the arsenal for a dry dock for the Indian ships; the work he has executed at Thomar, as well as the work he has done at Alcobaça and Batalha; besides he made a bastion at Mazagão so strong,' etc.—Raczynski's *Les Artistes Portugais*.

153. [153]Vieira Guimarães, *A Ordem de Christo*, pp. 184, 185.

154. [154]Foi erecta esta cap. No A.D. 1572 sed prof. E. 1810 foi restaur E. 1848 por L. L. d'Abreu Monis. Serrão, E. P^o. D Roure, Pietra concr^a. Muitas Pessoas ds. cid^ec.

155. [155]Ferguson (*History of Modern Architecture*, vol. ii. p. 287) says that some of the cloisters at Gôa reminded him of Lupiana, so no doubt they are not unlike those here mentioned.

156. [156]An inscription over a door outside says:

157. [157]One chapel, that of São Martin, has an iron screen like a poor Spanish *reja*.

158. [158]It has been pulled down quite lately. Lorvão, in a beautiful valley some fifteen miles from Coimbra, was a very famous nunnery. The church was rebuilt in the eighteenth century, has a dome, a nuns' choir to the west full of stalls, but in style, except the ruined cloister, which was older, all is very rococo.

159. [159]This reredos is in the chapel on the south of the Capella Mor.

160. [160]This aqueduct begun by Terzi in 1593 was finished in 1613 by Pedro Fernandes de Torres, who also designed the fountain in the centre of the cloister.

161. [161]It was here that Wellington was slung across the river in a basket on his way to confer with the Portuguese general during the advance on Salamanca.

162. [162]Terzi was taken prisoner at Alcacer-Quebir in 1578 and ransomed by King Henry, who made him court architect, a position he held till his death in 1598.

163. [163]Some of the most elaborate dated 1584 are by Francisco de Mattos.

164. [164]It was handed over to the cathedral chapter on the expulsion of the Jesuits in 1772.

165. [165]São Bento is now used as a store for drain-pipes.

166. [166]The Matriz at Vianna has a fifteenth-century pointed door, with half figures on the voussoirs arranged as are the four-and-twenty elders on the great door at Santiago, a curious arrangement found also at Orense and at Noya.

167. [167]There was only one other house of this order in Portugal, at Laveiras.

168. [168]Not of course the famous son of Charles V., but a son of Philip IV.

169. [169]In that year from June to October 45,000 men are inscribed as working on the building, and 1266 oxen were bought to haul stones!

170. [170]The area of the Escorial, excluding the many patios and cloisters, is over 300,000 square feet; that of Mafra, also excluding all open spaces, is nearly 290,000.

171. [171]Compare also the front of the Misericordia in Oporto.

Made in the USA
Las Vegas, NV
29 July 2024

93105819R00095